D0919503

Praise for *Gorillas Can Dance*

"*Gorillas Can Dance* comes at a vital moment in corporate history. With the lifespan of Fortune 100 companies decreasing rapidly, there's never been a more important time for large organizations to embrace the agile approach of their entrepreneurial disruptors. The great thing is that entrepreneurship is contagious and Professor Prashantham's insights allow corporates to get close to their startup counterparts."

—**Jeremy Basset,** founder, Unilever Foundry, and
CEO, Co-Cubed

"*Shameen Prashantham picked up on the corporate-startup collaboration trend very early, and he has tracked its evolution across industries and across continents for more than a decade. Combining thoughtful analysis with practical application, his insights into the why, how, and where of corporate-startup partnering will be valuable to companies that wish to be more agile and resilient in the digital era.*"

—**Julian Birkinshaw,** Deputy Dean, London Business School

"With DeepTech quickly becoming the third wave of innovation and startups increasingly attacking fundamental topics beyond what we are used to expecting, Shameen Prashantham's insights and practical examples are becoming more critical than ever for both corporations *and startups. When everything blurs, cooperation is the best solution for the survival and prosperity of the species."*

—**François Candelon,** Global Director,
BCG Henderson Institute, and
Senior Partner Managing Director,
Boston Consulting Group

"Gorillas Can Dance is a fascinating overview of collaborations between big corporates and startups. Based on more than a decade of research and observation, Shameen Prashantham's insider view from an outsider's perspective is filled with helpful examples and practical advice. An enlightening and engaging book that helps to lift the 'mist' around this space."

—**Celina Chew,** former President–Greater China, Bayer

"Professor Prashantham has studied Microsoft's pioneering partnerships with startups for many years in advanced and emerging markets. His thought leadership in Gorillas Can Dance provides actionable insights on corporate-startup collaboration for companies that want to be entrepreneurial and innovative."

—**James Chou,** CEO, Microsoft for Startups–North Asia

"I am a passionate believer in the benefits startups and social entrepreneurs bring to the global economy and to society. Through my own work with Microsoft's Global Social Entrepreneurship Program, and as

founder of Live for Good, I know that this value can only be realized through close partnership, enduring mindsets, and effective collaboration with a broad ecosystem of organizations. Shameen's framework reinforces that, when we connect startups with investors, enterprises, governments, and communities, amazing things can happen."

—**Jean-Philippe Courtois,** EVP and President, Microsoft Global Sales, Marketing, and Operations

"We have been featuring Shameen Prashantham's work at Thinkers50 for a number of years. The relationship between large corporations and entrepreneurial upstarts has always been fascinating and a vital part of economic growth. Shameen's insights and research shed vital new light on this."

—**Stuart Crainer,** cofounder, Thinkers50

"For over five years, I have been more than a close observer of how Professor Prashantham has transformed his skills and global perspective into a fruitful outcome in both research and teaching. I am also a witness of how he, as a typical CEIBS professor, has made a deep dive in China as an Indian British national to become a top-notch expert in Chinese enterprises management practices and theories. Therefore, on top of academic management knowledge, this book is also a must-read on the perspective of MNCs and startups in China that is solution-based and forward-thinking."

—**Yuan Ding,** Dean, CEIBS

"I've spent much of my career in roles focused on helping startups and corporations prosper together. Shameen Prashantham has collected a massive breadth of experience and has boiled it down into this entertaining read. Save yourself years' worth of grief and read this book."

—**Dave Drach,** Vice President–Innovation Sales, Techstars

"Great to see Professor Prashantham's focus on two of my passion areas – corporate innovation and social impact. The holy grail for any startup is to ultimately sell to an enterprise. Sounds simple, but it's a journey. The beauty is to do matchmaking that is a win-win. Given the situation we are in with COVID-19, there has never been a better time to be a social entrepreneur, especially for SDG goals for Agenda 2030. Professor Prashantham has hit the nail on these two very important topics relevant in the startup ecosystem. Gorillas can dance indeed!"

—**Shaloo Garg,** Global Lead,
Microsoft Global Social Entrepreneurship Program

"Startups are a severely underutilized competitive resource for corporations. Shameen Prashantham's book is a most needed contribution to filling this gap."

—**Gregor Gimmy,** founder,
BMW Startup Garage, and CEO, 27pilots

"Gorillas Can Dance is the essential playbook for entrepreneurs located in the office of a large corporation and for those hustling to make their big idea a reality from a small office. Through extensive interviews

and research across several contexts, Shameen Prashantham is able to comprehensively lay out the unique set of opportunities and challenges for large corporations seeking to innovate through partnerships. More importantly, in many instances, including with Walmart, Shameen was there seeing it happen. This book is an absolute must-read for entrepreneurs at either end of the table."

—**Ben Hassing,** Chief Executive, Ecommerce, Coles Group

"Shameen Prashantham, through his research over the years, has gained expertise on the topic of corporate-startup partnering. He has developed a global research program covering not only the United States, Europe, and Israel, but also Asia – particularly China and India – and, more recently, Africa. His insights in this book, based on knowledge-sharing with executives at CEIBS and public speeches, provide guidelines for corporations interested in partnering with startups. I wholeheartedly recommend this book to anyone interested in having a deeper understanding of corporate innovation and entrepreneurship."

—**Dipak Jain,** President, CEIBS, and former Dean, Kellogg School of Management

"Be it matured corporate players or newbies in the innovation ecosystem, looking to benchmark or understand its intricacies, the book provides the perfect prescription for everyone. Backed by years of research, including the most recent developments, this is a must-have reference guide for any innovation practitioner."

—**Sruthi Kannan,** Head, Cisco LaunchPad

"There are so many things that lead to cultural and institutional change in large multinational organizations. Only a thorough longitudinal study can shed light on the effort required. This book does just that."

—**Dan'l Lewin,** CEO, Computer History Museum, and former Corporate VP, Microsoft

"While most large organizations know that collaborating with startups should be a critical part of their innovation strategy, many will also admit that doing so effectively and on a global basis is a very different story. Shameen Prashantham's book helps bridge this 'knowing-doing' gap by providing fresh insights on how and where today's gorillas can dance with faster and more agile partners. A must-read for corporate innovators and entrepreneurs alike."

—**Felipe Monteiro,**
Senior Affiliate Professor of Strategy, INSEAD

"Shameen Prashantham has scoured the world, seeking the experiences of an impressive network of thought leaders across the entrepreneurial ecosystem. There is no set formula for how successful startup-corporate collaboration works; all we can do is keep learning from each other. This book provides both corporate innovators and game-changing startups the platform to do this."

—**Sheelpa Patel,** founder and Managing Director,
Mavens & Mavericks

"The major global challenges are simply too big for any company alone to address. It is imperative for the larger organizations to partner effectively with the more nimble startups to help create a better world for all. This book has some great insights on the how."

—**Paul Polman,** former CEO, Unilever,
and cofounder and Chair, IMAGINE

"A general pattern of organizational life seems to involve being nimble but inefficient in their youth, and lumbering but efficient as they age. How to keep the best attributes of both life stages has become a sort of holy grail for academics and consultants. Prashantham does a terrific job laying out what he has observed of partnerships between established and entrepreneurial firms as a mechanism that aims to hit this bliss-spot. Combining smooth prose with insightful observations, this book will be a great read for those who design and manage organizations as well as those who study them."

—**Phanish Puranam,**
Roland Berger Chaired Professor of Strategy
and Organisation Design, INSEAD

"Having spent most of my career trying to dance with gorillas, and now as a gorilla learning to dance, I can safely say that Gorillas Can Dance is an important addition to the strategic partnership canon and should be required reading for entrepreneurs on both sides of the table."

—**Martin Suter,** Global VP Digital Commerce,
Anheuser-Busch InBev

"With ecosystem approaches to innovation gaining traction, 'gorillas' and startups now recognize that they need to work with, rather than against, each other. It's not always going to be easy, but through a decade of keen observation, Professor Prashantham has uncovered the most important insights for both budding entrepreneurs and seasoned corporate executives."

—**Wern-Yuen Tan,** CEO, Pepsico APAC

"Corporate innovation as we know it is dead. Current corporate innovation is delivered through skunkworks and through learning new dance moves with startups. In his book, Professor Shameen Prashantham has captured the fine details of dancing with gorillas and how to redesign modern large corporations to survive and thrive in this new world."

—**Tzahi (Zack) Weisfeld,** Vice President and GM Ignite: Intel for Startups

"Based on over 15 years of international research, Shameen Prashantham's insightful work on partnering between established corporations and startups breaks new ground in identifying the why and how of effective alliance building. Rich in examples and practical advice, this work will be recommended reading for any corporate manager or startup executive looking to build scale and deliver innovation through partnerships."

—**Jonathan R. Woetzel,** Director, McKinsey Global Institute

"Shameen Prashantham is one of those rare academics who can combine theoretical rigor with in-depth company examples to yield highly practical insights and frameworks. Gorillas Can Dance is a great example of this combination and is essential reading for both large companies and their startup partners."

—**George S. Yip,** Emeritus Professor of Marketing and Strategy, Imperial College Business School, and member of the Thinkers50 Hall of Fame

GORILLAS CAN DANCE

SHAMEEN PRASHANTHAM

GORILLAS CAN DANCE

LESSONS FROM MICROSOFT AND OTHER CORPORATIONS ON PARTNERING WITH STARTUPS

WILEY

Library of Congress Cataloging-in-Publication Data

Names: Prashantham, Shameen, author.
Title: Gorillas can dance : lessons from Microsoft and other corporations on partnering with startups / Shameen Prashantham.
Description: Hoboken, New Jersey : Wiley, [2022] | Includes index.
Identifiers: LCCN 2021021545 (print) | LCCN 2021021546 (ebook) | ISBN 9781119823582 (hardback) | ISBN 9781119823605 (adobe pdf) | ISBN 9781119823599 (epub)
Subjects: LCSH: New business enterprises. | Partnership. | Success in business.
Classification: LCC HD62.5 .P646 2021 (print) | LCC HD62.5 (ebook) | DDC 658.1/142—dc23
LC record available at https://lccn.loc.gov/2021021545
LC ebook record available at https://lccn.loc.gov/2021021546

COVER ART & DESIGN: PAUL MCCARTHY

SKY100291111_081321

To my children, Diya and Aditya.
I hope the ideas in this book play a small role in contributing to
a more innovative and sustainable world for your generation,
and the ones to follow.

CONTENTS

CONTENTS

FOREWORD

I have been an entrepreneur for my entire life. After a few successes and a failure, I started to invest in early-stage startups. We became frustrated with the investment process, which we felt was especially detrimental to entrepreneurs. Out of that frustration we founded Techstars in 2006 and we created a better business model for entrepreneurs, investors, corporations, and communities.

In the Techstars model we take a cohort of 10 startup entrepreneurs who come together under one roof for three months to develop their concept, receive guidance and mentorship from experienced entrepreneurs, and refine their product and business model to pitch to investors. We coined the term "accelerator" and today Techstars has replicated that first accelerator in Boulder, Colorado, to nearly 50 geographic locations, across multiple verticals, and in partnership with some of the largest corporations in the world.

I provide this short history of Techstars not as a tribute to what we've accomplished but as a point in the timeline of Shameen's inspiring book that you now hold in your hands. Professor Prashantham began his journey documenting corporate-startup partnering in 2003 when Microsoft was first understanding disruption to its business model. Technology companies like Microsoft and others were vulnerable to "two people in a garage somewhere" inventing a technology that would make them irrelevant.

Companies outside of technology – manufacturers, distributors, or retailers, for example – would appear (in 2003) to be immune from business model disruption from startups but as Shameen clearly demonstrates, all global corporations face an imperative to innovate. As retired CEO of Ford, Mark Fields said, "When I first joined the company, a long time ago, we were a manufacturing company. As we go forward, I want us to be known as a manufacturing, a technology, and an information company.. . . That's where we're heading."

Today, while it's largely understood that every corporation must somehow become innovative and entrepreneurial, there's not as much understanding about how to do that. Part of the difficulty in partnering between startups and corporations is figuring out what to do: Do you buy a technology? Create an accelerator within your company? Develop a presence in entrepreneurial hotspots like Silicon Valley? Or deploy scouting teams in other entrepreneurial hotspots throughout the world? All of these tactics have been tried, but what will work for your company and how can you make it happen? More importantly, how can you get your leadership team to be on the same page? *Gorillas Can Dance* provides an excellent overview, with relevant case studies and examples, that will help gain alignment from leadership and management on corporate-startup partnering.

But part of the problem in partnering stems from very real obstacles in mindset, operating procedures, and resources that corporations and startups have within their DNA. A result of these obstacles is that corporations often view startups as risky – will the startup deliver on their commitment or will they just be a distraction? And for the startups, the questions about working with corporations are equally vexing – Can they trust the corporation to not take advantage of them?

Fortunately, for both startups and corporations, Shameen has spent the better part of the past two decades interviewing managers in a wide range of companies in China, India, Israel, Kenya, South Africa, United Kingdom, the United States, and other locations to provide more than imperatives and obstacles. The game-changer in creating corporate-startup partnerships that matters, that makes an impact, is the mindset of participants: entrepreneurial, collaborative, and global.

Professor Prashantham has effectively articulated what we experience and have understood at Techstars: it's not enough to understand that corporations and startups can partner to accelerate innovation, nor is it enough to understand the challenges and obstacles that make partnering difficult. The key is the mindset of the individual. Are you open to new ideas from diverse people, from diverse cultures? Are you willing to make sacrifices in personal or corporate gain to achieve a greater vision? Do you see the world as a blank canvas waiting for your creativity and potential to expressed?

The mindset is about choosing authentic engagement with others in a way that provides hope for the future.

I believe we are in the very early stages of harnessing the ways in which entrepreneurship can be applied to global problems. It requires partnering between corporations, startups, communities, governments, nonprofits, universities, and a multitude of organizations. With the insights of *Gorillas Can Dance*, we now have a roadmap to help. As Shameen concludes, "Who knows? Perhaps working together may become so commonplace that a time will come when not many will need to be reminded of its potential, or even schooled in the nuances of the process."

David Cohen
Co-founder and Chairman, Techstars

PREFACE

One of the best decisions I've ever made was to muster up the courage to ask the late Professor C. K. Prahalad, a respected strategy professor at Michigan University, a question at the 2006 Academy of Management conference in Atlanta. I explained to him that I had begun researching how start-ups were partnering with large corporations; I was curious to know if he thought this was a promising phenomenon or just a passing fad. His response was unequivocal: "Startups must learn to dance with the large gorillas."

Thus came the phrase "dancing with gorillas" into my life.

I kept following this phenomenon. Microsoft proved to be a particularly fascinating example, and I was fortunate to be able to study its startup partnering activities as an independent academic. I was able to make observations over an extended period of time – a decade and a half – and across several locations including China, India, Israel, Kenya, the UK, the United States, and South Africa, among others (see "About the Research"). Importantly, corporate-startup partnering was part of that company's organizational transformation.

There were several other companies that I studied, too. Initially, the cases I came across resulted from ad hoc activities and happy accidents. Eventually, spurred by the growing ubiquity of digitalization, more systematic and deliberate efforts were made, initially by technology companies and later by ones from traditional sectors like automotive, banking, and retail.

In the process, a new notion was added to my lexicon: "gorillas can dance."

By observing the phenomenon of large corporations partnering with startups over time, I've been able to better understand that the capability to partner with a highly asymmetric organization takes time and effort. By taking a deliberately global perspective I've been privileged to gain insight into how partnering practices are adapted to, and adopted from, different contexts.

Corporate-startup partnering has become an integral part of corporate innovation, reflecting a greater openness in companies' efforts to innovate. And while there are other ways of engaging with corporate innovation – including intrapreneurship and corporate venture capital – the fundamentals of the partnering perspective that this book deals with offer a useful perspective that is relevant to be incorporated in those other efforts.

This book shares some of the lessons I observed in the corporations that partner effectively with startups. It is written for the gorillas – the large corporations seeking to make their partnering efforts more effective. A key lesson for managers is that partnering with startups is great on paper, but not easy to do.

An important insight that I got as I studied many companies is what I call the "paradox of asymmetry"; that is, corporates and startups seemed to be attracted to each because they were hugely different and had things that the other wanted. Yet these very differences – or asymmetries – were what got in the way of effective partnering. This helped me better understand what distinguished corporates that were more effective than others in partnering with startups; they make deliberate efforts at overcoming the downsides of asymmetry while tapping the upside. Thus partnering with startups sounds like a great idea on paper for large corporations; making it work, however, is not so simple.

The book opens with an account of Microsoft and culminates with an outline of the book's six chapters, with two each in three parts: Why, How, and Where. Each part highlights an important mindset: entrepreneurial, collaborative, and global, respectively. An Epilogue at the end briefly highlights the importance of all three mindsets, which represent an important takeaway that transcends this book's specific focus on corporate-startup partnering.

Thinking about these mindsets, as I have been completing this manuscript, has prompted a fair bit of reflection about the intersection of globalization and entrepreneurship, which in essence is what partnering between large multinationals and entrepreneurial startups represents.

Such reflection has been greatly influenced by the Covid-19 pandemic.

While this book has been well over a decade in the making, the home stretch of the writing effort to complete the manuscript took place against the unprecedented backdrop of the havoc wreaked, including on my travel plans to China, by the Covid-19 pandemic. As a result, I unexpectedly found myself progressing this book in my hometown of Vellore, in southern India. This meant that, after many years, I was back in the house I'd grown up in as a child.

That building was built over 250 years ago by the East India Company as an indigo factory. The East India Company was a "born global" – the epitome of globalization and entrepreneurship of its era. Many years later, the building was sold to the Reformed Church of America, where the Scudder family – a prominent medical missionary family – lived at the turn of the nineteenth century. In 1900, Ida S. Scudder, a third-generation medical missionary, started a one-bed dispensary in that building – quite literally, a startup – that eventually became the Christian Medical College (CMC) Hospital. Today, with more than 2,500 beds and a fine medical college, it is one of India's top teaching hospitals and a non-profit organization that assiduously seeks to serve the poor. Later, the building came to house the offices and director's residence for an organization founded in 1970, the Christian Counselling Centre (CCC), which has continued the tradition of non-profit service.

Arguably, this building offers diametrically opposing illustrations of how global and entrepreneurial mindsets can intersect. At one extreme, scholars such as Jeffrey Sachs suggest that, at least from the perspective of the country that is included in its name, the East

India Company represented exploitative globalization. By contrast, organizations like these non-profits in Vellore that came into existence in this very building were also arguably conceived and built on the basis of global and entrepreneurial mindsets, but with an ethos of service that is very different.

Of course, for most for-profit organizations today, the optimal balance will lie somewhere in between these extremes. But in a post-Covid world, there may be merit in leaning more toward the Vellore non-profits' mindset than that of the East India Company, an erstwhile vehicle of imperialism. And it is collaboration – between dissimilar actors – that may be the lynchpin that helps to harness the benefits of entrepreneurship *and* globalization.

This is why I am particularly gratified to observe corporations like Microsoft, Unilever, and others explicitly incorporate a focus on the United Nations' Sustainable Development Goals (SDGs) in some of their startup partnering activities. Corporate-startup partnering thus holds promise for social impact. This prospect – and the accompanying urgency – has only increased with the debilitating social and economic effects of the Covid-19 pandemic. I truly believe that as corporations and startups partner together more effectively for mutual benefit, there can be outcomes – economic *and* social – that enhance well-being, productivity, and meaningfulness in life. But this is easier said than done, and it is my hope that the lessons in this book will help a little to make that a reality.

Shameen Prashantham

PROLOGUE

MICROSOFT'S STARTUP PARTNERING JOURNEY

Microsoft's one of the few companies we were able to partner with that actually worked for both companies . . . Bill [Gates] and Microsoft were really good at it because they didn't make the whole thing in the early days and they learned how to partner with people really well.

– Steve Jobs[1]

MICROSOFT: A CASE STUDY IN STARTUP PARTNERING

In October 2010, Microsoft organized an event, billed as the One Summit, at its Silicon Valley campus in Mountain View, California. While Microsoft was well known for its partner-related events and activities, this summit for startups was a first for the company. The event marked the soft launch of a program called BizSpark One, a partnering initiative through which Microsoft partnered with 100 of the most innovative startups that used its technologies, selected from over thousands that had signed up to its BizSpark program launched in 2008. The majority of the startups in that room were from North America and Western Europe.

Fast-forward to April 2019. Walmart CEO Doug McMillon was in Shanghai, China, and one of the local initiatives that he spent time learning about was Omega 8, a partnering program through which that retail giant could work with local startups to solve their pain points. A few startups that had gotten to work with Walmart in China through this program demonstrated their solutions. Apart from the apparent prowess of those startups, the win-win outcomes for them and Walmart, and the high-level executive attention the program had attracted, there was something else that was striking: most of those Chinese startups were alumni of the Microsoft Accelerator program.

I was fortunate to be present at both those meetings as an academic researcher. For well over a decade, as part of my ongoing research program I have studied how Microsoft (and many other corporations discussed in this book) partnered with startups. For me, Microsoft's journey of partnering with startups across time and locations is an excellent case study for three reasons.

First, Microsoft took startup partnering seriously, yet had to work hard to figure things out – therefore there was plenty for me to study, over time and across space. Partnering has been in Microsoft's DNA, as acknowledged by Steve Jobs. Yet, even Microsoft has had to work hard at startup partnering. A key point of the story is that Microsoft's current status as a partner of choice for many digital startups didn't happen overnight; it has been effort*ful*, not effort*less*.

Second, I was fortunate to gain access to relevant Microsoft managers across several regions, over a considerable period of time – therefore I could observe an unfolding journey. My exposure to Microsoft began in June 2003 during a fortuitous visit to its headquarters in Redmond, Washington. Since then, many Microsoft managers, startup partners, and other ecosystem members have been generous with their time and stories with me over the years, as I embarked on a study of corporate-startup partnering. Spanning over a decade and a half, my research on Microsoft covers multiple geographies including China, India, Israel, Kenya, South Africa, the UK, and the United States, among others. On occasion, I have even found myself telling Microsoft managers stories about the past that they weren't aware of!

Third, it is a story about a learning journey – and thus offers lessons for all companies that are committed to partnering with startups, even traditional ones. Today, startup partnering is relevant to corporations in all industries. As seen, traditional companies like Walmart could partner with startups *alongside* a technology company like Microsoft. Moreover, in this era of digitalization, all companies are becoming software companies, as Microsoft CEO Satya Nadella often says. Everyone can learn from the Microsoft story.

Before getting into my narrative, I wish to make it clear that I am a neutral observer; despite the warm professional relationship I have had with many current and former Microsoft managers, I deliberately declined taking on any commercial or consulting role while my research was ongoing, a stance that has been graciously accepted by all my informants. (This holds for all the other companies I've studied for this book, as well.)

In presenting my account of Microsoft's startup journey, I describe three broad phases (see Figure P.1). The first culminates with the launch in 2008 of BizSpark, Microsoft's large-scale programmatic initiative to engage with young startups; that was also the year Bill Gates exited day-to-day operations at Microsoft, leaving Steve Ballmer fully in charge. The second phase covers subsequent startup partnering initiatives that had a global footprint, including an accelerator program originating in Israel, and were brought under a single umbrella, Microsoft Ventures, in 2013. The third begins around 2014, when Satya Nadella became CEO, when startup partnering had become increasingly "mainstreamed" into Microsoft's corporate strategy.[2]

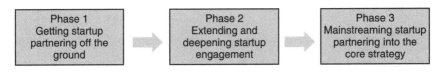

Figure P.1   Three Phases of Microsoft's Startup Partnering Journey

PHASE 1 GETTING STARTUP PARTNERING OFF THE GROUND

Recognizing the Imperative to Partner with Startups

Following my first contact with Microsoft in 2003, the year it became the most valuable company in the world,[3] I had the opportunity to talk to Microsoft managers who were reaching out to the software developer community. Their goal was to co-opt independent software vendors (ISVs) as Microsoft partners. If these companies built their software products on top of Microsoft tools, then there was a win-win situation every time that company sold its offerings, since Microsoft technology would, in effect, be bundled with it. A prominent name that kept coming up in my interactions with these managers was that of Dan'l Lewin.

Back then, Lewin was a relative newcomer to Microsoft – a Silicon Valley insider who'd been around for a couple of years in a company that many viewed as a Silicon Valley outsider. Lewin's professional background made him better suited than most to connect Microsoft with the Valley. Lewin had worked at Apple as a member of the original team that designed, built, and marketed the Macintosh, an initiative that Steve Jobs described as intrapreneurship, and was hand-picked by Jobs when he left Apple to set up NeXT Inc.[4] In the years that followed, Lewin got involved in entrepreneurial ventures of his own, and had credibility in the Silicon Valley startup community. Later, in late December of 2000, he contacted Steve Ballmer and offered to help Microsoft build bridges with Silicon Valley, based on Ballmer's speech committing Microsoft to web standards, which he believed were going to be critical to realize the company's goal of becoming a software enterprise powerhouse; he says: "I sent Steve Ballmer an email, and I said, 'If you're serious about . . . want[ing] to engage the start-up and venture capital community, I'd be interested in talking.'"[5]

Ballmer acted swiftly. In January 2001, Lewin was hired as an officer of the company and, as a corporate vice president, had execu-tive and site responsibility for the company's operations in Silicon Valley and the mandate to change how the company engaged the venture capital community and entrepreneurs and to resolve techni-cal and business conflicts with the industry. In the aftermath of the dot-com boom and the lingering US Department of Justice (DOJ) anti-trust settlement, this was an important hire for Microsoft.

To better understand why Lewin's arrival at Microsoft in 2001 was significant, it is useful to take a step back and look at what Micro-soft had been dealing with in the runup to Lewin joining the com-pany. I am not a business historian, but looking back, developments at Microsoft in the late 1990s suggest that certain seeds were sown then that had a long-term impact.

The second half of the 1990s had been a complex period for Microsoft in at least three ways. First, the Internet had produced a "tidal wave"[6] that Microsoft was late to catch, but eventually did. Second, there was turbulence as the company had to deal with an antitrust lawsuit brought by the US DOJ.[7] Third, as noted in a memo known as the "Halloween papers,"[8] Microsoft faced the threat of being disrupted by the open source software movement. The last-mentioned was particularly crucial given the emergent platform strategy that culminated in the 2002 release of .NET, as Microsoft sought to transform itself into an enterprise software company in the post-dot-com era. The platform "evangelists" were seeking to get B2B independent software vendors (ISVs) to work on Microsoft platform technology and create enterprise solutions. Startups constituted a potentially important set of platform adopters, but there was a sense of disconnectedness between Microsoft and startups, notably in Silicon Valley, before Lewin arrived on the scene.

Operating out of Microsoft's Silicon Valley campus in Mountain View, California, Lewin went about establishing Microsoft's worldwide venture capital and startup community engagement efforts.[9] Lewin and his team began the groundwork for a partner program that would become BizSpark (discussed later) and related Microsoft Innovation Centers[10] across six continents in over 150 locations. This was going to be a marathon, not a sprint. Lewin had a formidable network in Silicon Valley, and in the early days of my research, Silicon Valley entrepreneurs took Lewin seriously but were still reserving judgment about Microsoft. Microsoft's power, because of its user base, was undeniably considerable; it couldn't be ignored. But the company was not perceived as being "cool." At a Microsoft event in California, one Silicon Valley entrepreneur quipped to me during the lunch break: "That was like watching my dad dance . . ." Microsoft may have been grudgingly respected, but it certainly wasn't loved in Silicon Valley.

But further afield, Microsoft managers were getting the message that attracting great startups onto their platform was important. Essentially, this was a period of learning for Microsoft as it figured out how to partner with startups. In the mid-2000s this was happening within the generic framework infrastructure of partnering with ISVs, since a partner program customized for startups – which would appear as BizSpark – was still in the future.

Beginning to Partner with Start-ups (within a Generic Partner Framework)

Microsoft's partnership with a startup called Skelta was one of the early striking examples that I came across of a mutually beneficial partnership that took place even *before* there was a startup-friendly partnering program – with the emphasis on being more of a partner than a vendor.

In 2004, an early decision made by the founders' of Bangalore-based Skelta was to build its business process management (BPM) software products on Microsoft's .NET platform technology. They were thus betting on Microsoft's user base among enterprise customers that also constituted Skelta's target market. Having attracted a returnee with extensive experience in software product companies, Sanjay Shah, to be the CEO of the new venture, Skelta aggressively pursued a close working relationship with Microsoft's subsidiary in Bangalore.

During 2005, Microsoft India was highly supportive because it felt that Skelta had proved to be a valuable and loyal partner. Skelta was given significant exposure to thought leaders within Microsoft and enhanced Skelta's visibility in Microsoft beyond its India operations. Shah knew that Microsoft managers in India were pleased to have, in Skelta, a good example for internal and external audiences of its efforts to partner with Indian companies. As noted by Rajiv Sodhi, COO of Microsoft India, who was then the Microsoft manager who had been instrumental in fostering the relationship with Skelta under the auspices of the ISV program,

> Skelta fostered a very strong link with Microsoft India on multiple levels. They quickly recognized that Microsoft is a big company and will have its own agenda. And so smart people like them very quickly align themselves to this [agenda] because then, they have the whole subsidiary standing behind them. What happens as a result is that it's not a very distant point in time when they start getting elevated to global levels.[11]

In 2006, Skelta received an award from Microsoft recognizing it as an ISV "making waves."[12] This reflected Skelta's progress, with support from Sodhi and other Microsoft managers, including one who had moved from the India subsidiary to global headquarters, in building bridges with actors in other parts of the Microsoft ecosystem, including at the corporation's global headquarters. This enabled Skelta to gain go-to-market support from Microsoft in the United States and also led to Skelta's building a partner network comprising other fellow Microsoft partners to act as their resellers in international markets around the world, including in Europe. In all, 80% of Skelta's revenues accrued through international business, with the bulk of this resulting from Skelta's engagement with the Microsoft global ecosystem.

In 2007, a Microsoft conference in Beijing showcased an example of good practice in reaching out to young firms by tailoring the existing ISV apparatus to local conditions. The person behind this, Vaqar Khamisani, was an entrepreneurial Microsoft manager in Pakistan, who had found that promising small enterprises needed rather more structured guidance than the ISV partnering program allowed for. He therefore proactively modified that program into a "journey" of sequenced activities through which small firms could develop technical and market capabilities that would ultimately make them far more effective in leveraging the Microsoft partnership.[13]

What is perhaps most impressive about the Skelta-Microsoft partnership, and the work of managers like Khamisani, is that these occurred prior to the commencement of more systematic partnering efforts that were specifically targeted at startups. When a more structured partner program for startups did emerge, many more Microsoft managers were galvanized into partnering with startups. That initiative was BizSpark, launched in 2008.

Establishing a Customized Startup-Friendly Partner Program

The 2008 launch of the BizSpark program was a major milestone in Microsoft's journey of partnering with startups. The program's stated goals were to "develop and support a global ecosystem of start-ups, learn how best to provide value to these partners in the rapidly changing technology industry, and foster innovation, opportunity and economic growth around the world."[14] It was the crystalliza-tion of a programmatic way to partner with startups on a large scale, and entice them onto Microsoft's technology platform by provid-ing software, along with support and visibility, virtually for free to privately held startups that were less than three years in existence and made less than $1 million annual revenue.[15]

Pulling off the BizSpark launch called for two key sets of actions. First, Lewin made robust efforts to persuade Ballmer of the impor-tance of BizSpark, got his boss to underwrite the program, and navi-gated the challenges of introducing a complex program like this in the middle of the company's financial year. Second, to understand their perspective, Lewin created a team to engage with the entrepre-neurial community and promote platform technologies such as the .NET platform to startups.

Dave Drach, who was part of that early Microsoft team, described to me the interactions they had with Techstars, a startup accelera-tor in Boulder, Colorado. Through his relationship with Brad Feld, Lewin and a small team met with the very first Techstars cohort, and talked to startups for feedback as to why they were using open source rather than Microsoft technology. They were told that startups couldn't deploy Windows server software because it was not available with the appropriate license rights to run web-based software. Feedback from startups at other accelerators was consistent. The bottom line was that even if they wanted to, startups could not license Microsoft software without a special service provider's license agreement (SPLA), which was only available to the telecom industry though a dedicated sales force. Then the team worked on figuring out how to address this issue and came up with a scheme to limit the use rights via a click-through license from a special website and to limit the market focus through partner (e.g. VCs) nominations of private companies less than three years old with less than $1 million in revenue.

Within less than a year of BizSpark's launch, more than 15,000 startups had signed on.[16] The following year, this number was over 35,000,[17] and five years from the launch of that program, the number stood at more than 85,000.[18] BizSpark was strategically important to Microsoft because it had simultaneously achieved two things. First, it paved the way for harnessing the potential of getting startups onto Microsoft's platform technologies. Second, the provision of free software tools helped stave off the threat from the open source software movement. (Since then Microsoft has become much more of a supporter of open source,[19] a shift that Lewin and his team advocated.)

While BizSpark was a breadth program, depth engagement was still going to be needed, and the early success of the BizSpark program created a large pool of startups that had chosen to adopt Microsoft platform technology. As one entrepreneur said to me, "We are taking a big bet on Microsoft . . . we are betting the farm on their technology." From this pool, Microsoft now had the opportunity to partner more closely with a select group of promising startups. And this was exactly what Microsoft sought to achieve through the BizSpark One program.

PHASE 2 EXTENDING AND DEEPENING STARTUP ENGAGEMENT

Engaging in Selective One-to-One Partnering

In 2009, a new depth program called BizSpark One began to take shape. This initiative was an invitation-only "depth" program for the 100 most innovative startups, hand-picked from the member base of the BizSpark "breadth" program. As Lewin put it, "The idea behind BizSpark One is to cast a finer net using Silicon Valley best practices, and then lift the net up to find the startups that are most likely to succeed in the market and shape the industry's future."[20]

This elite startup partnering initiative was managed by Microsoft's Corporate startup engagement team, led by Matt Clark (who reported to Lewin), based in its Silicon Valley campus in Mountain

View, California. The program provided startup members with a designated corporate account manager from that team in order to build a one-to-one relationship with Microsoft over a 12-month period, with the end goal being joint go-to-market strategies. The account managers' role was to help startups gain access to the right people and resources from relevant business units within Microsoft, as well as the corporation's wider partner ecosystem.

These efforts being driven by Lewin's team were indicative of broader strategic changes within Microsoft, with the mobile Internet and cloud computing becoming of strategic importance, ultimately leading to, especially vis-à-vis cloud computing, a business model change over time. S. Somasegar who was then a senior vice president in the server and tools business, commented:

> Whenever there is a platform shift that happens – cloud computing being one of the biggest platform shifts that we have seen thus far – figuring out ways to engage with different parts of the ecosystem to drive adoption and usage of the platform is critical to the success of the platform. One of the important components of the ecosystem was startups. We wanted to ensure that we started to engage with the startup ecosystem both as a way to learn how to make our platform more relevant to startups as well to get feedback as startups starting to use our cloud platform.

The BizSpark One program was in effect seeking to foster the development of startups that could be put forward as examples for the thousands of other startups vying to partner with Microsoft, as well as turn into potentially significant partners in the future. Since all of the selected startups came from the BizSpark partner program pool, they were all young (less than three years old) and had built their software offerings on Microsoft platform technologies. As Matt Clark observed: "Startups are the next generation of partners for Microsoft. Our whole business will rely on how well they succeed. BizSpark One extends the BizSpark program. We try to find the highest potential startups and provide technical and business support that helps them grow and succeed."[21]

In 2010, when I attended the One Summit, a soft launch for the program in Mountain View, California, it was apparent that, for many of the startups selected to be on the program, there was a strong sense of being fortunate to have the opportunity. The majority of these came from North America and Western Europe. (One Chinese startup, Gridsum, did benefit greatly from BizSpark One, as discussed in the next section on emerging markets.)

In 2011, at Microsoft's annual Worldwide Partner Conference (WPC) in Los Angeles, which took place about eight months after the One Summit, some of the BizSpark One success stories were showcased at this event, which brought together approximately 15,000 delegates from the company's formidable partner ecosystem. As the then-president of the server and tools business, Satya Nadella gave a stirring speech about the importance of cloud computing.[22] Indeed, a few BizSpark One startups were finding that betting on the cloud was paying off for them. For example, at the 2011 WPC, StorSimple, a Silicon Valley startup offering cloud-integrated storage solutions,[23] was named BizSpark Startup of the Year. It was later acquired by Microsoft.[24]

The 2011 WPC was also significant for another BizSpark One startup, called Calinda. This French startup's efforts to enter the US market received a big boost when it was showcased along with a few other BizSpark One startups in a booth at the WPC that would have otherwise been well beyond their means. Through the networking that occurred at that event, it signed up its first resellers in the US market, who were themselves members of Microsoft's partner network. A magical moment at the 2011 WPC happened one evening when I was sipping drinks outside the venue with these entrepreneurs: Microsoft's BizSpark One team had arranged for these startups' logos to be flashed on a big neon screen outside the convention hall. The entrepreneurs excitedly grabbed their phones to take pictures and post on social media. The mood that night was electric.

However, there wasn't a happy ending for everyone. Later in 2011, a BizSpark One startup called Huddle began to publicly position itself as a rival to Microsoft.[25] This came as a bit of a surprise to Microsoft, since this British company had been previously showcased as a poster child of BizSpark One. It was not the only startup whose relationship with Microsoft soured or became indifferent. Some startups were simply not proactive enough to grab (or create) opportunities for creating value within Microsoft's ecosystem. Others built good relationships with the startup engagement team but found the going hard once they started interacting with the (less sympathetic) business units – which is where the real opportunities for joint value creation are.

Israel provided a noticeable difference in the composition of the BizSpark One portfolio of startups between the One Summit in October 2010 and the WPC in July 2011. A manager called Tzahi (Zack) Weisfeld at Microsoft Israel had been proactively looking for ways to promote startup partnering in his locale. He and his team found Lewin's efforts through BizSpark One to be highly relevant to Israeli startups. A set of Israeli startups became an important subset of the BizSpark One portfolio. Indeed, with corporate involvement and support from leaders like Lewin and Somasegar, Israel would play an influential role in Microsoft's startup partnering journey.

Adopting New Corporate Innovation Practices

In late 2011, Weisfeld met with Satya Nadella (head of Microsoft's server and tools division at the time) and highlighted the need for deep engagement with startups. Weisfeld cited Paul Graham's blog post "Microsoft is Dead"[26] and recommended additional formats, such as corporate accelerators, to work with startups. Weisfeld and his team at Microsoft's research facility in Israel had recognized the potential for working much more closely with promising startups through an accelerator model. Managers in Microsoft's research unit in China and India warmed to the idea. Executives like Somasegar were highly involved in and supportive of this initiative as it unfolded.[27]

In 2012, Microsoft launched accelerators in Tel Aviv, Bangalore, and Beijing, housed within its research facility in each location. All of these milieus had promising startup ecosystems. The format of the accelerator program was that startups would be co-located for four months (initially six, in China) during which time they would have access to cloud computing and other technology infrastructure, mentoring, and opportunities to build networks with Microsoft managers and partners. The accelerator program would conclude with a demo day attended by Microsoft managers as well as select partners and investors. In 2013, using the same template, accelerators were launched in three important European startup ecosystems: Berlin, London, and Paris. And the following year, an accelerator was established in Seattle, Microsoft's own backyard. Global responsibility for running all the Microsoft accelerators was given to Weisfeld, who continued to be based in Israel.

Although the early accelerators explicitly focused on offering free credits of Azure, Microsoft's cloud computing service, a technology-agnostic attitude was adopted to the selection of startup partners. That is, it was not deemed problematic if startups preferred other cloud solutions such as Amazon's AWS. The first Microsoft accelerator I visited was the one in Beijing. I recall vividly my astonishment at seeing Apple equipment on the startup's tables in their co-working space. Mouth agape, I turned to my host, David Lin, the then-director of the Beijing accelerator. Lin smiled and said, "We want startups to know that we are interested in their success." Although it was clear that Microsoft was incentivizing the use of its cloud tools, at that stage Microsoft did not make working on its own technology a precondition for joining its accelerators. This suggests that Microsoft was working hard to win the hearts and minds of startups.

During one research field trip to India, I observed a Wednesday afternoon session at Microsoft Accelerator, which had the strong support of CFO Amaresh Ramaswamy and the leadership of a former entrepreneur, Mukund Mohan. Initially, there were a couple of partners – one from Nokia and another from SAP – who gave brief talks about how they might be able to support the dozen or so startups represented in the room. Next, the startups engaged in some peer sharing with three startups, demonstrating some of the progress they had made – for example, one entrepreneur demoed his work-in-progress app – and received feedback from mentors and the other entrepreneurs. Finally, everyone trooped to a local pub for beer and pizza. Chatting with the entrepreneurs in that informal setting, I could sense a palpable buzz among them.

On a visit to the Tel Aviv accelerator, I noticed that an event for startup alumni was going on in the adjacent room. When I met managers and entrepreneurs at the London accelerator I was struck by the upbeat mood of the entrepreneurs who felt Microsoft's cloud offering was valuable to the startups there, a view echoed by a senior marketing director, Helen Litvak. On yet another field trip I met the heads of the Bangalore, Beijing and Tel Aviv accelerators who had come together to compare notes and share their learnings with each other.

Thus I observed positive vibes among Microsoft managers and entrepreneurs across multiple locations. The period and nature of engagement was not unlike other accelerators, but what appeared to make it work was the caliber of the startups, involvement of Microsoft executives, and the willingness of Microsoft partners from its wider network to engage with the startups as well. I was left with the impression that Microsoft was taking startup partnering seriously; it wasn't just paying lip service.

Tapping Emergent Startup Ecosystems

Before wrapping up the second phase of the story, it seems worth noting that the action was heating up in emerging markets, notably China and India – and Microsoft's strong presence in those markets was a great advantage.

As a company, Microsoft has historically taken emerging markets seriously, as seen from the scale and scope of its operations in China and India, and regular visits from global top managers. Not surprisingly, this is the case when it comes to startup partnering as well. The Skelta example from India demonstrates that although it required strenuous efforts from both managers at Microsoft India and the leaders of the startup, it was not impossible for an Indian startup to "dance" with Microsoft, even before BizSpark. And with the launch of BizSpark (and of BizSpark One), more such opportunities presented themselves, as illustrated by the case of Gridsum.

Beijing-based Gridsum was founded by Qi Guosheng, a young computer science graduate from Tsinghua University.[28] While at college, Qi had spent a summer interning at Microsoft's research facility in Beijing. When he founded Gridsum after graduating, he used Microsoft technology to build software products, the quality of which impressed Johnny Xu, a Microsoft China manager working with startups. Gridsum became the first (and, for a while, only) Chinese entrant into BizSpark One. For Microsoft China's sales force, Gridsum became an attractive example of how a Chinese company could leverage Microsoft technology to build software products. And thanks to BizSpark One, Gridsum was also able to attract global attention from Microsoft.

In 2011, when Steve Ballmer visited Beijing, he gave a talk at an event that had two speakers – Ballmer and Qi. Thus Gridsum was showcased as an example of how a startup in an emerging market like China could have a mutually beneficial relationship with Microsoft.[29] However, despite the examples of Skelta in India or Gridsum in China, most of the action during BizSpark One was in the West. For example, Microsoft produced a video showcasing some of the most promising BizSpark One startups; they were all from North America or Western Europe.[30]

In 2012, by contrast, the launch of accelerators in Bangalore and Beijing, on the heels of the original one in Israel, gave tremendous impetus to Microsoft's startup partnering efforts in the world's two largest emerging markets. When first launched, the Indian accelerator readily adopted the Israeli model of a four-month curriculum, but in China, with its linguistic differences and unique ecosystems, it was felt that a six-month program was required. Eventually Chinese cohorts also adopted the same four-month program.

The timing of the launch of the Bangalore and Beijing accelerators proved to be fortunate, as both China and India were witnessing the beginnings of the rise of the mobile Internet. (In China, for example, 2011 was the year that WeChat was launched, and it began to take off the following year.[31]) Microsoft was able to engage with some interesting startups and "catch 'em young." For instance, Testin was a startup created in Beijing in 2011 to provide software testing services for mobile apps. Testin was part of the first cohort of Microsoft's accelerator in Beijing in 2012. It has since gone on to extend the Microsoft partnership with China to the United States, where it has an office in San Francisco, apart from also building partnerships with several other multinationals.[32]

In 2013, Microsoft reiterated its interest in a wide range of emerging markets when it launched the Microsoft4Afrika program,[33] which included small and medium-sized enterprises (SMEs) as one of its target audiences, with a view to helping them develop digital skills (and thereby become potential customers of Microsoft software). In South Africa, with input from advisors like Catherine Young, managers such as Warren Larkan actively promoted Microsoft's partnering with smaller firms. The BizSpark program was creatively augmented in conjunction with a government program that led to a more elaborate offering of support to startups. Also, to comply with South African government policy, Microsoft launched a depth partnering program for a small number of software startups that qualified in terms of black-ownership criteria and high innovation potential.[34]

Also in 2013, Microsoft's efforts around community building (notably, the breadth program, BizSpark), accelerators (depth), and seed funding (e.g. a small fund associated with Microsoft's search engine, Bing) were brought under a single umbrella called "Microsoft Ventures."[35]

PHASE 3 MAINSTREAMING STARTUP PARTNERING INTO THE CORE STRATEGY

Scalerator: Shift Toward Later-Stage Startups

In 2014, Steve Ballmer, under whose watch the BizSpark and Accelerator programs had thrived, stepped down as Microsoft CEO. Satya Nadella succeeded Ballmer. Big changes followed. Microsoft Office software was made available on Apple's iPads for the first time[36] and a significant write-off was made on the Nokia smartphone acquisition.[37] Given that even prior to becoming CEO Nadella had championed cloud computing – which was of great relevance to startups – Microsoft's startup managers I spoke to at the time expressed hope that startups would continue to be taken seriously.

By 2015, there was an upsurge in interest in startups among corporations as valuations rose and several so-called unicorns – startups with a valuation of $1 billion – emerged, not only in advanced markets but also in emerging markets like China and India.[38] Thus Microsoft's move into accelerators looked like a prudent move. The rise of cloud computing was also having a profound impact on start-ups, which were no longer constrained by the need to incur upfront expenditure on software infrastructure. The emergence of startup accelerators and other enablers around the world was accompanying the growth of startups in the ecosystems where Microsoft Accelerators already had a presence. That same year, Microsoft launched BizSpark Plus alongside its in-house programs, through which it engaged with over 200 startup accelerators around the world.[39]

The 2016 Global Accelerator Report identified Microsoft accelerators in China, India, and Israel as the leading ones in their respective countries. Weisfeld found that Nadella's vision for Microsoft resonated with his efforts in startup engagement; he once remarked to me, "Microsoft accelerators were 'growth mindset' in action," referring to Nadella's fondness for Professor Carol Dweck's concept regarding the human capacity to believe that change and improvement in one's capabilities is possible and hence strive for it.[40] He observed, "Ten years ago, Microsoft was not seen as relevant or in the loop with the entrepreneurial community," and added that he and his team found it immensely satisfying that Microsoft had come a long way in being supportive of startups: "There's just something about working with startups and entrepreneurs. It's a very emotional journey, but both experiencing and helping them through those ups and downs make it a very giving experience."[41]

In 2016, talking to Ravi Narayan, who was part of Weisfeld's global team, I sensed a shift in thinking regarding the type of start-ups that Microsoft should be welcoming to its accelerators. Although there was no doubt in Narayan's mind that Microsoft's accelerators had added immense value to startups, including in terms of helping them raise funds[42] – in fact, Microsoft was viewed as one of the best accelerators in both China and India and some global rankings[43] – it seemed that it was time for a change. The focus was switching from early-stage to more mature startups.

The rationale was that one of the ways that Microsoft was especially well placed to add value to startups was by helping them sell to Microsoft's enterprise clients – but this typically meant that the startup would have to be somewhat mature to be able to provide workable solutions. Moreover, it seemed that early-stage startups now had other options, such as more conventional accelerators, to turn to. Rather than helping an early-stage startup get to a series A round of funding it seemed more prudent to attract B2B startups that already had reached, or were close to, this milestone and to then propel such startups to scale up by helping them get enterprise customers. In subsequent discussions with other members of the global team based in Israel, it became apparent that Microsoft was going to transform its accelerators into "scalerators."

In 2017, Microsoft launched a new accelerator in Shanghai – China is the only country that has two accelerators – and, sure enough, the focus was explicitly on more mature startups. The transition from accelerator to scalerator seemed to be a natural transition as Microsoft became aware that one of its key ways to add value to startup partners was to help them connect with corporate clients, and this was more likely to be feasible when the startups were relatively mature and so were their offerings. James Chou, who led the accelerator's operations, had assembled an impressive set of startups, all of which had some traction including, in most cases, series A funding. Meanwhile, the Bangalore accelerator had a new leader, Bala Girisaballa, who also was targeting more mature startups.

In 2018, a new avatar of Microsoft's programmatic startup engagement, Microsoft for Startups, was announced.[44] Shortly before that, I had visited Tel Aviv and gotten a further update from Amir Pinchas, who had worked closely with Weisfeld from the start, that a big reorganization was in the cards. Not long after, Weisfeld and his influential team in Israel moved on. When I got an update on the new program, Annie Parker, the then-global lead, was based in Sydney, Australia – the site of the newest addition to the Microsoft accelerator program. She confirmed that what I had observed in my interactions over the previous couple of years had now become official strategy: the focus was on scaling up relatively mature startups. Microsoft for Startups also included a corporate venture capital arm,[45] Microsoft Ventures (later renamed M12[46]).

Perhaps most interestingly, a major feature of startup engagement was a big focus on co-selling startup solutions built on Microsoft's cloud technologies.

Aligning Incentives to Co-Sell with Startups

The Co-Sell program is a key feature of the ScaleUp program, which is what the Microsoft Accelerator program became under the Microsoft for Startups umbrella announced in 2018. What this means is that startup offerings could contribute to a co-sell repository. Microsoft incentivized its salespeople to co-sell partners' offerings just as much as to sell Microsoft's own. The sales force has became incentivized to increase consumption of Microsoft's Azure cloud service, and co-selling startup partners' Azure-based offerings was entirely consistent with this strategy.

The Microsoft journey with startup partnering thus reached an intriguing stage – from business as *un*usual to business as usual. That is, partnering with startups had become tightly aligned with the core of the company's cloud-first strategy. The decisive reorientation of startup engagement to co-selling in 2018 was arguably the culmination of an evolutionary process over a period of more than a decade – notably kickstarted by the BizSpark program introduced in 2008. Dave Drach, who had been part of the original BizSpark team, commented to me: "BizSpark was originally established to get startups on the platform. Now, everyone gets it. So, since that original problem has been solved, the question is: how to yield more value? The answer: through deep engagement yielding more business impact. Satya Nadella has made Azure core to Microsoft's strategy and is concerned with how to make it work for startups."

During 2019, I came across various instances of Microsoft helping its current and alumni startup members to connect with large corporations, such as Walmart and Merck, in a way that was consistent with the new emphasis on co-selling solutions. In essence, Microsoft began connecting members of its startup community with that of more recent entrants to startup partnering in a way that was win-win for the two large corporations as well as the startups. That is, Microsoft could help its startup partners get a corporate client while the latter would be able to quickly get access to high-quality startups. As noted at the outset, in 2019, Walmart's CEO Doug McMillon was given a first-hand account of how Walmart was working with startups that were alumni of Microsoft's accelerator program.

Partnering with Social Ventures

In February 2020, the Microsoft Global Social Entrepreneurship Program, a new global initiative specifically targeted at social entrepreneurs, was launched. My account of Microsoft's startup partnering journey concludes with this announcement by Jean-Philippe Courtois,[47] EVP and president, Microsoft Global Sales, Marketing, and Operations, warranting a final observation regarding social impact.

Even prior to the formal launch of this new initiative, social enterprises had appeared on the corporation's radar.[48] This was evident during my research field trips to Africa. The Microsoft4Afrika initiative had been an avenue through which Microsoft was engaging with African startups, as I learned from Muhammad Nabil, the then head of ISVs and Startups Recruitment. These included social enterprises. During a field visit to Kenya – where Nadella had launched Windows 10 – I learned about Microsoft's efforts to partner with Twiga Foods, a social enterprise that was linking traditional fruit growers with retail outlets, and was using Azure technology.

Microsoft had engaged with social enterprises in other regions as well, such as the Indian subcontinent. To illustrate, Sehat Kahani is a Pakistani startup founded by Dr. Sara Saeed (CEO) and Dr. Iffat Zaffar (COO) that uses telemedicine to provide remote medical advice to patients while at the same time tapping the underutilized capacities of women doctors. In part through partnering with Microsoft,[49] this social enterprise was able to scale its mobile app and gain traction owing to the Covid-19 pandemic, which greatly increased the need for telemedicine.

Through its Global Social Entrepreneurship Program, Microsoft would partner with social enterprises around the world that used Azure "to help create a sustainable, accessible and equitable world"[50] by offering Microsoft Philanthropies grants, connections to other organizations, go-to-market support, and free access to Microsoft technologies including $120,000 of free Azure cloud and $1,000/ month of GitHub Enterprise.[51] Shaloo Garg, Global Lead, Global Microsoft Social Entrepreneurship Program, stated, "Our #1 operating principle for this program is simple. We want 'Founders' to be the center and their success is what drives us. When we designed this program, our key driver was to offer core components like Technology, Grants, Corporate Innovation (co-sell to enterprise customers) to help drive startup success. And we are absolutely jazzed about it."

Three startups were announced as the initial participants: OmniVis, which had built a smartphone-based cholera detection system; Seabin, which tackles marine litter such as microplastics; and Zindi, which generates AI solutions for Africa through its web platform.[52] Success would be measured both by profitability and social impact, including commitment to the ethical and responsible use of AI.[53]

Potentially, initiatives such as Microsoft's social entrepreneurship program have an important role to play in the post-pandemic 2020s decade as the world economy rebuilds and resumes its efforts to achieve the 2030 Sustainable Development Goals.[54]

LESSONS FROM THE MICROSOFT STORY

There are three important facets of Microsoft's startup partnering journey that are worth paying attention to:

1. Co-aligning with strategy – which relates to the *why* of corporate-startup partnering
2. Co-innovating with startups – which relates to the *how* of corporate-startup partnering
3. Co-evolving with ecosystems – which relates to the *where* of corporate-startup partnering

First, in terms of the *why*, two key observations can be made. There is an *imperative for partnering* with startups. Large corporations need to be entrepreneurial to cope with disruption and competitive dynamics in an era of digitalization – and one way this is manifested is through partnering with startups. Indeed, in the Microsoft case, managers like Dan'l Lewin, Zack Weisfeld, and James Chou, among many others, were especially key in driving startup partnering efforts. That said, there is also *challenge in partnering* because of the sheer differences between large corporations and startups. As seen in the Microsoft case, a concerted effort was required in order to better understand startups' circumstances, through talking to the startup community.

Second, in terms of the *how*, again a couple of points are worth making. It is important to identify a *partnering process* that is systematic and addresses the asymmetries between large corporations and startups. In the Microsoft case, a format that was developed that worked well was a cohort-based model that brought a set of high-potential startups together for a prespecified period of time. It is also important to build a *partnering capability* vis-à-vis startups. In the case of Microsoft, there was clearly a capability that had been built, which made it possible to sustain its startup partnering efforts. Key managers like Zack Weisfeld, Bala Girisaballa, and Dave Drach went on to facilitate corporate-startup partnering at other organizations in their post-Microsoft career.

Third, in terms of the *where*, for multinational corporations there is scope for *partnering globally* with startups. In the Microsoft case, important activity took place in a range of settings: North America, Western Europe, and Israel, as well as emerging markets – with strong leadership from headquarters. As Dan'l Lewin observed, "The direction from which all the actions were taken in the market (the subsidiaries) was crafted by the Corporate team (which I lead)." Emerging markets like China and India have continued to be leveraged for startup partnering. Finally, there is scope for *partnering for good* with startups. This was vividly seen in the case of Microsoft's work in Africa, but also elsewhere. By formalizing its efforts to engage with social entrepreneurs Microsoft has demonstrated an intent to contribute towards achieving the 2030 SDGs.

WHAT THIS BOOK IS ABOUT

In sum, the Microsoft story helps us understand the "why," the "how," and the "where" of corporate-startup partnering.

This gives the structure for this book.

This book is about one way in which large corporations can be entrepreneurial: by partnering with external startups. Specifically, it is about key principles and practices that have been distilled from the entrepreneurial actions of managers who helped their corporations engage with startups. To be clear, opening an innovation lab here and organizing a hackathon there won't make a difference. This is about substantive programmatic interventions that could ultimately underpin a more fundamental change of the organization as a whole becoming more entrepreneurial.

This book tackles corporate-startup partnering in three parts (see Figure P.2), with two chapters each.

Why: Co-aligning with Strategy

Chapter 1, Why Entrepreneurship Matters for Large Corporations, deals with the *imperative for partnering* with startups. Corporations need to be entrepreneurial in order to renew themselves in the face of a fast-changing environment. In the face of disruption, some of which may emanate from startups, large corporations have the opportunity to collaborate with startups. There is scope

WHY	HOW	WHERE
(Co-aligning with strategy)	(Co-innovating with startups)	(Co-evolving with ecosystems)
• Imperative for partnering	• Partnering process	• Partnering globally
• Challenges in partnering	• Partnering capability	• Partnering for good

Figure P.2   Overview of *Gorillas Can Dance*

for these very different sets of organizations to combine what each is good at – corporations' efficient use of existing resources and capabilities with startups' agile development of new capabilities and ideas – in a way that is consistent with the corporation's strategic priorities.

Chapter 2, Why Partnering with Startups Isn't Easy, highlights the *challenge in partnering*. While there is a potential for a win-win, it is not straightforward for large corporations and startups to work together naturally. Organizational differences, as well as a power advantage in favor of the large corporation, mean that "business as usual" is unlikely to work in terms of making corporate-startup collaboration feasible or meaningful. Thus the very differences that make these partners attractive to each other may in fact make it difficult for them to work together; effective startup partnering requires recognizing these asymmetries.

How: Co-innovating with Startups

Chapter 3, How to Partner with Startups Systematically, sheds light on the *partnering process*. Entrepreneurial managers within the large corporation have to make a robust effort to make startup partnering work. Doing so entails working out systematic programmatic interventions that help overcome the sheer asymmetries between corporations and systems. Corporations need to discover what formats work more effectively for them. The key is to develop a clear partnering process that will make it more likely that corporations and startups can collaborate in a way that realizes the potential of a win-win partnership.

Chapter 4, Building the Capability to Partner with Startups, is about developing the requisite *partnering capability*. Beyond figuring out a process that works, corporations need a new partnering capability to refine, replace, and add partnering practices over time. Carving out dedicated teams for startup engagement helps build the capability to repeatedly put in place systematic partnering processes and practices. This may take time, but for a corporation that takes startup partnering seriously, the investment of effort is worth it, and indeed essential.

Where: Co-evolving with Ecosystems

Chapter 5, Partnering with Startups Around the World, is concerned with *partnering globally*. For a multinational corporation, there is scope to partner with startups across multiple local milieus. This could range from established clusters in the West like Silicon Valley to outlier ecosystems such as Israel in the Middle East and emerging markets, such as China, India, and, increasingly, Africa. Multinationals like Microsoft have thus been able to harness globalization by tapping entrepreneurial talent around the world, making sure that they adapt practices to local contexts, adopt new practices in locations like Israel, and develop a portfolio of locations that include emerging and developing markets.

Chapter 6, Partnering with Startups as a Force for Good, is exactly about that – *partnering for good*. In addition to jointly creating economic value, there is scope for corporate-startup partnering to have a social impact. This is particularly so in locations like Kenya, for instance, that have traditionally been underserved but have both a growing appetite for entrepreneurship and many socially relevant problems to solve. From the corporation's perspective there is scope to not only build goodwill but also, if it takes a long-term view, reap the benefits of development in those regions, as the demand for their services grow – and the 2030 Sustainable Development Goals are achieved.

The chapter outline is summarized in Figure P.3.

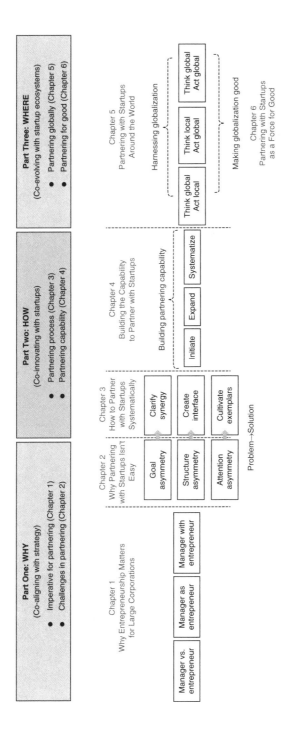

Figure P.3 *Gorillas Can Dance* Chapter Outline

PART ONE

WHY

CHAPTER ONE

WHY ENTRE-PRENEURSHIP MATTERS FOR LARGE CORPORATIONS

When large companies started to work with startups, people initially thought this whole startup thing was "just a trend." I don't think it's a trend at all. It's a fundamental transformation in the way that business innovation occurs.

> – Dave Drach, Vice President–Innovation Sales, Techstars[1]

WHY PARTNER WITH STARTUPS

In the mid-2000s, during the early stages of my research on "dancing with gorillas" – startups partnering with large corporations – I was hard-pressed to find examples of active efforts to make this work. Within a decade, however, things had changed dramatically, with numerous corporations actually having managers with the word "startup" in their job title. The gorillas, it would appear, have been learning to dance.

My research, over 15 years, has involved over 400 interviews with corporate managers, startup entrepreneurs, and other individuals involved in corporate-startup partnering (see "About the Research"). My field interviews have taken me to the Tel Aviv Stock Exchange, where a company called The Floor connects fintech startups, to Zurich, where the stock exchange there is similarly connecting startups with large corporations, and to London, where I met a Silicon Valley–based fintech startup called Crowdz in the Barclays accelerator that is seeking to transform supply chain finance for SMEs, as well as to Munich offices of BMW Startup Garage and Nissan's Infiniti Labs in Hong Kong, where startups are helping these automotive giants to adopt new technologies while at the same time exploring ways to scale their own innovations by dancing with gorillas. I've also conducted many research interviews in emerging markets in Asia, notably China and India, as well as Africa.

Consistent with my observation through field interviews that there was growing interest from large corporations in engaging with entrepreneurship, one BCG study showed that by 2015, nearly half (44%) of the top 30 companies in seven industries had incubators or accelerators, up from 2% in 2010.[2] Such engagement was only expected to grow. Unilever's State of Innovation white paper reported that 80% of corporates believe that engaging with external startups can have a positive impact on corporate innovation, and predicted that by 2025 corporations and startups will be working under the same roof.[3]

There has been an upsurge in efforts by large corporations to partner with startups. In many cases, corporations are specifically seeking to work with startups possessing some form of digital capability. This is true of both information technology (IT) corporations and ones in more traditional sectors. Some corporations – notably some IT companies – started their journey of startup partnering earlier than others. These include companies like Microsoft, IBM, Intel, and SAP, many of which were traditionally not seen as natural allies for startups. Non-IT companies such as Bayer, Nissan, Unilever, and Walmart have, subsequently, come to engage with digital startups. There has been a dramatic rise in managers in corporations and entrepreneurs in startups talking to each other.

Why has this happened? There are three points worth making. First, often the starting point for engaging with startups is in fact a perceived threat from these very organizations – managers in large corporations may be disrupted by startups' entrepreneurs. Second, when considering how to respond to disruption, some managers in large corporations seek to become entrepreneurial themselves, exhibiting proactive, innovative, and risk-taking behaviors. Third, one way that managers manifest their entrepreneurial orientation is by partnering with external startups. Consistent with the notion that innovation can be more open, drawing upon external actors in its ecosystem, large corporations increasingly see the potential for a division of entrepreneurial labor with startups, since they are good at exploiting existing capabilities while startups are adept at exploring new capabilities.

In sum, while entrepreneurs can be a *source of disruption* for managers in large corporations, when managers behave entrepreneurially and engage with the wider ecosystem, startups can be a *source of co-innovation*. To get a fuller picture of how managers have come to reach out to entrepreneurs, this chapter considers three aspects of how their paths have collided (see Figure 1.1).

Figure 1.1 Managers and Entrepreneurs

MANAGERS VERSUS ENTREPRENEURS: THE CHALLENGE OF DISRUPTION

The starting point is consistent with the late Harvard Business School professor Clayton Christensen's argument that entrepreneurs' startups can be a source of disruption for managers in large corporations; some startups' success may come at the expense of incumbents, that is, existing established corporations.[4] Today's large companies that were once entrepreneurial (when they were young) are now being disrupted by startups pursuing new opportunities. By developing new business models, often predicated on digital technologies such as cloud computing, big data, the Internet of Things, and artificial intelligence, the startup can change the rules of the game and adversely affect the incumbent corporation's economic performance. Famously, Amazon disrupted booksellers like Barnes & Noble, Netflix disrupted Blockbuster, Airbnb disrupted hotel chains like Hilton and Marriott, fintech startups are disrupting traditional banks – the list is virtually endless. Thus, in a sense, startups' entrepreneurs have become the nemesis of corporations' managers.

The disruptive effects of startups follow from the opportunities they pursue. Professor Howard Stevenson of Harvard Business School, who introduced the Entrepreneurial Management course for the first time in the 1980s, offered a simple but powerful insight: entrepreneurs differ from managers in that their starting point is an opportunity, not resources.[5] Whereas the more traditional "administrative" management of professional managers in corporations is attuned to optimally using resources that are already controlled, entrepreneurial management involves the pursuit of the identified opportunity. In so doing, the "work" of the entrepreneur is, to a large extent, assembling relevant resources such as people and money.

Even more so in the era of digital innovation, startups' entrepreneurial opportunities cause disruption because they result in business model innovation. At the turn of the century, the dot-com boom reached its peak and then receded – dramatically. But whatever we learned about the risks of irrational exuberance, it was clear that the Internet had changed the world forever. Companies like Amazon were redefining the way that commonplace products like books were sold to buyers of books. The difference was that there could now be new business models – the "how" connecting the "what" (the product) with the "who" (the market). The role of digitalization has continued to grow in leaps and bounds over the past couple of decades, and industries have had to contend with new trends.

Even before Covid-19, many managers were anxious because of disruption – much of it driven by digitalization. Industries from automotive to banking and retail are being disrupted by startups that pursue new opportunities, with a nimble organizational culture, and pursuing business model innovation that are changing the rules of the game in their industry. According to one McKinsey study, 84%

of executives believed that innovation was critical to business success – and at the same time, 80% thought their companies' business models were at risk.[6]

Addressing digital disruption has become one of the defining strategic imperatives of contemporary corporations. There is a growing recognition among corporate managers that business as usual is not good enough to cope with disruption that most industries are facing, especially due to the rise of digitalization. One implication of the prospective adversarial relationship between entrepreneurs (startups) and managers (corporations) is that, inasmuch as startups need to hone administrative management skills as they mature and scale, corporations also need entrepreneurial management skills to combat disruption.

In other words, managers need to become more entrepreneurial.

MANAGERS AS ENTREPRENEURS: RESPONDING TO DISRUPTION

The challenge of disruption does not arise because large corporations aren't good at what they do – it's precisely *because* of it. As the late Professor James March of Stanford University noted, companies are engaged in two types of activity: (1) exploitation that involves leveraging capabilities to do what the company is good at and

(2) exploration that is about developing new capabilities to pursue new activities or ways of doing things.[7] Typically corporations become really good at exploitation, and because this contributes to economic success, managers tend to focus primarily on this, thus crowding out exploration. By contrast, startups focus on exploration, and when their innovation – including of business models – changes the rules of the game, they disrupt large corporations.

That said, notwithstanding the general (and correct) perception that managers focus on the optimal management of resources, some managers have been known to be entrepreneurial – that is, to demonstrate an "entrepreneurial orientation." Entrepreneurship scholars have spent considerable effort understanding the nature and effects of such an orientation,[8] and while this idea has multiple dimensions, three are particularly noteworthy:

1. Proactiveness: This refers to behavior that takes the initiative rather than waiting for something or someone else to do so.
2. Innovativeness: This is about finding creative, unconventional solutions to problems; there may be aspects of product, process, or business model innovation in the activities of entrepreneurs.
3. Risk-taking: This entails carrying out actions despite the probability of failure; experienced entrepreneurs mitigate risk by, for instance, sharing risk with others, and at the same time recognize and accept that their venture is risky to a greater or lesser extent.

Indeed, there is a long tradition of intrapreneurship – the pursuit of entrepreneurship within established corporations – a topic whose popularity has waxed and waned over the years. In the late 1940s Lockheed Martin had a "skunkworks" division that pursued a new product development initiative (exploration) without interfering with the company's daily operations (exploitation).[9] In the 1960s an unconventional adhesive at 3M eventually led, in the early 1970s, to the development of that company's famous yellow sticky notes; 3M famously encouraged employees to use 15% of their time on projects of their own that could help the company. 3M's Dr. Spencer Silver developed the adhesive that would eventually form the basis of the ubiquitous yellow sticky note by accident and then took a personal initiative to identify a use for it, a process that took years, with the involvement of another intrapreneur, Art Fry.[10] In the 1980s Steve Jobs was heavily involved in an intrapreneurial project that led to the creation of the Macintosh. In an interview with *Newsweek*, Jobs pointed out that the idea of taking the "startup garage" into a large corporation setting was exactly what he had done with the Macintosh at Apple.[11] In the 1990s, Ken Kuturagi, a mid-level engineer who tinkered with his young daughter's Nintendo, had the audacity to pursue a side project using his spare time to work on what eventually became the PlayStation.[12]

These celebrated examples of bottom-up intrapreneurship would probably have not very easily come to fruition in a more top-down setting, especially if higher-ups had gotten wind of these ideas when they were nascent. Julian Birkinshaw of London Business School, my coauthor on the "dancing with gorillas" article,[13] would often remark that large companies tend to have a "corporate immune system" that typically quashes novel ideas that don't fit the norm.[14] Hence, intrapreneurs nurturing ideas until they become credible to share has been historically vital. Bottom-up initiatives seen in far-flung subsidiaries at the periphery of multinationals are often like that, as Birkinshaw's early research showed very vividly. For example, an NCR subsidiary in Scotland worked under the radar to demonstrate its technical prowess to headquarters in the United States that led to an expanded mandate.

Common to all of these attempts to generate internal entrepreneurship was an internal focus; these activities were essentially driven by intrapreneurs seeking to leverage resources from within the company. There has been a growing sophistication in the way that intrapreneurship efforts are pursued as corporations seek to systematize the identification and cultivation of intrapreneurs, rather than relying on happy accidents as in the case of 3M's Post-It notes or Sony's Playstation. Various companies have intrapreneurship programs that systematically call for new projects to be pitched, with successful pitches being supported for a period of time and then evaluated to see if a project warrants continued success. Google famously took a leaf out of 3M's intrapreneurship playbook to empower employees to use up to 20% of their time on their own ideas that were relevant to the company; Gmail is one of many innovations to result from these efforts.[15]

Today, many companies have sought to develop systematic ways of promoting intrapreneurship. Samsung's C-Lab offers an example of this.[16] Cohorts of intrapreneurs are given resources and time off to pursue ideas that hold some relevance to the corporation. In some cases, successful intrapreneurial projects are spun off into independent entities – and the originating corporation might even invest in them. Intrapreneurship has the advantage of providing some risk mitigation to the individuals involved – even if the project fails, they still have a job. In some cases, as with Samsung, the end result when everything goes to plan is a spun-off business (that may get funding from its corporate venture capital arm). For instance, TagHive, which was founded in Seoul in 2017 to develop smart toys and mobile solutions for children, resulted from the Samsung intrapreneurship program. Samsung is a strategic investor in the startup.[17] In other cases, the team derives satisfaction from seeing the project being adopted by a business unit and commercialized in a way that generates revenues for the corporation and, usually, some form of reward for the intrapreneur.

Nowadays even subsidiaries may launch systematic intrapreneurial programs. For example, Intel China's Ideas2Reality (now rechristened GrowthX) program is a fascinating example of subsidiary-based entrepreneurship with a systematic programmatic structure (as opposed to being an ad hoc or one-off initiative). In 2015, following the Chinese government's call for promoting mass entrepreneurship, the leadership of Intel China subsidiary's charged Kapil Kane, Director of Innovation, with the task of fostering an entrepreneurial mindset among their large pool of engineering talent.[18]

I ended up playing a cameo in influencing the thinking that went into Kane's efforts. An MBA student of mine who was interning with Kane told him about my dancing with gorillas research. When we met over lunch in Shanghai and exchanged notes, it quickly became apparent to me that Kane's thinking – which struck me as refreshing – was consistent with the spirit of intrapreneurship. I readily agreed to give a talk, sharing thoughts from my research (in particular, about intrapreneurship) at his next meeting with Intel China engineers.

I titled my talk "Entrepreneurship Inside," encircling these words on my title slide with Intel's swooshes to mimic the "Intel Inside" logo. Kane, who had essentially been an intrapreneur even in his previous roles at Apple and Intel, got the point immediately, resonating greatly with the notion of intrapreneurship. Typically, it takes intrapreneurs to facilitate the intrapreneurship of others by initiating and running such programs. Such individuals need to have a good understanding of both the external environment and the internal realities (including politics) that provide both resources and constraints. Organizations with a culture that makes intrapreneurs feel empowered and valued are more likely to remain competitive in the face of discontinuous change.

In the weeks that followed, with further input from others, Kane created a systematic intrapreneurship program to support internal teams with promising projects that leveraged Intel's technology and had market potential. Interestingly, some of these internal teams have found that they can accelerate their progress greatly by partnering with *external* startups. For example, one Intel team was working on a facial recognition technology to operate doors, and were on the lookout for an OEM partner to co-develop the solution and bring it to market. Curbing the normal instinct to partner with another large corporation, Kane helped this team connect with an external startup in Hangzhou. As he explained to me: "Typically, large corporates look to other large corporates to co-develop because they both speak the same language and feel safe working with each other. However, after I helped this team connect with an external startup in Hangzhou, the ensuing collaboration brought the project to fruition within three months."

Intel China's experience shows that while intrapreneurship programs hold promise and will continue to be an important part of company's corporate innovation toolset, value can also be created by engaging with external startups. Indeed, some intrapreneurs may choose not to restrict their focus to the inside of their organizations; they may attempt to help their corporations to be entrepreneurial by partnering with external startups.[19] In the twenty-first century, there has been a growing recognition of the importance of open innovation and an ecosystem mindset. Startup partnering has emerged as an integral component of companies' pursuit of innovation-related activity in conjunction with external partners. This allows new possibilities such as a startup creating new applications based on the large corporation's core technology or even the two partners working jointly on new offerings. In other words, some intrapreneurs look *outward* to engage with external startups, resulting in a third perspective: managers *with* entrepreneurs.

MANAGERS WITH ENTREPRENEURS: PARTNERING WITH EXTERNAL STARTUPS

There has been growing recognition among corporate managers that external entrepreneurs can be co-opted as allies rather than viewed exclusively as competitive disruptors. And typically, the managers leading the charge in terms of external startup engagement at corporations are intrapreneurial themselves. That is, their act of entrepreneurship within a large corporation is to build bridges with startups.

This makes eminent sense, as large corporations have become mindful of the value of complementing internal R&D efforts with external collaborations, which Professor Henry Chesbrough and others refer to as "openness" in innovation.[20] The importance of this openness is reiterated by the need for an ecosystem mindset highlighted by Professor Ron Adner[21] and others. Even though Microsoft eventually did not fare well in mobile telephony, the observation at a press conference regarding the strategic alliance with Nokia that companies were engaged in a "war of ecosystems" was on point.[22] Orchestrating ecosystems of partners has become one of the strategic imperatives of the digital age. Startups have emerged as an important constituent of corporations' innovation ecosystems.

Corporate-startup partnering can be viewed as a "division of entrepreneurial labor" between corporations and startups. My first teaching job, following my doctoral and post-doctoral research, was at Glasgow University's business school, which is named after the father of modern economics, Adam Smith, one of the most esteemed professors in its history. Smith's insight into the division of labor revolutionized the study of economic activity. The eminent international business scholar, Professor Peter Buckley, and I have worked together to apply this perspective to corporate-startup partnering.[23]

The starting point is that the threat of, and response to, disruption reflects an underlying tension: that between exploration and exploitation. Large corporations are good at exploitation: they tend to stay on the path they are pursuing and have experienced success on. But success in the present could come at the expense of growth in the future. By contrast, innovative startups tend to be adept at exploration: their focus is on new possibilities based on capabilities that they are building. While on the one hand there can be conflict as a result (manager *versus* entrepreneur), on the other there is also the potential for collaboration (manager *with* entrepreneur) – whereby startups' competence in exploration is combined with corporations' adeptness at exploration. That is, while being entrepreneurial is important, one doesn't have to do everything oneself. Corporations can leverage what they are good at in tandem with what startups are good at. This division of entrepreneurial labor can be viewed in terms of the three

	Corporation	Startup
Proactiveness	Exploiting an existing market	Exploring a new niche
Innovativeness	Downstream – advantage of largeness/oldness	Upstream – advantage of smallness/newness
Risk-taking	Flexibility deficit needs to be addressed	Legitimacy deficit needs to be addressed

Figure 1.2 The Corporate-Startup Division of Entrepreneurial Labor
Source: Adapted from Buckley and Prashantham.[24]

aspects of entrepreneurial behavior noted previously: (1) proactiveness, (2) innovativeness, and (3) risk-taking (see Figure 1.2).

In terms of proactiveness, there may be the scope to combine a startup's exploration of a new niche market with a corporation's exploitation of existing markets. In relation to innovativeness, the large company's expertise in downstream (marketing) activities could be pooled with the upstream (innovation) capabilities of startups. In terms of risk-taking, the large corporation's legitimacy can benefit startups while their flexibility could help large corporations.

Clearly, numerous corporations have caught on to the prospect of such a division of entrepreneurial labor, and many have begun partnering initiatives targeted at startups.[25] This includes traditional corporations. For example, at Unilever, the FMCG giant, a manager named Jeremy Basset was the intrapreneur whose efforts led to establishing the Unilever Foundry program that helps generate solutions, including around digital marketing, from startups.[26] Such efforts are different from the practice of corporate venture capital (CVC). Rather than taking minority equity stakes, these intrapreneurs co-innovate with startups via project-based innovation engagement in the form of pilots or R&D projects without investing in them.

Indeed, many of the companies that I studied, such as BMW and SAP, did have their own CVC arms. However, the startup partnering efforts that I studied – such as BMW Startup Garage or SAP Startup Focus (since replaced by other initiatives) – were devoid of equity investment. Through these initiatives, the companies engaged with a wider pool of startups than a CVC team typically would, which gave them the flexibility to include some earlier-stage startups than those that a CVC unit would typically invest in.

In the case of BMW, the creation of the Startup Garage program was reflective of strategic imperatives, in terms of digital disruption, faced by the automotive industry. Gregor Gimmy, a co-founder of the program, was originally from Germany but had returned from Silicon Valley, where he had been an entrepreneur and consultant in the design firm Ideo. Gimmy's contrarian thinking made its mark on the BMW Startup Garage in aspects such as its startup-friendly visual identity and outreach through being a keynote speaker in multiple startup ecosystem events.

In the case of SAP, the Startup Focus was a top-down initiative that followed from key strategic imperatives. SAP had made the strategic decision to develop platform technologies such as the HANA platform. In 2012, the SAP Startup Focus was launched as an initiative to partner with startups and bring them onto SAP's platform. This was a huge change for a corporation known around the world for providing ERP solutions to some of the largest companies in the world. It was entrusted by the chairman to the then-CTO, Vishal Sikka, who operated out of Silicon Valley. Eventually, a vice president, Manju Bansal, led the program, also from Palo Alto. By locating the initiative in the world's most innovative startup ecosystem, SAP was sending out a signal of the seriousness of its intent. Bansal made strenuous efforts to connect with colleagues worldwide.

The big concern, of course, is that in the absence of boundary spanners like Bansal, when such initiatives are located away from headquarters and mainstream business units, they have little tangible effect on the organization. This is why spanning boundaries within the corporation becomes important. People like Bansal and Gimmy were thus crucial in acting as a bridge between the corporate and startup worlds. They needed to be relatable by startups as well as trusted by corporations. This underlines the importance of having entrepreneurial individuals – including perhaps former startup entrepreneurs – in crucial bridging roles. Also, it could help a lot to pair such individuals with a corporate veteran, which was exactly the case with Gimmy, who co-founded the BMW Startup Garage with Dr. Matthias Meyer, a BMW insider.

Although some of these entrepreneurs have aggressively promoted their modus operandus as being superior to CVC, I tend to view non-equity partnering and CVC as complementary tools in the corporate innovation toolkit. Some partnering efforts – for instance, Bayer and Telefonica – do have provisions to have some equity participation. But the bigger point is this, which was articulated eloquently to me by an expert on CVC, Gerald Brady of Silicon Valley Bank: "The bit that companies need to get right is *partnering*. You can't be investing without partnering. You can partner without investing."

Thus, irrespective of whether an equity- or non-equity-based approach is employed, what is key is to work with startups as *partners* – an idea reiterated by Jeremy Basset, the intrapreneur at Unilever whose efforts led to establishing the Unilever Foundry program: "I learned that it didn't really matter what ideas we came up with; someone in the world was already doing something in that space. Today, growth is enabled, not so much through joint ventures or acquisitions but through genuine partnerships."[27]

SCOPE FOR WIN-WIN COLLABORATION

A key message in this chapter is that seeking to be intrapreneurial doesn't preclude engaging with external entrepreneurship – in fact, it is a powerful way in which an intrapreneur can help to turbocharge corporate innovation. As noted, there is scope for a division of entrepreneurial labor: collaborating based on complementary strengths for mutual benefit. Each partner has strengths that the other lacks. This can lead to three interrelated benefits: legitimacy, learning, and leads (see Figure 1.3).

	Benefits for Corporation	Benefits for Startup
Legitimacy (with respect to each other)	Building culture of a partner of choice; winning hearts and minds	Increases access to funding because investors take them more seriously
Learning (within the partnerships)	Access to novel ideas, business model innovation	Improves technical knowhow
Leads (in the interfirm network or ecosystem)	Greater value creation offered by leveraging its interfirm ecosystem	Enhances market access, especially in B2B markets

Figure 1.3 Benefits of Corporate-Startup Partnering

Legitimacy

For a startup it is easy to see that there is credibility by association when it partners with an established large corporation. Having "alumni" status from a Microsoft Accelerator has been helpful to startups around the world in numerous ways. First, some entrepreneurs have told me that this has made it easier to attract *key employees*. Second, many entrepreneurs have mentioned that prospective *investors* have taken them more seriously as a result of their association with a large corporation. Third, doors to prospective *customers* – especially enterprise customers – have opened more readily.

Perhaps somewhat counterintuitively, even large corporations can gain legitimacy benefits from becoming adept at startup partnering. As engaging with startups becomes more pervasive, corporations are increasingly competing with one another for the hearts and minds of the best startups. Gaining a reputation as a partner of choice for startups therefore holds an attraction to a large corporation. Such reputation is multidimensional and more likely to arise when startups perceive corporations as fair and trustworthy, sincere about engaging meaningfully with startups (not merely paying lip service), and competent at managing the partnering process.

Learning

Although startups are often strong in the niche that they specialize in, they are often able to expand their knowledge base by partnering with large corporations. First, they may gain access to certain complementary know-how, and understand the corporation's technology roadmap in those areas. Second, getting into close proximity to a large corporation gives them valuable exposure to well-established business processes and a high degree of professionalization – which young firms typically lack but aspire to eventually acquire. Third, they are likely to obtain a deeper understanding of how the wider interfirm ecosystem network works.

From a corporation's point of view, there is the scope to complement its core areas of know-how in various ways. First, it may obtain access to expertise in complementary niches that results in useful applications added to its core offering. Second, they may be able to plug some gaps in their know-how by incorporating the startup's know. (In such cases, at a certain point, the corporation might decide to acquire the startup.) Third, the corporation may learn new business models from its startup partners. All of this can be synthesized to yield more integrated offerings that result in new business leads and thus revenue-generating opportunities, as noted next.

Leads

From a startup's perspective, new business opportunities may arise in partnership with the gorilla or other members of the ecosystem in multiple ways. First, the gorilla itself may become a customer of the startup, commissioning a proof-of-concept project or similar. Second, there may be joint go-to-market opportunities involving the gorilla's and the startup's complementary competences. Third, possibilities may arise for a startup to combine resources with other ecosystem members and, together, pursue new sales opportunities and business growth.

For large corporations, there can be augmented services and offerings by combining their core capabilities with those of the startup partners. First, they may be able to meet certain needs of customers that they couldn't do previously, thereby enhancing their revenue-generating potential. Second, they may have new sales opportunities because of new business models adopted from the startup partner. Third, they might even be able to target new business areas or hitherto unreached customers, thanks to novel capabilities learned from startup partners.

But . . . Partnering with Startups Is Attractive – But Not Straightforward

A common refrain I have heard – from both corporate managers and startup entrepreneurs – is that there is scope for a win-win relationship between their organizations. Yet, almost in the same breath, those who have attempted these partnerships also say, "it's not so easy." Despite the growing interest in partnering with startups as a tool of corporate innovation, many corporations are still figuring out how to make it work. One study by Arthur D. Little revealed that 83% of the corporate managers surveyed deemed collaborating with startups to be of long-term importance, but only 28% considered themselves to be highly experienced at startup engagement.[28] Getting there will call for gaining expertise in how to engage with startups.

In fact, one of the reasons why the phrase "dancing with gorillas" seems to have resonated with so many people I have come across is that it seems to connote a sense of danger that startups feel vis-à-vis large corporations – and large corporations, on their part, also have to work hard at overcoming the barriers that exist between them and startups.

When I met BMW Startup Garage's co-founder, Gregor Gimmy, in Munich, he explained to me that he had to put in a great deal of effort to make the partnering initiative's logo, website, and even office décor sufficiently different from BMW's standard corporate branding in order to be startup-friendly. That illustrates the huge differences between corporations and startups. Of course, the fact that several large corporations have still bothered to make the effort to find ways to partner effectively with startups underlines the prospect of win-win collaborations. In BMW's case, the disruption of the automotive industry had prompted a desire to collaborate with innovative startups around areas like cybersecurity, connectivity, autonomous driving, electrification, and the shared economy.

But this required recognizing that there are *asymmetries* between corporations and startups that mean that, on the one hand, the great differences between them make them attractive to each other as complementary partners and yet, on the other hand, these *very* differences mean that working together is not straightforward.

Chapter 2 takes a closer look at the asymmetries between corporations and startups.

WHY PARTNERING WITH STARTUPS ISN'T EASY

It's very difficult for a large organization to stimulate the same sort of incentives and flexibility that exist for an entrepreneur. We come from this background of "plan and perfect." We research things very well. When we launch things we really invest in them. . . . This is the antithesis of what is needed in an entrepreneurial environment.

– Jeremy Basset, Founder, Unilever Foundry[1]

SCOPE FOR WIN-WIN . . . BUT ASYMMETRIES TO OVERCOME

While on paper there is excellent scope for a division of entrepreneurial labor between large corporations and startups, there is also a challenge.

Asymmetries pertain to the very basis for potential win-win collaboration, stemming from large corporations' well-oiled exploitation of existing capabilities at scale while startups are well placed to pursue exploration with agility. As Professor James March argued three decades ago, established organizations tend to incrementally improve the capabilities that have served them well (exploitation), while younger firms build new ones to be able to be competitive (exploration).[2]

Ironically, these differences give rise both to the potential for mutually beneficial relationships *and* to considerable asymmetries between corporations and startups that impede the prospect of collaborating with each other. Even if there is enthusiasm to dialog with startups *precisely because* large corporations are more adept at exploitation and startups at exploration, there are deeply embedded differences that cannot be changed overnight, and stand in the way of successful partnering.

Of course, what I describe might sound like a caricaturization of large organizations. However, while it is true that some large corporations have made considerable progress in recent years in making adjustments to work with startups (described in Chapters 3 and 4), it is not always smooth sailing even for the managers driving startup engagement in those companies. Moreover, it is certainly the case that for managers working in corporations that are laggards when it comes to startup partnering, it is important to have a deep understanding of corporate-startup asymmetries. Otherwise, these companies will continue to watch from the sidelines and not make inroads into the challenging but rewarding journey of startup partnering.

The upshot is that despite the intent to engage with startups, I've found that all too many corporate managers bump up against long-seated ways of *planning*, *organizing*, and *executing* that pose barriers to partnering with startups. Corresponding to each of these three facets, three asymmetries are especially relevant:

1. Goal asymmetry (relating to planning)
2. Structure asymmetry (relating to organizing)
3. Attention asymmetry (relating to executing)

Each of these asymmetries comes in the way of achieving the three mutual benefits of legitimacy, learning, and leads, discussed in Chapter 1 (see Figure 2.1). In this chapter we take a look at how this happens in order to form the basis of understanding the "how" of corporate-startup partnering in Part Two (Chapters 3 and 4) of this book.

	Goal Asymmetry (Planning)	Structure Asymmetry (Organizing)	Attention Asymmetry (Executing)
Legitimacy [Vis-à-vis startup ecosystem]	Lack of commonality with startups	Lack of connectivity to startups	Lack of confidence in startups
Learning [From the partnership]	Learning styles seen as incompatible	Learning opportunities seen as inaccessible	Learning outcomes seen as ineffective
Leads [Within the wider interfirm ecosystem]	Ecosystem eligibility has restrictive norms	Ecosystem networking has limited touchpoints	Ecosystem partnering has stringent criteria

Figure 2.1 Three Asymmetries That Impede Corporate-Startup Partnering

GOAL ASYMMETRY

To start with, consider differences arising from the approach that large corporations take while *planning* – which is in marked contrast to that of startups. As noted previously, large corporations' managers are primarily geared toward managing resources whereas startups' entrepreneurs focus on pursuing opportunities. Large corporations adopt a more formal (and inflexible) approach to planning based on longer decision horizons compared to startups. Furthermore, managers and startups have different approaches to pursuing goals – the former start with the end and figure out the means, whereas the latter may well do the opposite. And there is a much greater emphasis on control and coordination, with a view to mitigating execution risk. These differences – goal asymmetries – play out in ways that suppress the benefits of legitimacy, learning, and leads, resulting in the potential for partnering with startups not being clearly recognized or understood (even if a vague sense of the benefits exists).

Lack of Commonality with Startups

Corporate managers' focus on managing resources optimally (as opposed to entrepreneurs' pursuit of opportunities) leads to an emphasis on efficiency-oriented goals. This tends to favor engaging with similar, rather than dissimilar, others. From the perspective of dealing with other organizations, a "similar other" might be another big corporation or even a smaller company that has, over time, harmonized its way of working with that of the large corporation in question. Working with such companies – as opposed to dissimilar others – would be consistent with the goal of efficiently exploiting a company's existing capabilities; and this could come in the way of naturally building *legitimacy* vis-à-vis the startup ecosystem.

In my view, this distinction echoes what Professor Robert Putnam of Harvard University describes as bonding and bridging ties.[3] Bonding ties are those with people who are similar to us, bridging ties with those who are dissimilar. Similarity depends on the context: in relation to sports, it might be age or gender (at the risk of stereotyping, I am more likely to have common sporting interests with other males than females), whereas in relation to food, it might be culture or ethnicity (I am more likely to have common culinary tastes with fellow Asians than non-Asians, for instance).

Bonding and bridging ties are good for different things: bonding ties (which tend to be stronger and have many mutual connections) are conducive to building trust, whereas bridging ties (which tend to be weaker and have few mutual connections) are useful for yielding novelty, in terms of information, ideas, and opportunities. When pursuing efficiency in operations, a company is likely to gravitate toward bonding ties with similar others that speak the same language and approach planning in a similar way.

Partnerships between corporations and startups are essentially bridging ties. That is, these organizations are vastly dissimilar from each other in ways that are relevant to innovation – including their size in terms of employees, organizational complexity, and availability of resources.

Thus these relationships have the benefits of bridging ties – the opportunity to do new things that would be difficult on their own or even with other bonding ties. But these relationships suffer from challenges stemming from the very differences that yield novelty.

Thus the starting point in understanding goal asymmetries – because of large corporations' focus on efficiently pursuing their goals – is a simple one: they don't see commonality with startups. And while of course this is the very reason for wanting to partner with them, the lack of commonality means that establishing legitimacy in the eyes of the startup community will likely involve going against the grain, a challenge that not all managers who talk about the prospect of partnering with startups realize.

Incompatible Learning Styles

The pursuit of efficiency translates into a planning style that Jeremy Basset, who set up Unilever's startup partnering program, describes as "plan and perfect" – and this could be problematic in terms of *learning* outcomes via corporate-startup partnering.

Corporate planning processes are detailed and time-consuming. By contrast, startups are in a hurry; if they don't get a response to a collaborative partnership within days, they could die – or at least, that is the sense of urgency with which they operate. For large corporations, even when they are acting fast (by their standards) to deal with the challenge of disruptive innovation, their planning horizons are typically much longer than those of startups, for whom the disparity can be frustrating. One entrepreneur I interviewed recounted how exasperating it was to deal with a large Californian multinational that most industry observers would in fact have described as a fairly fast-moving corporation. This entrepreneur described the manager he was dealing with as "a know more" because, as he put it, "all this guy wanted to do was know more about this process of ours or that solution we had . . . while himself moving really slowly. We wasted three months of our precious time dealing with this slowpoke."

This difference makes it difficult for corporations and startups to work together collaboratively in a manner that yields learning outcomes of mutual benefit. Professor Saras Sarasvathi makes an intriguing distinction between how managers and entrepreneurs approach the pursuit of goals, which underlines their differences in planning and, by implication, learning styles.[4] She says that for managers, decision-making tends to be causal; the end is decided first, and the means follow, whereas, by contrast, for entrepreneurs, decision-making tends to be effectual; the means are the starting point, and the end follows. To elaborate, corporations are staffed by managers – and this is very evident in the work of middle managers in particular – who think in a very linear way. They start with objectives and proceed to assemble and leverage the means that will help them to achieve their ends. Their approach to decision-making can be described as being *causal*. By contrast, the entrepreneurs of startups often go about things in exactly the opposite way. They start with the means at their disposal – such as expertise and contacts – and then work backwards to identify the ends that they *can* pursue. Their approach to decision-making can be described as being *effectual*.

Each approach can work well on its own, but when these disparate approaches collide – which likely occurs when managers from large corporations and entrepreneurs from startups engage – then there could be potential difficulties. At the risk of overgeneralizing, managers operate in an environment lacking flexibility. Corporations are focused on specific objectives – chiefly involving the optimal use of existing resources – making it difficult to be agile or flexible. Corporate managers have low motivation to experiment with new ideas. While this is one of the reasons that agile startups become interesting to work with, it means that compatibility of goals – and by extension, of learning styles – is not self-evident. Thus, in terms of learning through partnerships, corporate managers and startup entrepreneurs have fundamentally differing orientations. As such, goal asymmetry can impede learning outcomes – one of the potential benefits of corporate-startup partnering.

Restrictive Norms for Ecosystem Eligibility

The strong desire for control reflects a certain inflexibility in the planning process, which, ironically, is one of the features of large corporations that partnering with startups is meant to help reduce. As Professor Ron Adner notes, managers' emphasis is all too often on managing execution risk; what gets missed out on is the role of the wider interfirm ecosystem.[5] The emphasis on control and coordination may encourage a tendency to focus on vertical relationships, which are associated with supply chain operations or acquisitions, rather than the horizontal partnering that helps generate business *leads*.

One executive of a major US automotive corporation once said to me, "Your ideas about partnering with startups are fascinating, but in a company like mine we are far too obsessed with control to be able to be a true partner." He went on to relate to me how the company had just acquired an attention-grabbing startup in the mobility space. Within a couple of years another executive from this company was narrating to me how that acquisition had unraveled. To be honest, I wasn't totally surprised. Now, to be clear, the moral of the story isn't that acquiring companies is futile; rather, it is that many corporations have a propensity for controlling others that goes against the grain of what it takes to make collaborative horizontal relationships work – especially vis-à-vis startups. The DNA of large corporations' strategic planning processes means that their default position is to view startups as outsiders.

Even though many companies have begun talking about ecosystems and open innovation, their planning procedures are still geared toward vertical rather than horizontal relationships, predicated on control. Even when there is scope within the planning processes of corporations to explore horizontal relationships, it is relatively difficult for startups to be eligible for horizontal relationships – such as a co-innovation alliance, for instance – within the wider ecosystem. Some startups I have studied have found that when they approached a large corporation with a proposal to collaborate, they were more likely to be considered for specific time-bound vertical supply chain roles – such as niche, project-based services – than as a horizontal partner on the basis of its intellectual property.

Thus although the importance of ecosystem thinking is taking root in many large corporations, their planning processes and orientation toward control mean that certain prospective partners are "outsiders" that don't readily "fit" into their scheme of things vis-à-vis orchestrating an interfirm network or ecosystem. The greater propensity for top-down vertical partnerships with actors that conform to their network orchestration norms tends to have an exclusionary effect on startups as potential partners. The emphasis is on control over creativity.

Although there have been dramatic changes in many corporations, I keep coming across very traditionally bureaucratic corporations whose planning processes are so tightly controlled that they favor working with highly similar organizations – if not in size then in terms of ethos and the willingness to essentially execute on requirements provided. There is nothing wrong with having top-down vertical relationships with exchange partners in the supply chain. However, doing this to the exclusion of horizontal links to dissimilar ones – such as startups – that have the potential to provide novel information and ideas is a missed opportunity.

In addition to reducing the appetite for taking risks, formal planning processes that lack flexibility also potentially accentuate an all-too-human tendency: people tend to resist ideas and solutions that are "not invented here" (NIH). One startup I studied seemed to find that managers within large corporations generally viewed a startup as an outsider, a feeling that partially resulted from a sense of feeling threatened. This startup had made progress in a mobile telephony software that had the potential to address an emergent trend in the industry, and had done so more rapidly than the large incumbent corporations. Yet the reactions of the large corporations that resisted the chance to partner with this startup indicated a sense of feeling self-indicted if they agreed to the collaboration. That is, working with that startup would be an admission of having failed to come up with the technology themselves. A senior manager in that corporation admitted to me, "This startup has complementary expertise we can use, but getting them on board will require some tact to assuage the concerns of the engineers who will think they should have done this themselves."

✳ ✳ ✳

In sum, the goal asymmetry between corporations and startups, resulting from their considerable differences in planning, adversely affects all three potential benefits of partnering with each other: legitimacy, learning, and leads. Thus even if there is a vague sense that engaging with startups would be useful – or fun – managers quickly recognize the sheer dissimilarity between themselves and entrepreneurs, resulting in *resistance* to engage, which is likely to be reciprocated by the startups as well.

STRUCTURE ASYMMETRY

Having looked at three aspects of planning (goal asymmetry) that come in the way of recognizing the potential for startup partnering, consider differences in *organizing* (structure asymmetry). An organization's structure has a big impact on how planned strategy is executed because it directs the flow of information and interactions between individuals within the organization as well between those inside and outside the organization (e.g. customers or partners). Following from the way they plan – which, as noted, tends to be based on formal, long-term procedures that are controlled and coordinated – large corporations organize themselves in a way that is oriented toward exploitation, and is hierarchical and siloed. In contrast to startups, corporations have multiple business units or divisions with clearly defined hierarchical and specialist roles. These organizational differences reflect size and scale, as well as the age of these sets of companies. Hence, even if there is some level of recognition of the potential for a win-win relationship, there are still other problems stemming from differences in organizational structure that impede the benefits of legitimacy, learning, and leads.

Lack of Connectivity to Startups

Normally, partly because of differences in structure, the paths of corporations and startups don't cross naturally. This can get in the way of corporations developing *legitimacy* as a potentially promising partner in the eyes of the startup community.

Large established companies usually have structures that are inflexible and siloed, with hierarchies ossifying the inclination toward doing more of the same (that is, exploitation rather than exploration). External-facing units are typically involved in engaging with prospective or existing enterprise customers driven by sales targets or with operational partners that tend to have mature routines. Even organizational units in large corporations that do engage actively with external audiences, notably customers and suppliers, usually exclude startups. In a business-to-business (B2B) selling context, often large corporations are dealing with more mature organizations (even established SMEs but usually not startups), while in a business-to-consumer (B2C) setting the question of engaging with startups doesn't even arise. As such, when it comes to reaching out to a new audience such as the startup community, without interventions, there has traditionally been a lack of conduits that allow corporations to readily build connections with startups.

Furthermore, while these days one might hear of hackathons and corporate accelerators – and these could well be part of the solution to partnering with startups (as will be discussed in Chapter 3) – all too often such activities appear to be casual, faddish efforts that do little to help corporations to develop legitimacy with the startup community. This is because the way large corporations organize in the form of formal, bureaucratic, and hierarchical structures allows for little, if any, meaningful outreach to the startup community.

In the very early stages of my research, even Microsoft – which today is heavily engaged in startup engagement – didn't have a readily accessible organizational structure through which startups could procure their software. The experience that most startups had several years ago when contacting resellers (distributors) of Microsoft was that their calls weren't returned because they were mere startups; those resellers preferred dealing with more mature business customers, which were perceived to be more stable and thus a more reliable source of recurring revenue.

While things are very different at Microsoft today, this still remains the state of affairs in many traditional corporations. Not that long ago, I was speaking about corporate-startup partnering at a breakfast seminar organized by *The Economist*. During the Q&A session, a senior manager at a prominent Fortune 100 US corporation said to me, "My biggest problem is that I don't know where to start if I want to dialog with startups . . . I get what you're saying about working with startups, I really get it . . . but what should my first move be?" We will get to the specifics of the startup partnering process in Chapters 3 and 4, but for now the point to note is that in the normal course of things, large corporations' organizational structures lack natural conduits or pathways to engage with the startup community.

One exception is the notion of a "scouting unit," which some corporations have put in place as a listening post and conduit to engage with startups. Two locations where I have found this phenomenon to be especially prominent are Silicon Valley and Israel. More recently, some of these efforts have been closely linked to the sort of startup partnering initiatives that are discussed in the next chapter. But until recently, the few scouting units that existed were few and far between and, as mentioned, restricted to one or two prominent locations. And these too were vulnerable to be being faddish efforts that weren't taken seriously back at headquarters.[6]

As such, the organizational structures of large corporations preclude ready interaction with startups, and thus constitute an impediment to building legitimacy in the eyes of startups.

Inaccessible Learning Opportunities

Even if corporate managers recognize that there could be some win-win scenario in working with a startup, one of the classic difficulties arising from the way large corporations are structured – hierarchical and specialized – is that it is difficult to identify role counterparts within these very disparate sets of organizations, which in turn makes it difficult to harness *learning* outcomes.

This is a problem that does not exist as much when two large corporations work together. A vice president of marketing in one organization can readily identify his or her counterpart in another organization, and is more likely to have their email replied to or phone call returned. 'Twas ever thus: as long ago as the mid-1980s, Professor Yves Doz of INSEAD highlighted the difficulty posed by the lack of role counterparts between large corporations and startups.[7] (He was writing about an early instance of corporate venture capital at the time.) Of course, one exception to the difficulty of corporations and startups working together is the case of pharmaceutical corporations working with biotech startups. But that was a specific case, one that was highly technical. Beyond this, good examples of regular partnering between corporations and startups were hard to find when I began my research.

Part of the challenge, beyond the obvious disparity arising from size and scale of the operations of corporations and startups, is the degree of specialization in roles. Within large corporations, there are more specialists, with delineated responsibilities. By contrast, although startups will also likely have some division of labor among its employees, the boundaries tend to be much more fluid, and individuals – especially those in key positions of responsibility, notably the entrepreneur – tend to wear multiple hats. So leaving aside the differences in the organizational chart between a corporation and startup, the different ethos and limits of responsibility of individuals in each type of organization are likely to make it difficult for individuals from each company to sit across the table and feel like they are genuinely talking to a counterpart.

A corollary of this situation is that startups are often frustrated when trying to proactively reach out to a large corporation because it often proves difficult, if not impossible, to find the "right" person within that organization to talk to. I can no longer remember the number of times I have come across exasperated entrepreneurs who've felt that they'd wasted up to three months (sometimes more) to get through to someone in the large corporation who had sufficient authority – and an ecosystem mindset – to be interested *and* able to start making things happen in a partnership. And in those relatively rare instances, especially early on in my research, it seemed that the startup had essentially lucked out in finding an unusually entrepreneurial manager within the corporation who could, and was willing to, take an interest in dialoging with the entrepreneur. But such instances were typically one-offs that were hard to replicate with other managers in the large organization.

The result of this difficulty in finding counterparts is that forming interorganizational relationships between corporations and startups is not straightforward – which means that the prospect for co-learning is impeded because opportunities to do so don't arise readily.

Limited Touchpoints for Ecosystem Networking

The prospect of gaining valuable *leads* (that is, mutually beneficial opportunities for driving revenue growth, directly or indirectly) typically involves going beyond some initial point of contact between a corporate manager and startup entrepreneur to engage some other entities, internal or external, in the corporation's ecosystem. For instance, a particular internal business unit might have a need that the startup's offering is ideal for, or a partner organization could be a suitable distributor of it. However, the differences in organizational structure between a corporation and startup make it harder to yield leads.

The main difficulty stems from the fact that the organizational structure in large corporations tends to be siloed; in general, managers in a given business unit tend not to be intimately aware of what other units are involved in at a given point in time. Therefore the prospect of a startup having more touchpoints with other internal and external units of the corporation doesn't readily materialize. Due to the siloed organizational structure, there is typically a lack of managers who can "span boundaries" across these units in a way that results in a startup's offering being better utilized by the wider corporation and its ecosystem in mutually value-creating ways.

As a result, what I often found in my research was that even when a startup was able to find an interested manager to enter into a dialog with, getting traction with the wider corporate network did not prove easy. This is not to say that boundary-spanning managers do not exist in large corporations; indeed, these are often the intrapreneurs who work hard to make things happen. The key point being made here, however, is that this situation tends to be the exception rather than the rule; even when such managers show up on the scene, it's often due to *their* own volition. Indeed, in the early stages of my research when I found startups that had had a productive partnership with a large corporation, it was precisely because a proactive entrepreneur had been fortunate enough to connect with an entrepreneurial, boundary-spanning manager inside that corporation – whose actions were *not* the norm. In other words, successful dancing with gorillas typically happened despite, not because of, the large corporation's siloed organizational structure.

The end result of a corporation's siloes is that even if a startup was able to manage to establish some form of communication with the corporation, not only is there the problem of a lack of counterparts, as noted previously, but also limited touchpoints for subsequent networking with other business units and partner organizations in the corporation's wider ecosystem. One frustrated entrepreneur once remarked to me, "The problem with trying to do something meaningful with a large partner is that there are so many people and stakeholders on the inside who don't really talk to each other . . . and so it takes one hell of an effort for us, with our limited time and knowledge of the company, to reach out to these different folks." Once again, we see that one of the very reasons a large corporation would want to partner with a startup – in this case the siloed structures that stifle agility – comes in the way of smooth interactions between these vastly dissimilar organizations.

* * *

In sum, the structure asymmetry between corporations and start-ups, which follows from big differences in their approach to organizing, impedes the potential benefits of gaining legitimacy, learning, and leads because even if there is recognition of the potential value of corporate-startup partnering, the sheer *disconnectedness* between these two sets of organizations reduces the feasibility of partnering in a meaningful way.

ATTENTION ASYMMETRY

Having considered three aspects of organizing (structure asymmetry) that impede opportunities for corporate-startup partnering, it is important to also look at *executing* (attention asymmetry). Managers are typically incentivized to pay attention to executing tasks in the here and now, and it makes sense in that effectively exploiting current capabilities is what helps a firm to generate revenue and be profitable. A problem arises, however, if managerial attention being paid to the everyday (exploitation) crowds out consideration of the future (exploration). This is one of the struggles of large corporations in addressing the threat of disruption. In contrast, as noted, startups tend to be more focused on the future – thus, on exploration. But this very difference can be problematic for corporate-startup collaboration, stemming from the focus of managers' attention.

Lack of Confidence in Startups

In addition to a lack of commonality and connectivity with start-ups (as seen previously), corporations may have a lack of confidence in startups. Following from the way large corporations plan and organize, managers' attention is predominantly *immediacy-focused*, and so managers are less likely to pay close (and therefore discerning) attention to prospective external partners outside the ambit of their immediate exchange relationships. Managers often do not have sufficient awareness of startups because of the way they normally channel their managerial attention, which thwarts the prospect of building *legitimacy* vis-à-vis the startup community.

This awareness problem may not be one of complete ignorance of the fact that "there are startups out there" as much as a more nuanced one of not knowing how to *discern* among startups in order to become aware of *which* startups are worth talking to. That is, corporate managers see thousands of startups "out there" but aren't sure which ones are particularly worth engaging with as partners. These managers may show up at the odd startup event and become bewildered by the large number of startups they come across. In the absence of familiarity with startups, a typical response I have heard from corporate managers who are new to the game of startup engagement is, "Boy, there sure are a lot of startups out there! Which ones should I prioritize talking to?" Thus, in this context, a lack of awareness primarily refers to a lack of discernment.

While some startups may be able to send "signals" of their promising quality by demonstrating some initial traction from investors or customers, it is still a challenge for a corporate manager from a highly structured well-oiled environment to figure out which startups are worthy of his or her consideration. But being able to figure out the "right" startup to talk to is not easy. The inability to be discerning can be problematic because the harsh reality is that most startups will fail. (On their part, as previously indicated, startups have a different "unawareness problem": they know which large corporations are out there, but they may struggle to find the right individuals to talk to, given the lack of readily apparent counterparts.)

Thus the immediacy-focused manager with little experience of dealing with startups may dabble tentatively and then *lose confidence in startups* because they are not aware of which startups to talk to. This sets in motion a vicious cycle of backing away from startup engagement, thus scuppering any possibility that might have existed to develop legitimacy in the eyes of the startup community.

Ineffective Learning Outcomes

Another issue that comes in the way of effective corporate-startup partnering – in particular, *learning* outcomes – pertains to the *scarce attention* that corporate managers devote to startups. This observation is less an indictment of managers than an issue of asymmetry in numbers: there are many more startups clamoring for the attention of a large corporation than there are managers to give attention to startups. From the corporation's perspective, it is a one-to-many situation. From the startup's perspective, it is a many-to-one situation. Thus corporate managers trying to engage with startups are often dealing with a portfolio of startups, and run the risk of spreading their scarce managerial attention too thinly across the startup partners.

Alternatively, a corporate manager could seek to prioritize across startups in their portfolio in order to focus their attention on technologically promising startups with a strong fit as partners. However, especially when little experience of dealing with startups has been accumulated, it is not easy to exercise the right judgment. Indeed, one of the striking challenges in corporate-startup partnering that I have uncovered in my research pertains to how attention is given and gained. The result of insufficient attention being given to the most deserving startups – the most promising ones with the best fit as partners – could be that there is little to show, by way of learning outcomes, from these partnerships.

A lack of positive outcomes in terms of corporations gaining novel technology and opportunities through startups (and vice versa) has a damaging impact on the morale of both parties. Many a time I have heard managers as well as entrepreneurs say, "Never again!" after a disappointing experience of corporate-startup partnering. Beyond the immediate partnership in question, this could fuel a more widespread sense of skepticism about startup partnering within the large corporation, and further undermine confidence in startups.

The risk aversion associated with strategic planning plays out in the execution of strategy as well. For a brand manager running a multimillion brand, the prospect of taking a chance on working with startups understandably provokes anxiety unless the prospect of a win-win is patently obvious and beneficial. Thus, even if there is an attempt to overcome structure asymmetry, managers running business units (BUs) may still not be persuaded to engage with startups meaningfully. They may conclude that partnering with startups is a distraction at best and a major risk at worst.

Stringent Criteria for Ecosystem Partnering

Finally, an important factor that impedes the generation of *leads* to new business opportunities is the *reliability-oriented attention* that corporate managers typically devote to their everyday responsibilities.

Similar to the orientation toward control and coordination while planning, when it comes to execution, managerial attention is directed toward ensuring reliability. This reliability-oriented attention is devoted to avoiding problems or fixing them when they arise. This means that even when managers engage with external actors – suppliers, buyers, and other partners – they will tend to work with tried-and-tested companies, and this is reflected in procedures adopted within the wider ecosystem, for instance, in relation to go-to-market strategies and to procurement from third parties.

The attention to reliability promotes derisking and leads to an avoidance of unproven or immature solutions, and incentives for a corporation's sales force to co-sell startup solutions might be insufficient for this to actually transpire. Procurement norms tend to favor working with mature companies with an established track record, which is something that startups don't have, by definition. Getting a coveted supplier number is often virtually impossible because managers' attention is focused on ensuring reliability – and startups are viewed as a source of execution risk.

What all this points to is that, in essence, startups are seen as a risk. When engaging with startups, corporations typically have one major concern: whether the startup is trustworthy in the sense of having the competence to deliver on their commitment; in colloquial parlance, *Will they screw up?* For their part, a basic concern for the startup is whether the large corporation is trustworthy in the sense of having the benevolence to not take unfair advantage of them; in colloquial parlance, *Will they screw us over?*

Thus even if startups have some form of engagement with a corporation, it is not easy for them to gain attention from the wider ecosystem. Skepticism about a startup's ability to deliver can make it difficult for a startup to be taken seriously by business units and other partners of the corporation. The end result is that attention is directed toward preserving reliable existing offerings rather than risky prospective ones. The most common explanation I am given for this by corporate managers is that they have no incentive to bother with exploration. In other words, managers behave like managers.

This is perfectly understandable – but not very helpful, in relation to helping the large corporation to become more entrepreneurial.

* * *

In sum, the attention asymmetry between corporations and startups, which follows from differences in executing, comes in the way of realizing the potential benefits of gaining legitimacy, learning, and leads because dissatisfaction in the outcomes through partnering between these two sets of organizations leads to *skepticism* about the prospect of partnering in a meaningful way.

THE PARADOX OF ASYMMETRIC PARTNERING

Thus, we are faced with the paradox of asymmetry, a double-edged sword: the very differences between corporations and startups that make it *attractive* for these companies to work together *also* make it *difficult* for them to engage with each other. On the one hand there is the perception of a win-win opportunity for corporations partnering with startups. But on the other, there is the more complicated reality that the sheer asymmetry between corporations and startups makes it difficult for these entities to work together.

Compounding the challenge is the vast difference in power between corporations and startups. It's not just that these organizations are different in size and structure; startups are typically power-disadvantaged vis-à-vis the corporation. Power follows from the possession of critical resources that are desirable to another party. All else being equal, by virtue of having more resources (including brand recognition and reputation), more options to choose from in terms of prospective startup partners, and more degrees of freedom to act, the large corporation can normally be expected to have the power advantage over startups.

In sum, their vast interorganizational differences – which make large corporations and startups attractive to each other as partners – also constitute a major impediment to them working smoothly together. Organizational characteristics such as size, structure, and power create interorganizational asymmetries. As a result, connecting with the right people within a large corporation is not easy for startups. In many respects, it comes back to the distinction between the manager and entrepreneur. Ultimately, it is the people within companies who engage in the process of capability development. What managers (and entrepreneurs) do matters greatly in finding ways for corporations and startups to work together.

The key for startup partnering is to find systematic ways to overcome the asymmetry between these very different types of organizations.[8] We turn to this in Chapter 3.

PART TWO

HOW

Chapter 3 How to Partner with Startups Systematically

Synergy

Interface

Exemplar

Chapter 4 Building the Capability to Partner with Startups

Initiation

Expansion

Systematization

CHAPTER THREE

HOW TO PARTNER WITH STARTUPS SYSTEMATI-CALLY

If companies don't talk to startups they are at risk. . . . The bit that companies need to get right is partnering.

– Gerald Brady (Silicon Valley Bank)

A THREEFOLD STRATEGY TO OVERCOME ASYMMETRIES

As seen, while there are potential upsides to startup partnering in theory that some (perhaps, many) corporate managers recognize, in reality there is a paradox: *the very differences that make it attractive for these companies to work together also result in barriers to collaboration*. It is, at one and the same time, desirable *yet* difficult for large corporations and small startups to work together. The crux of the problem is the sheer asymmetry – in terms of goals, structure, and attention – between large corporations and startups. Broadly, corporations and startups differ in terms of organizational culture and power and such differences combine to give rise to three asymmetries that get in the way of smooth partnering.

As I have described earlier, companies like Microsoft have had to put in a lot of effort to figure out what works and what doesn't. Common to all of these companies that have taken startup partnering seriously is a *collaborative mindset*. Managers with a collaborative mindset do three important things: they leverage networks actively, discerningly, and reflectively.

Leveraging networks actively is about taking the initiative to connect with others. Proactive managers are not put off by interorganizational asymmetries. This is particularly true of the intrapreneurs who point their company to entrepreneurs outside their organizational boundaries, as seen in Chapter 1. They are likely to be inclined to find a way to overcome the asymmetries with respect to startups.

Leveraging networks discerningly comes about through the ability to recognize that different network partners are good for different things. An important part of such discernment is being cognizant of the opportunities, and challenges, associated with forging partnerships with dissimilar actors. Partners that are different than us are potentially a valuable source of *novelty* – in terms of information, ideas, and opportunities. At the same time, building trust with dissimilar others can be hard work. Managers who have a nuanced understanding of different types of collaborators can see the distinct advantages that digital startups have over other types of partners. Thus even though many corporations are by now very seasoned at partnering with fellow large companies, the ones that see the value of startup partners and leverage networks discerningly will also recognize that with startups it cannot be business as usual in terms of how they engage with other large companies (which represents the comfort zone for many managers). They see the need to understand the distinctive process of partnering with startups.

Leveraging networks reflectively comes from the realization that collaborators are an important source of learning – for instance, about new innovations and models. This is true of traditional corporations enhancing their digital capabilities as well as digitally native corporations that experience valuable learning outcomes through engaging with startups as part of their efforts to orchestrate vast partner networks. This is probably the single biggest reason why the companies that take startup partner seriously – and aren't merely paying lip service – think it is worth striving to overcome the three asymmetries that we've talked about.

In sum, when a company is oriented toward collaboration then it is likely to seek ways to overcome asymmetries with startups rather than walk away from the exciting but challenging prospect of partnering with these very different organizations. What then is the solution to dealing with these asymmetries? My research has uncovered a three-stage process: (1) clarifying synergies, to overcome goal asymmetry; (2) creating interfaces to overcome structure asymmetry; and (3) cultivating exemplars to overcome attention asymmetry (see Figure 3.1). This chapter discusses each process, in turn.

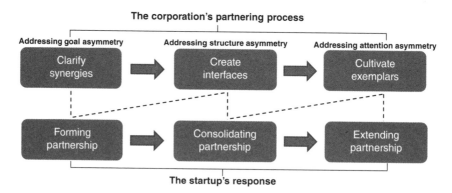

Figure 3.1 The Synergy-Interface-Exemplar Framework of Corporate-Startup Partnering

CLARIFYING SYNERGIES

The first thing that needs to be done is that the nature of the "win-win" – a term that is often used without very much precision as to what it means – needs to be specified. That is, while we know that corporations and startups have the potential to leverage the complementarity of their capability sets, it is important to crystallize a bit more clearly what that actually means. To keep things simple, at a broad level, two types of synergies are worth thinking about (see Figure 3.2):

1. Building block-based synergies (startups sell *with* corporations)
2. Pain point-based synergies (startups sell *to* corporations)

	Building block	Pain point
Typical focus	Developing new software products on the corporation's platform technology	Providing a digital solution to solve a problem, improve a process, or exploit an opportunity
Nature of the win-win	Startup sells *with* the corporation Typically revenue-sharing business model – for the large corporation (for every license of the startup sold, one of the corporation's underlying technology is sold)	Startup sells *to* the corporation Highly focused solutions that add direct value to the corporation Helps better justify the effort to engage with startups
Examples	Microsoft Azure, SharePoint, .Net SAP HANA IBM Cloud AWS cloud services	Unilever – digital marketing BMW – driving experience Bayer – digital health SwissRe – fintech

Figure 3.2 Building Block and Pain Point Synergies in Corporate-Startup Partnering

Building Block-Based Synergy

One type of synergy is building block-based. This is about win-win outcomes occurring when a startup uses a large corporation's building blocks – usually, an underlying technology – to develop its own offering, such as a new software application. The initial impetus for companies like Microsoft and SAP to actively engage with startup partners emanated from a motivation to capitalize on building-block synergies with its partners. The rationale for this synergy is straightforward: it comes down to revenue sharing. From the large corporation's perspective, its underlying technology is bundled with that of the software, generating revenues for it whenever the startup generates a sale. From the startup's point of view, when the large corporation gets involved, it brings to the table its clout in terms of brand recognition and marketing muscle. Thus the end game is the prospect of "selling together"; potentially, the best offerings from startup partners can be promoted by the large corporation's sales force to the mutual benefit of both partners.

Pain Point-Based Synergy

Another type of synergy is pain point-based. Here, the large corporation seeks to tap the expertise of digital startups to address its pain points arising from, for instance, a lack of specialized capabilities to deal with those issues. To illustrate, at Unilever, a South African manager for Knorr sought a solution to address the challenge of providing consumers with recipe ideas, using Knorr products; a digital startup partner was able to come up with a solution based on text messaging that worked even in markets where smartphone penetration was relatively low. The motivation for many traditional-sector corporations to engage with external startups in this way ought to be clear. The end game in this type of synergy is the prospect of startups "selling to" corporations that become early adopters of the technology while the startup gains a valuable new client. As a vivid illustration of this partnering logic, BMW described their startup partnering program, based on a pain point synergy, as a "venture client" model whereby the large corporation becomes a client to the startup or venture.

Although there is currently a divide between tech companies (pursuing building block-based synergies) and non-tech or more traditional companies (pain point-based synergies), this distinction may well blur over time. Already, there are instances where technological companies have found it useful to look for solutions for their pain points; for example, a multinational making mobile phone components reached out to a startup to tap its expertise in low-end handsets that had been elusive to develop in-house. And, as Microsoft CEO Satya Nadella notes, with traditional firms increasingly operating like software companies in an era of accelerated digital transformation,[1] they too may have building block synergies to pursue.

In sum, there are distinct synergies – building upon core technologies versus offering digital skills that are lacking – and as these become visible to all concerned, resistance resulting from issues highlighted in Figure 2.1 (such as a lack of perceived commonality, incompatible learning styles, and restrictive ecosystem eligibility norms) begins to erode because the nature of the potential win-win is made clear and transparent.

Fine-Tuning Synergies in the Digital Age

Three considerations must be given attention in order to specify and fine-tune the specific nature of the synergies that corporations pursue through startup partnering.

How aligned is the synergy with our digital strategy? Companies – whether traditional or digitally native – have an increasingly software-related digital aspect to them. This transformation has been turbocharged by the rise of phenomena such as artificial intelligence, cloud computing, the Internet of Things, and related technologies.

Technology companies have undoubtedly been impacted by digital's rise. To illustrate, in Microsoft's case, the impact has been profound, with cloud computing becoming a core part of the company's overall strategy. Promoting its cloud service, Azure, to independent software vendors (ISVs) – including startups – became an important focus within the division of Microsoft, Developer and Platform Experience (DPE), that houses the startup engagement function. In other words, technological building blocks have been fundamentally impacted by the cloud, and this must be factored into startup partnering efforts.

From the perspective of traditional companies as well, many now see themselves as increasingly digitally enabled firms – and again this process has become more rapid with the rise of cloud computing. Microsoft CEO Satya Nadella often says: "Every company is now a software company."[2] This notion is echoed in a quote from Ford's former CEO Mark Fields, who has commented on this phenomenon: "You know, when I first joined the company, a long time ago, we were a manufacturing company. As we go forward, I want us to be known as a manufacturing, a technology, and an information company. . . . That's where we're heading."[3] Thus it makes sense to pursue digitally relevant pain points when engaging with startups.

On their part, startups have been profoundly affected by such developments. The economics of cloud computing are especially well-suited to resource-constrained startups. By using cloud-based services that are based on a pay-as-you-go model, startups can save on their IT expenditure by avoiding the expensive fixed costs associated with setting up computing infrastructure. Indeed, cloud computing is one of the major reasons for the surge in the creation of digitally enabled startups around the world during the past decade (the 2010s). A quote attributed to LinkedIn CEO Jeff Weiner makes the point succinctly: cloud computing "makes it easier and cheaper than ever for anyone anywhere to be an entrepreneur and to have access to all the best infrastructure of innovation."[4]

In sum, it makes sense for the synergy to be closely related to a company's digitalization strategy.

Which strategic horizon is our focus? The timeframe of the synergy could vary across what McKinsey has referred to as three horizons for strategy making – the first being the existing business, the second on transitions the company is making, and the third to a future or emergent new business.[5]

The greater the emphasis on the first horizon the more likely it is that *incremental* innovation is associated with the synergy sought. The greater the emphasis on the third horizon the more likely it is that *radical* innovation will be pursued. There are dramatically different implications in terms of the type of startup that will be engaged with, the duration of the engagement, and the resources that will be committed – all of which decisions will profoundly affect the design of the partner interface, which is the next step in the partnering process.

Many of the examples in my study pertain to horizons one or two. When Unilever pursues startups to address pain points to improve its digital marketing prowess, for instance, the focus is arguably on horizon one, whereas when BMW looks for startups to improve its autonomous driving technology or cybersecurity the focus may well be on horizon two (or three).

Startup partnering can be effective in either case; the important thing is to have clarity not least for the sake of making clear to startups what the corporation's expectations are in its quest for a win-win partnership.

It can also be helpful in terms of ensuring a shared internal understanding of the agenda at hand. If a middle manager who is actually running a startup partner program is not on the same page as the senior or top manager in terms of the strategic horizon being pursued then there can be frustration for all concerned. One of them is likely to seek incremental innovations in horizon one that the other, if they are more interested in more radical change oriented toward horizon three, will see as insufficiently meaty.

Horizon three-based startup engagement tends to involve some equity investment, and corporate venture units (as opposed to the non-equity startup partnering units that we are primarily talking about) may be better placed to place smallish bets (investments) on promising startups whose technologies may have a future impact on the firm. Indeed, when a highly promising startup with a product or business model that will transform future business growth is identified, it is possible that the corporation will make an outright acquisition of the startup and create a new business line on that basis.

Of course, a judicious mix of horizon one, two, and three initiatives could coexist and be pursued through startup engagement – but again, the important thing is to have clarity about this, both for internal and external audiences.

Are there elements of the other synergy? It is certainly plausible that some synergies will have characteristics of both building blocks and pain points.

A primarily building block-based synergy may have a pain point dimension. For example, Qualcomm worked closely with a startup in Bangalore, India called Mango, which was developing a complementary piece of software for low-end handsets used in rural areas of developing countries. In working with Qualcomm, Mango clearly had to use its large partner's technological building blocks so that its offering was compatible with that of Qualcomm. Nevertheless, there was also a pain point dimension in that low-end handsets was an area where Qualcomm had not made as much progress as it had hoped and working with Mango was also an opportunity to alleviate that pain point. The implication was that Qualcomm deployed a lot of resources to make the partnership work, which I would expect would be more than was usual in the case of a more "standard" building block scenario.

A predominantly pain point-oriented synergy may also involve building blocks. As traditional companies become more and more software-centric it is plausible that in some cases they will also require startups that are addressing their pain points (say, cybersecurity) to also utilize their building blocks to ensure that the startup's offering or solution is tightly compatible with their own. Already some traditional companies work closely with a major IT vendor, say Microsoft or SAP, and in those cases startups working on their pain points will likely be best placed to make a tangible difference in solving them if they were to use those vendors' building blocks. The implication is that the large corporation may have to provide more hands-on guidance or direction to startups on technical matters than might normally be the case when a startup is addressing a large corporation's pain points.

That said, the distinction between "selling with" synergies (building blocks) and "selling to" synergies (pain points) still offers an important way of thinking about the specific win-win being jointly pursued. Hence it is helpful to be clear about the *predominant* nature of the synergy. Making things relatively simple and explicit can make a big difference in moving forward with clarity.

CREATING INTERFACES

Once the synergy has been clearly identified, the next step is to establish an interface – a first port of call for startups wishing to engage with the large corporation. Nowadays, while many companies do have startup partnering programs, albeit with varying degrees of efficacy, there are still many that don't. (And this book is mainly for them.)

Without an effective interface (like an explicit and visible startup partnering program), startups can waste precious time running from pillar to post as they seek to identify the right unit and decision-maker within the startup. An effective interface can help startups navigate the vast ocean that a large corporation represents. Such units typically have managers whose KPIs are directly linked with startup engagement and may even have the word "startup" in their job title – such as "Director – Startup Engagement."

Broadly, there are two types of interfaces that I have identified in my research:

1. Cohorts (involving groups of co-located startups for a period of time in a structured program)
2. Funnels (involving a built-in contest, without co-mingling, for joint opportunities)

Cohort-Based Startup Partnering Interface

A cohort involves a time-bound program, usually for a few months, that brings together a set of startups that jointly follow a set curriculum before they are able to graduate. The rise of corporate accelerators, in particular, put the spotlight on cohorts.[6] Typically running for three to four months, these interfaces bring together a batch of startups (say, 8–12) and provide a set curriculum of inputs to help "accelerate" the startup's ability to get its offering to the market. In parallel, there is typically a large amount of mentoring support; in fact, Techstars, who has worked with numerous corporations to establish accelerators, terms this phase of the process "mentor madness." The startup is given opportunities to engage with various managers from the corporation, some of whom act as mentors or subject matter experts, and in the course of their discussions sometimes hitherto-unseen possibilities for a joint project between the corporation and startup emerge.

Funnel-Based Startup Partnering Interface

A funnel involves startups competing for limited collaboration opportunities that may result in a pilot project to solve a pain point of the company or go-to-market activity for solutions utilizing the corporation's building blocks. Typically, there is little, if any, co-mingling between the startups vying for these partnering opportunities, as they get screened out at successive stage gates. BMW's Startup Garage program is a good example of a funnel. Calling it a "venture client model," one of its co-founders, Gregor Gimmy, consistently voiced his belief that one of the best ways for a large corporation to tap external innovation was to become a client of a new venture (hence the term "venture client"). Through an INSEAD teaching case and various writings, this idea has been widely shared. Another prominent startup partner program with a distinct funnel-based format that emerged was Unilever Foundry. Featured in a London Business School teaching case, this program allowed startups to pitch solutions to deal with specific requests posted by Unilever brand managers.

One way of thinking about the difference between cohorts and funnels is to contrast the experience of being in an MBA class (or other program of on-campus formal study) and the process of looking for a job thereafter. Getting into an MBA class (cohort) is typically competitive, but once in, barring a terrible calamity, everyone who starts the program finishes it, and an important part of the experience is the engagement among co-located peers during a prespecified period of time. This is the nature of startup cohorts, albeit on a shorter time scale (say, three or four months). By contrast, in the subsequent funnel-like job search process, which is highly competitive and may involve MBAs from other schools, many fewer come out at the other end of the process (with a job) than begin it. In fact, one may have no knowledge of or interaction with the others jostling for the positions on offer. This is akin to innovation challenges through which corporations progressively screen out startups until they find the ones they want to work with.

Of course, the use of cohorts and funnels may intersect. For instance, there is usually a rigorous selection process (a funnel) that precedes entry into a cohort-based interface. Also, at some point down the line, it is plausible that the survivors of a largely funnel-based process may be brought together for a cohort-type experience, perhaps in the form of a boot camp or partner gathering of some sort. However, in my research, I have generally found startup interfaces to clearly emphasize one or the other dominant design. The resulting dynamics are rather different. Clearly, in the case of cohorts, the opportunity for interaction among startup founders as peers, as well as with mentors and various corporate managers, is a key part of the process. This can lead to serendipitous outcomes. By contrast, in a funnel-like setup, the focus is very sharply on deliverables such as providing a solution that solves a pain point or co-selling a solution that uses the corporation's building blocks. This can be efficient, but it precludes the prospect of accidental discoveries or alliances in which, say, two startups pool their resources and work together with the corporation in an unexpected way.

As such, then, each interface is good for different things: cohorts bring with them the prospect of serendipitous outcomes while funnels have the virtue of promoting greater predictability. Through experimentation, brainstorming, and unanticipated interactions, cohort participants may identify previously uncon-sidered opportunities. By contrast, by delivering tangible precon-ceived outcomes, funnels can be highly efficient. Thus one basis for choosing between a cohort and funnel is the corporation's urgency and appetite for ambiguity. Funnels deliver quicker pre-dictable outcomes while cohorts could yield unanticipated (but slower) results.

It should be pointed out that corporations that are deeply com-mitted to startup partnering and do this on a large scale may include both cohort- and funnel-based interfaces in their toolkit. Thus, if resources and inclination permit, the same corporation could run both a cohort, such as an accelerator (perhaps in a certain region or for a specific need), and a funnel, such as a foundry that solicits startup solutions that are relevant for the corporation.

Four Types of Interface

Combining the two types of synergies (building blocks and pain points) we've talked about with these two types of interfaces (cohorts and funnels) yields four types of interfaces.

A prominent example of a *building block cohort* is the Microsoft Accelerators program, which has been absorbed into the broader Microsoft for Startups program. As previously noted, Microsoft has accelerators in multiple locations such as Bangalore, Beijing, Berlin, London, Paris, Seattle, Shanghai, Sydney, and Tel Aviv. Cohorts of about a dozen or so startups enter the accelerators for four-month periods, during which time they work through a curriculum of entrepreneurship input, discuss their plans with mentors, and interact with the corporation's managers.[7] Bayer's G4A accelerator program is an example of a *pain point cohort* through which that corporation can engage with digital startups developing healthcare-related technologies. A small cohort of startups would be invited to Berlin to undergo a 100-day accelerator program at Bayer's facilities.[8] Over time, the program has attracted startups from Asia, Europe, and Africa.

An example of a *building block funnel* is SAP's erstwhile program Startup Focus.[9] By introducing this initiative, SAP, an expert in dealing with Fortune 500 companies but with relatively less exposure to engaging with startups in its past history, was able to engage with promising startups developing new applications on its platform technologies like HANA. In so doing, the corporation sought traction for such offerings with its enterprise customers. Managed by a team based in Palo Alto, California, the program offered technical assistance for enterprise-centric solutions to the selected startups. Perhaps even more appealingly for the startups, a further subset whose solutions had been validated – this was a stage gate in the funnel process – would receive go-to-market support. The BMW Startup Garage[10] is an example of a *pain point funnel*. Through this program, BMW offers startups the opportunity to become an early venture client of theirs. That is, after screening startups through the funnel for technical quality and strategic fit through a stage-gate process, a small set of startups would be able to become a supplier of BMW on a specified project.

	Cohort	Funnel
Building blocks (Often IT corporations)	*Typical approach:* • Brings together batches of startups for a fixed period • Peer and mentor interactions • Incentives to use its technology building blocks *Key strength:* Prospect of unexpected opportunities and serendipity *Example:* Microsoft Accelerator (later ScaleUp) Program	*Typical approach:* • Progressively screens out start-ups using the corporation's technology building blocks • Go-to-market assistance usually provided in the ecosystem *Key strength:* Prospect of tangible and predictable partnering outcomes *Example:* SAP Startup Focus (later merged with SAP PartnerEdge)
Pain points (Often non-IT corporations)	*Typical approach:* • Brings together startup cohorts for a fixed period • Peer and mentor interactions • Scope for learning from the startups' digital capabilities *Key strength:* Increased odds of serendipity and peer learning that may lead to new opportunities *Example:* Bayer Grants4Apps (G4A)	*Typical approach:* • Opportunities for startups to address the corporation's identified pain points • A competitive stage-gate process *Key strength:* Generates focused solutions, justifying the effort to engage with startups *Example:* BMW Startup Garage

Figure 3.3   Types of Corporate-Startup Partner Interfaces

Of course, there is a step further that managers working at the interface need to ensure, which is to help startups navigate the corporation and forge links with relevant business unit managers who have the wherewithal to provide meaningful joint activity – for instance, a brand manager in Unilever or an innovation department in BMW – to startup partners. Just because there is an interface does not mean that internal boundary-spanning is easy; but having interface managers with a mandate and incentives to enable corporate-startup partnering certainly increases the odds of this happening. And in this way the problems noted in Figure 2.1 (lack of connectivity, inaccessible learning outcomes, and limited ecosystem touchpoints) become less problematic.

Design Choices When Building the Interface

Decisions have to be made on at least three aspects of the interface:

1. Who is the target audience?
2. How long is the engagement?
3. Who owns the interface?

Who is the target audience? One of the important decisions that needs to be made is what type of startups the corporation is seeking to attract.

Various criteria can be applied. In some instances, industry domain expertise may be vitally important. For instance, some of the pharmaceutical companies I have studied are primarily interested in health tech startups – that is, startups with a deep understanding of the healthcare industry and possessing strong digital capabilities that it knows how to utilize for creating value vis-à-vis a certain facet of healthcare. Other companies, however, may take a deliberately broader approach to welcoming startups with a view to being exposed to diverse bodies of domain expertise. As a broad rule of thumb – which is by no means a hard rule – I have noticed companies with cohort-based interfaces taking a broader approach in terms of industry domain expertise while funnel-oriented interfaces tend to be more narrowly focused on one or a few industry domains.

Irrespective of the domain, another more fundamental design choice relates to whether to work with early-stage or more mature startups. There is a clear tradeoff here. The advantage of working with early-stage startups – ones that are typically in the initial months of operation and are using seed funding – is that there is greater scope to shape the focus of the startup in a manner that aligns with the strategic needs and priorities of the large corporation. One executive who is keen on early-stage startups put it this way: "I want to meet a promising startup before I read about it in *Inc.* magazine." Others, however, would much rather partner with more mature startups in order to increase the odds of getting access to solutions that will work – and that the startup will be around a year or two later to be able to provide support services as needed.

Indeed, some companies have noticeably shifted in the focus of their engagement from early- to later-stage startups. Microsoft is a case in point. When their accelerator program was introduced in 2012, the focus was on early-stage startups. However, within five years the emphasis had shifted to more mature startups. In part, this was because in many ecosystems around the world there were "regular" accelerators that were doing a good job for early-stage startups and Microsoft felt that they were best placed to support more mature startups with strong solutions and offerings. By 2018, when the accelerator program was brought under the newly created "Microsoft for

Startups" entity, it was rechristened as the Microsoft ScaleUp program to underline the new focus on helping mature startups grow big. A related issue pertains to how many startups to work with in parallel; in many corporate accelerators I have observed, the range tends to be 8–12 startups.

How long is the engagement? Another issue concerns the duration of the engagement with startups. I have found that corporations typically gauge the optimal duration for them through a process of trial and error. Duration, by definition, is well-defined in a cohort interface, especially a corporate accelerator. That's because there are usually start and end dates, often marked by an event at each end – a launch or inauguration event at the start and a demo day or graduation at the end.

The typical duration of accelerators I have observed is three to six months. In some cases they may be briefer (say, eight weeks) and in other cases more like nine months. An example at the upper end of this range is Wayra, the corporate accelerator established by Spanish telecom giant, Telefonica. The former head of Wayra in the UK, Gary Stewart, explained that since they emphasized business development, it would be important for startups to have more than the usual three months, which typically isn't enough time to secure a business deal. Their rationale for this longer duration is to allow startups more time to navigate that large company and make inroads into business units with a view to generating mutually beneficial opportunities. More typically, however, I find that accelerators adopt 12- to 16-week programs with three phases:

explore possibilities; crystallize an opportunity; and execute and prepare for demo day.

The best corporate accelerators are generally not easy to get into – some even joke it's harder than getting into Harvard – but for startups that get in, the inputs provided are for the cohort, a process that makes peer interactions important. Without doubt, the choice of mentors in corporate accelerator programs is key, both the internal ones who are likely to be vitally important in helping the startup connect to meaningful opportunities with the corporation, and the external ones (say, a subject area or serial entrepreneur) who can provide valuable feedback to validate the startup's decisions or raise red flags (or, often, both). Need-based workshops on topics like product-market fit and go-to-market selling can be helpful, especially when tailored to the specific needs of the startups in the cohort.

Although funnel-based approaches may have less precise start and end points, it is still important to be clear about the likely duration. My observation of funnel programs is that in many cases these too last for three to six months in terms of finding and screening potential solution providers to identified pain points. In some instances, a tight timeline could be specified for the delivery of an actual solution. The Omega 8 interface requires selected startups to deliver their proof of concept (PoC) project within 60 days.

In addition, there may well be short "sprints" lasting for a few days – in some cases, even weekend activities or programs lasting for about a week. Weekend events may take the form of "hackathons." Week-long events, such as Google LaunchPad, could provide a condensed "taster" or boot camp to startups. Such short bursts of activities could help identify startups that the corporation will engage with for a longer period (say, three to six months).

It is important to specify the duration of the engagement for several reasons. First, this helps in the estimation of financial resources that must be committed by the corporation. Second, it offers clarity regarding the time involved for the participating startups. Third, it affects the development of a curriculum for the program. Finally, it influences the manner and extent of engagement from mentors, both internal and external, to support the process.

Who has ownership of the interface? An important decision with potentially significant political and practical implications relates to who within the corporation is ultimately in charge of the interface. One important related decision concerns whether there will be a specific, designated team to manage the interface. In many companies that are taking startup partnering seriously, this is the case. However, the question that then arises is who does the leader of this team report to? And which organizational unit's budget covers the interface?

In its early days, Infiniti LAB, the startup partnering unit of Nissan's luxury brand, was funded through the global brand marketing budget. By contrast, BMW's Startup Garage was funded through the R&D budget. Not surprisingly, in the beginning when I spoke to the founders of each program, their rhetoric and emphasis was rather different – more diffuse in terms of objectives in the case of Infiniti and more specific in the case of BMW. (This perhaps also reflects the different interfaces – cohort in the case of Infiniti and funnel in the case of BMW.)

It is also important to understand that over time the startup partnering unit may change hands in terms of which entity has ultimate responsibility. In traditional companies, there is increasingly a unit that overseas digital transformation, and there seems to be a trend – at least in many of the companies I have studied – to relocate the startup engagement unit to such a unit. This makes eminent sense when digital transformation is being taken seriously at the highest levels of the company's leadership. However, the intrapreneurs driving startup partnering will likely still have to work hard to ensure that their work retains high visibility and is viewed as a genuine source of value creation, not merely innovation theater.

Finally, the owners of the interface may choose not to do some or all of the interfacing work by themselves. As noted later on, in Chapter 4, there is scope for third-party specialist intermediaries to help connect corporations and startups. In some cases, they may undertake the bulk of the management of the interface while in other cases they may be utilized for specific aspects of the partnering process, such as scouting for innovative startups.

CULTIVATING EXEMPLARS

In my research I found that a major factor differentiating corporations that were highly effective at startup partnering from those that were less so was their proclivity for nurturing success stories or exemplars. When the synergy is building block-based the exemplar showcased would have effectively used the large corporation's platform technologies well and had a successful joint go-to-market outcome. If the synergy is pain point-based then the exemplar would have successfully solved some problem of the corporation and likely had its solution successfully piloted. In this way, it can be demonstrated that the startup partnering process does in fact work, while at the same time providing insight into how to improve things. Importantly, corporations get a sense of what success looks like in *their* specific context, and provides a basis for prioritizing and directing managerial attention to the sort of startups and partnerships that will yield mutually enriching outcomes.

Exemplars come in different forms (see Figure 3.4). In some cases, the engagement between corporation and startup is a one-off and the duration of the engagement is relatively short – and yet, the win-win outcomes are so clear that they are still worth showcasing.

I learned about an exemplar that resulted from a short one-off engagement, during an event involving managers from the three

	One-off engagement	Repeated engagement
Relatively short period of time	Useful as "quick wins" to gain buy-in from other startups and internal stakeholders	Likely to arise when startup partnering relates to an urgent strategic priority area
Relatively long period of time	Likely when the domain of partnering (in terms of topic or geography) is relatively new	The superstar exemplars that end up being the most showcased success stories

Figure 3.4 Types of Corporate-Startup Partnering Exemplars

East Asian subsidiaries – China, Japan, and South Korea – of a well-known Western pharmaceutical multinational. The representative from Korea spent virtually the entire time allocated to him to describing one Korean startup that was making waves, which had worked with that company in Seoul in a one-off accelerator program in an intense burst of activity. The Korean team worked especially hard to provide hand-holding to the startup as well as their internal colleagues. This was especially significant for that team because those were early days for them in startup partnering, and that was their first big success story.

At the other end of the spectrum, a partnership may progressively result in several points of contact and an ongoing collaboration over an extended period of time. Indeed, in some cases, these startups may become high-potential candidates for investment or acquisition. As previously noted, early in my research I came across a Bangalore-based venture called Skelta that had partnered successfully with Microsoft not only in India, but also in the United States and multiple other markets. Skelta had clearly garnered a lot of attention, initially from Microsoft's India subsidiary and eventually from global headquarters. I found this to be a recurring pattern at Microsoft. At Microsoft's BizSpark One Summit, it was relatively apparent that certain startups were being showcased as exemplars. Indeed, after spending the entire day observing that event, I came to the view that "showcaseability" – if such a word doesn't exist, then it should! – is a desired attribute in startups from the perspective of the large corporation. Back then, the challenge was to attract high-quality startups to work with it because Microsoft's coolness quotient in Silicon Valley was not very high in those days. Even today, Microsoft aggressively talks up its success stories.

And other combinations and permutations may arise, such as a one-off engagement that is relatively lengthy or repeated but rapid engagement in a short time period, as seen in Figure 3.4. The point is that managers running startup interfaces should continuously seek to cultivate these exemplars both because of the enhanced external and, vitally, internal credibility that this lends to their startup partnering efforts. Also, importantly, by reflecting on what works and doesn't, including the nuances of different ways in which a win-win partnership works, this will help them better understand which startups to focus more of their limited managerial attention on. This is an important learning process that helps corporations to address the asymmetry of attention that impedes corporate-startup partnerships.

Cultivating exemplars early on is helpful from two perspectives: overcoming skepticism to the idea of corporate-startup engagement with both (1) external audiences and (2) internal stakeholders.

External validation. Having success stories validates the intent and ability of the corporation to partner with startups in the eyes of external audiences, notably the entrepreneurial ecosystem. Not unlike a school highlighting successful alumni in order to attract other high-quality applicants, showcasing exemplars is an important way to win the hearts and minds of prospective startup partners. This is especially important because, as startup partnering has become mainstream, corporations are often competing to access the same pool of entrepreneurial talent. Being able to point to success stories can make it much easier to address some of the queries – and quell some of the anxieties – that startups may have when a corporation announces a new partnering initiative. Although by now startup partnering is a well-established reality in many industries, some startups might still be wary of getting "trampled" while dancing with gorillas. Startup partnering success stories can mitigate this concern and help the corporation in question build "street cred" as a reliable partner.

Internal validation. Also, perhaps more importantly, having success stories helps address the skepticism that the startup engagement team may encounter *inside* its own corporation. Clearly, the startup interface, be it a cohort or funnel, can help deliver joint value for the partners involved only when there is genuine engagement (selling with or selling to), and this requires active participation by internal business units and other relevant teams. Yet, as noted in Chapter 2, risk-averse managers in corporations are often reluctant to give it a shot. The ability of the startup interface team to showcase exemplars can be an antidote, to at least encourage a few managers to be brave early adopters and eventually (as discussed further in Chapter 4), startup partnering can become more firmly established in the company.

Of course, while early wins are important, it goes without saying that it is important not to cultivate exemplars merely for the sake of it, or to declare victory too quickly based on one or two lucky flukes. Rather, the process of cultivating exemplars should be an intellectually honest process – with a healthy tolerance of failure, especially early on – that attempts to genuinely figure out how to make the startup partnering process work for both parties. In so doing, a clearer understanding of which startups are worthy of the company's scarce limited managerial attention will emerge. And in this way, the attention asymmetry between corporations and start-ups can be suitably addressed over time.

In either case – signaling interest in engaging with external startups or convincing internal managers – it is useful for corporations to become adept at showcasing successful startup partners. Various forums and media can be used for this purpose, including keynotes by top executives, newsletters, and social media posts. When there is growing evidence that genuinely win-win partnerships – and here, the watchword is genuine – are achievable, skepticism on both sides resulting from factors highlighted in Figure 2.1 (lack of confidence in startups, learning outcomes perceived as ineffective, and stringent criteria for ecosystem partnering) will start to reduce.

Increasing the Odds of Cultivating Exemplars

Corporate managers can increase the odds of cultivating exemplars by paying attention to three useful things – prioritizing among startups, recognizing the risks how showcasing startups may backfire, and nurturing an alumni network.

Who do we prioritize to get the most attention? Managers working with startups should be mindful from an early stage to increase the odds of having success stories.

This calls for being intentional about which startups to pick. As discussed previously in relation to designing the interface, consideration needs to be given to whether to partner early-stage startups (ones with seed funding) or more mature ones (ones with a series A round funding, for instance). There is a tradeoff: more mature startups are more likely to deliver a win-win outcome but early-stage startups are more malleable to be shaped in a way that suits the corporation's agenda.

Importantly, managers need to be intentional about which startups to *prioritize* in terms of the allocation of resources. Arguably the most important resource is managerial attention, since other resources that startups get flow out of this – the more attention they receive from managers the more likely they are to get access to resources from the corporation. And since managers have a finite amount of managerial attention to give the startups they are working with, inevitably they must prioritize. An important consideration in deciding which startups to pay more attention to is the likelihood of success of the startup as a partner to the corporation.

Of course, exemplars may vary in terms of their impact on the large corporation: in most cases, exemplars have an incremental (but useful) impact, and in a few cases, a more radical one – perhaps even becoming the basis for establishing a new business of the corporation. Early wins are more likely to be examples of the former. But over time, as the company builds its startup partnering capability, the odds of deriving more radical impact through exemplar start-ups increase.

What are the potential risks? Things don't always turn out well. It is entirely possible that today's collaborators might become tomorrow's competitors. That is, there can be a risk of helping a startup become so successful that it goes on to compete in some way with the large corporation – occasionally, in hostile ways. A case in point is Huddle, a software company founded in London, UK, which was one of the early exemplars showcased by Microsoft when it started getting serious about startup partnering. Despite being showcased as a poster child of the BizSpark One program, the British venture went on to position itself as a major competitor to one of Microsoft's offerings, SharePoint.[11]

Less dramatically, there is always the risk of overdoing the showcasing. This can be problematic in a couple of ways. One, the startup may be prematurely identified as a winner whereas things subsequently go south for the startup (and the partnership). Two, the exposure to external and internal audiences can, in fact, become distracting and counterproductive. Some of the more thoughtful managers in startup engagement are careful not to accept too many visitors, internal or external, and are careful to strike a balance between getting valuable exposure and avoiding harmful intrusion for startups.

In fact, some companies are coy about showcasing exemplars, in part because they impose a nondisclosure agreement (NDA) on startup partners. However, even in these cases, I find that the company is typically very clear about who the exemplars are. For example, even if the company doesn't name startup partners in public, they will very likely showcase these startups to internal audiences. (I have sat in on closed-door corporate meetings as an invited "neutral" external speaker where this has happened.)

That said, it is important to avoid paying lip service or going through the motions of innovation theater. Leaders of startup partner divisions or programs would do well to avoid the distractions of excessive visitors and publicity – unless there is some clear value to be gained. It is easy to go overboard with the showcasing of success stories, and discipline is required to make sure that one's eye isn't taken off the ball in terms of making meaningful efforts that contribute to undertaking startup partnering.

How do we stay in touch with alumni? Corporations that take startup partnering seriously are often good at remaining in touch with startups after their formal period of engagement has ended. I am always impressed when I see savvy startup partnership managers post about "alumni" startups on social media. This can be a powerful way of validating themselves as valuable partners to startups for both internal and external audiences. An alumni network is also a good source of referrals for recruiting other promising startups.

Another reason this is a good idea is because some startups may make it big *after* their engagement with the corporation. While managers want to showcase exemplars in terms of success stories that have had a productive partnership with the corporation (e.g. they have been very effective in solving a pain point for the corporation – and benefited in the process too), there is another type of success that warrants drawing attention to, namely external validation, for instance in the form of a big fundraising round. Often, this materializes after the formal engagement with the corporation has ended, and yet the partnership may well have helped the startup open new doors and achieve their success. Hinounou, a Shanghai-based startup integrating healthtech and insurance, was part of the Bayer G4A accelerator. Subsequently, it has achieved visibility, including attention from President Macron of France on a visit to Shanghai. Bayer has been savvy enough to continue to support the startup informally, through mentoring from senior managers, and has promoted its association with Hinounou through social media.

Yet another reason why staying in touch with alumni is a good idea is that there may well be scope to do further work with the corporation or with another company in its wider ecosystem. This means that there is scope to multiply the touch points between both partners in a way that is undoubtedly attractive to the startup but also efficient for the corporation in that it can gain more collaborative benefits without having to incur further search costs for a reliable and effective startup partner. An interesting outcome for both sides occurs when startups start engaging with business units of the corporation in multiple countries: the startup goes international in the process, while also giving the corporation more bang for its buck by partnering more extensively with it.

UNDERSTANDING THE STARTUP'S PERSPECTIVE

Of course, it takes two to tango, and the three-step (synergy-interface-exemplar) process just described will only work when the managers involved take the trouble to understand the startup's perspective (see Figure 3.1). This matters not least because "gorillas" (large corporations) are increasingly competing with each other for the hearts and minds of startups as they vie for the best new venture partners. When gorillas adopt the sort of systematic partnering discussed in this chapter it becomes more straightforward for startups to dance with them, which my research suggests involve three important steps: forming, consolidating, and extending.[12] From the startup's perspective each of these steps needs to combine proactiveness with caution.

Dancing with Gorillas: How Startups Partner with Large Corporations

Forming. The first step from the startup's perspective is to conceptualize the possibility of working with a given gorilla, and to be willing to reach out to them. This means that the startup will need to envisage fairly readily what a possible win-win relationship with that particular gorilla might look like. Thus the startup's efforts to form a relationship with a gorilla can be seen as its response to the perceived synergy that the gorilla offers its startup partners, which in turn would lead it to seek out a suitable partner interface within the gorilla's operations.

At the same time, the startup, which is typically the less powerful actor when partnering with a large corporation, is likely to be reassured that the gorilla is in fact committed to engaging with startups (as opposed to merely going through the motions as a public relations exercise). Thus a startup is more likely to respond favorably to the prospect of synergy when it perceives this to be sincere – and this is more likely when the synergy is self-evident or believable.

Thus, ensuring perceived clarity (and reasonableness) of the partnering synergy is important in order to attract high-quality startups.

Consolidating. Next, the startup would ideally seek to consolidate the already-formed relationship it has with a gorilla by achieving a tangible win that realizes the potential of a mutually beneficial relationship. This is plausible when it engages with the gorilla in question using the latter's startup partnering interface, such as an accelerator or contest to pitch its solution to a pain point of the gorilla. Without a readily available interface, it is often a hassle for the startup to find the right people within the large corporation with whom to establish some joint activity. Thus a startup is more likely to engage closely with an interface when it can see the clear prospect of undertaking some clearly defined joint activity – such as a proof-of-concept project – by using the gorilla's startup engagement interface.

That said, a startup may be simultaneously enthusiastic *and* cautious in dealing with a corporation. The startup may be concerned that the prospect of the plug being pulled midway through a project or even that, if it reveals too much of its expertise too fast, the gorilla may carry out the project by itself or in conjunction with some other partner. Startups are particularly sensitive to delays in projects since, especially in the initial stages, they can be very vulnerable to cash flow pressures, for instance, if quick decisions aren't made to action a project (and process payment for it, if this was agreed). Effective interfaces can make the process of consolidating the relationship more straightforward and fluent for startups – and also ameliorate the fear of being taken advantage of or not treated professionally.

Thus, ensuring that effective (and transparent) interfaces are created is important in order to enable high-quality startups to consolidate their relationship with the concerned gorilla.

Extending. Finally, startups that have consolidated their partnerships by achieving a tangible win – especially ones that are showcased as exemplars – would likely seek to extend their relationship with the corporation. This might entail expanding the scope of the original project, working on new projects, or engaging with other business units or subsidiaries of the corporation. For instance, a startup that has developed a successful proof-of-concept may now seek to move to the next stage of building a pilot for implementation or a primarily technical relationship may morph into a more commercial one. Alternatively, the startup may be on the lookout for additional projects with the gorilla. This may entail working with other business units, even subsidiaries in other markets.

However, the startup may retain a certain level of wariness because, still, the gorilla is likely to be perceived as the more powerful entity. Therefore the startup may also explore the prospect of working with other gorilla partners so that it is not overly dependent on the original gorilla that it initially partnered with. Gorillas that take a more open approach to their innovation network would then likely steer these exemplar startup partners to other potential partners within its network. And even if the startup moves beyond its orbit there is still often scope to maintain the relationship in some fashion by, for instance, conferring alumni status on the startup. This would be part of the gorilla's efforts to build and sustain a set of exemplar startup partners while keeping the door open to them; at a later stage they may return to the fold and revive their relationship with the gorilla.

Thus, ensuring that exemplars are cultivated actively (and with an openness to keeping in touch even when the startup moves on to other partners) increases the odds of high-quality startups extending their relationship with the concerned gorilla and its wider ecosystem.

In sum, for its part, a startup that understands the corporation's synergy-interface-exemplar approach well will be able to better align its own actions with those of the gorilla. Conversely, corporations' managers who are highly focused on the startup's perspective are ultimately the ones that are more likely to experience fruitful partnerships with startups. And in the process, corporate managers can gain a better handle on partner selection criteria when considering which startups to engage with because the synergy-interface-exemplar framework points to certain key considerations.

* * *

Understanding the synergy-interface-exemplar partnering process is important. But more needs to be done. The other part of the "how" of startup partnering is making sure that a competent partnering approach vis-à-vis startups becomes institutionalized within the company and outlasts the intrapreneur leading these efforts when he or she moves into another role or even to another company. Chapter 4 looks at how to build a startup partnering capability over time.

CHAPTER FOUR

BUILDING THE CAPABILITY TO PARTNER WITH STARTUPS

While our organization was very good at working with large partners, this was the first time we had engaged with partners at the opposite end of the spectrum. Talk about a learning curve for us! At first, most startups were actually a bit confused when we approached them . . .

– A large corporation manager[1]

LEARNING TO PARTNER WITH STARTUPS

It is one thing to understand a specific partnering process (such as the synergy-interface-exemplar framework discussed in the previous chapter), but quite another to be able to learn to partner with startups as a repeatable activity. Embedding the capability to partner with startups within the organization – that is, making it an institutionalized practice – calls for a broad-based process of learning a new capability. Only then can a corporation hope to attain valuable outcomes through startup partnering in a consistent and somewhat predictable fashion. Or to put it another way, without a startup partnering capability, partnering with startups may end up merely being a one-off activity, and no more than innovation theater, which is a waste of time for all concerned.

While cultivating the first exemplar (or set of exemplars) is undoubtedly valuable, it's also important to go beyond that so it doesn't seem like a fluke or one-off. This is where it becomes prudent to consider how corporations can build a new partnering capability.

Compared to in-house operations or even external acquisitions, *partnering* requires its own unique type of *capability*, as has been well established in the voluminous research on strategic alliances.[2] However, traditional alliances tend to be between similar types of entities. When Microsoft realized it was losing the smartphone game, it announced a strategic alliance with Nokia, which eventually led to the former acquiring the latter. Of course, that particular engagement did not quite have the desired outcome but the point to note is that this alliance involved two similarly large Western firms. This is true also of alliances forged for international market entry; typically a large foreign company will prefer to partner with a large domestic company. Thus when Starbucks entered India, it partnered with one of the biggest companies in that market, Tata. As such, consistent with the idea that birds of a feather flock together, it is somewhat more natural for large companies to form strategic partnerships with other large companies.

By contrast, as discussed, corporate-startup partnering involves very different entities coming together, and their asymmetry poses challenges for partnering. Even corporations with strong partnering capabilities in a general sense need to work hard to develop the competence to partner with *startups*. This often involves trial-and-error learning over time. Furthermore, corporations have to work hard to *be seen to be* good, reliable strategic partners to startups. This is important given the growing competition among corporations to attract the best startups to work with them.

Building any new capability is challenging and effortful (not effortless). This is true of developing the capability to partner effectively with startups. To be clear, several companies have taken partnering seriously over the years. In the 1980s and 1990s the globalization of companies' market and supply chain operations drove alliance formation; in many instances they had little choice but to ally with local partners. Some corporations even have alliance management departments that have accumulated valuable expertise in partnering over the years.

However, partnering with startups is a different ball game. Even companies that have a long history of working with young companies – for instance, large pharmaceutical companies partnering with biotech ventures – have had to adjust to working with digital startups whose expertise is far removed from their own.

Consider the case of Bayer, a traditional German pharmaceutical company that makes aspirin (and a host of other drugs) – and one that has taken partnering with digital startups seriously. Started in 2013 as a self-described "passion project" of a Bayer manager named Jesus de Valle, the initial focus was on providing small grants for the development of digital applications that were relevant to healthcare – hence the name Grants4Apps, abbreviated to G4A. Within a couple of years, a 100-day accelerator program was launched in Berlin for digital startups. Ongoing tweaking helped improve the interface. The following year, the cohort's scope was broadened. Specifically, startups from outside Germany as well as internal employees with startup ideas were invited to apply. And the year after that, further adjustments were made to link more tightly the expertise of the startups with Bayer's strategic areas of interest.[3]

This programmatic initiative expanded as it became adopted – with some adaptations – by other country subsidiaries including China, Japan, Russia, South Korea, and Spain. In parallel, there was an incubator at Bayer's global headquarters in Leverkusen, Germany, as well as managers in Silicon Valley seeking out prospective startup partners. By 2018, Eugene Borukhovich, the head of the operation, decided it was time to consolidate. The Leverkusen incubator was closed, and all existing activities were placed under one of three categories of the G4A digital health startup engagement team. Borukhovich described these three areas as follows: intelligence ("where to play" – understanding value pools, unmet needs, and strategic imperatives), partnerships ("who to play with" – including commercial deals with and early-stage investments in startups) and ventures ("how to win" – developing new revenue streams). Regarding the last-mentioned, Bayer G4A's first foray into identifying a new business opportunity was anchored in behavioral science and involved creating a team of entrepreneurs and intrapreneurs, with more cross-pollination between intrapreneurs and entrepreneurs foreseen. The program's mission was clearly defined as contributing to "digital health" and the branding dropped the expanded form – grants for apps – in favor of G4A.

Of course, sometimes companies may deliberately do something – say, a hackathon or startup challenge – as a one-off activity, and there may be good reason for that. But for those companies that see startup partnering as an important part of their corporate innovation arsenal, then demonstrating commitment to undertake these activities is vitally important.

The Bayer example suggests three sets of important managerial actions: (1) initiation, (2) expansion and (3) systematization, which this chapter discusses (see Figure 4.1).

	Initiation	Expansion	Systematization
Purpose	Making a start – even a relatively small one – to get corporate-startup partnering off the ground.	Galvanizing internal support to ensure that corporate-startup partnering is not merely a one-off.	Institutionalizing corporate-startup partnering within strategic priorities of the corporation.
People	Change-initiating intrapreneur(s) driving things forward to make a start, which may include: • Entrepreneurs hired in (including through acquisitions) • Managers previously seconded to startups • Entrepreneur-manager teams	Interface head (may or may not be the same intrapreneur involved at initiation), along with: • Internal champions (ideally senior managers) • Opportunity gen-erators (business unit managers) • Roving ambas-sadors (managers across levels)	By now, beyond dependence on a small number of individuals; involves continued efforts of interface specialists together with highly committed senior leaders who view corporate-startup partnering as integral to the future evolution of the corporation.
Process	Considerations involved: • Capitalizing on latent appetite to innovate • Allying with other gorillas • Selecting suit-able startups	Actions taken to ensure: • Repeating • Refining • Routinizing	Becomes embedded in: • Corporate innovation • Corporate culture • Corporate strategy

Figure 4.1   The Startup Partnering Capability-Building Process

INITIATION

Needed – A Bias for Action

The *purpose* of initiation is often just that: to make a start. Many successful startup partnering programs have arisen from a modest beginning. But even a small-scale start can be a useful (and realistic) way for an intrapreneur to get a foot in the door and initiate startup partnering, and represents a drastically better outcome than endless discussions and paralysis by analysis at the end of which nothing gets done. Getting started is often the hardest part – and in fact the greatest virtue of the 1.0 version of a startup partnering program is often simply the fact that something was attempted. In Bayer's case, it was a small contest to give away grants (with students as the main recipients) to create digital apps, and very rapidly the program evolved from that miniscule start, although the abbreviation for the original name – G4A for grants-for-apps – stuck. In other cases, the start might be a hackathon over a weekend. Beginning proceedings even with a bite-sized endeavor might be better than never-ending discussions with a view to starting with a bang that simply doesn't materialize. Of course, the danger to guard against would be remaining in the terrain of small-scale endeavors that go nowhere. Thus small-scale efforts that help a corporation get started clearly need follow-up activities that will keep the momentum going and lead to more substantial and enduring startup engagement activity.

Involving Entrepreneurial Individuals

A key challenge for corporations and startups to work together is that, in the end, collaboration comes down to *people* working with each other. While it is plausible that a CEO might mandate startup partnering, in the majority of the cases I have studied, there has been a passionate middle manager or two instigating the development of a startup partnering program. In such cases, these intrapreneurs may even take bold action in the early days and proceed without the explicit blessing of superiors.

To illustrate, when BMW's Startup Garage was initiated, the program's co-founder, Gregor Gimmy – an outsider to BMW – shook things up a bit by designing a new startup-friendly website and office space without going through the hoops of bureaucratic clearances typically required in a large corporation. His philosophy was that it was better to ask for forgiveness than permission. This philosophy, which he had picked up from his days in Silicon Valley before returning to his native Germany, led to proactive efforts in terms of building a separate brand identity and web presence for the Startup Garage. When he received a call from the communications department he thought he might be in trouble; but, in fact, it turned out that he was being congratulated for his innovative work.[4]

While senior management has an important role to play in legitimizing and mainstreaming startup partnering in a corporation, the inspiration and starting point may well come from middle managers who see the opportunity to engage with startups, and initiate the process in an entrepreneurial way. These individuals are, in effect, intrapreneurs themselves and they don't always start with the mandate or blessing to engage with startups. But when they gain sufficient traction and demonstrate the value of doing so, many of them have been able to persuade their corporate bosses to take startup partnering seriously. Zack Weisfeld who was a key figure in Microsoft's startup partnering efforts and now heads Intel's Ignite accelerator program, comments that partnering with startups helps bring a "growth mindset" into large corporations. He adds that this will only work when managers have empathy for the entrepreneurs they engage with, and are entrepreneurial themselves.

The challenge of being intrapreneurial is nontrivial. It is not everyone's path. But for those who are unwilling to be content with the status quo and can see the opportunity to enhance the prospect of their company creating and capturing value via open innovation, the prospect of startup partnering is certainly one to consider. Also, while the corporations I have studied often have one or two key individuals who helped get things going in terms of startup partnering – the individuals running the partner interface and thus becoming the "face" of their company within the entrepreneurial ecosystem – there are several others, perhaps less visible, who matter greatly. These include key members of the startup partnering team who work behind the scenes to lubricate linkages with various business units. They also include various corporate managers who end up engaging with the startups on some joint project. Furthermore, the various individual managers, in some cases spread across multiple divisions and locations, who champion the efforts made to engage with external entrepreneurs – and may become valuable allies for each other – are key to the process.

As Professor Howard Stevenson of Harvard Business School pointed out from the very beginning of his efforts to teach entrepreneurship in the classroom, managers and entrepreneurs have rather different orientations as individuals.[5] Thus a key challenge is getting these different types of individuals to work together. There are various tactics that can be used to address this – and companies that move faster in experimenting with these and ultimately develop a startup partnering capability will be better prepared for a world in which the continuing imperatives for agility and creativity on their part might well result in managers and entrepreneurs having to increasingly work together.

Hiring in entrepreneurs. First, it may be possible to tap entrepreneurs who become part of the corporation to engage with startups. Hiring entrepreneurs is an obvious way for corporations to find suitable people to handle startup engagement. However, this isn't always easy; many such individuals typically don't want to work for large corporations. One way around this problem is for corporations to take advantage of the acquisitions that they make of startups. Although typically a small numbers game relative to non-equity startup partnering, what this provides corporations with, apart from the intended objective, is access to entrepreneurs. Entrepreneurs from startups who remain within the corporation may, in fact, not find the role of being conventional managers to be attractive, yet know enough about the corporation's strategy to become suitable for the corporation's partnering interface with startups. Bringing onboard a temporary entrepreneur-in-residence could also help provide a bridging role between the corporation and external startups.

Exposing managers to startups. Second, providing internal managers with exposure to the startup world can help to equip them to play a role in corporate-startup partnering. In my research, I have regularly observed that when a startup co-founder had previously worked for a large corporation, he or she was astute in "dancing with gorillas," all the more so when the "gorilla" in question was their former employer. The former employee being able to lubricate smooth communication between the partners typically suits the gorilla too. However, this option is not always available. Therefore, corporations that are keen to develop a startup partnering capability might also consider letting select managers experience the startup world. For example, managers could be seconded to partner startups for an agreed period of time. This would give such individuals a deeper understanding of, and empathy for, the entrepreneurs the corporate managers work for. The CTO of a startup I studied that was partnering closely with IBM had actually been seconded by that corporation for a fixed period. Of course, such arrangements represent a departure from the human resource management norms of bureaucratic corporations, but with some imagination and flexibility, such a scheme could build a cadre of managers who get to understand the mindset and imperatives of startups better, and become a valuable part of the corporate-startup interface. This tack would also fit with a larger agenda of developing an entrepreneurial corporate culture.

Creating entrepreneur-manager duos. Third, having an entrepreneur-manager pair at the helm of startup partnering initiatives might be an effective way forward. One of the challenges that corporations face when dealing with startups is the need to simultaneously gain external credibility with the startup ecosystem *and* internal legitimacy with business unit managers or innovation specialists who, ultimately, will be the ones working with startups on tangible projects. Indeed, what I observed when I visited BMW's Gimmy in Munich was that he was a savvy operator who really wasn't taking reckless risks in the sense that he had a partner, Dr. Matthias Meyer, who was a longstanding BMW insider, and thus someone with a good handle on how people thought and behaved within the company. This meant that working as a pair allowed for complementary capabilities to deal with both internal and external audiences, and thus avoided rash risk-taking. Together, they were able to navigate internal organizational communication and processes, and only occasionally – for important things like its web presence – was decisive action taken in this way (prioritizing forgiveness over permission). Thus, two intrapreneurs with distinct yet complementary boundary-spanning skillsets can help the corporation to simultaneously pursue external and internal visibility and acceptance of its startup partnering efforts.

As such, it is important at the early stages that a start be made, even on a relatively small scale – and this is more likely to happen when entrepreneurial managers lead the way.

Considerations in Getting Started

In terms of the *process*, the key is to find a way to get started – and there are at least three ways to get a move on with startup partnering.

Capitalizing on the corporation's appetite to innovate. When there is a latent appetite for corporate innovation, then it is just that much easier for an intrapreneur to initiate startup partnering. Before launching the Unilever Foundry initiative, Jeremy Basset was part of two teams that sought to promote innovation. In 2010, he joined Unilever's New Business Unit, which sought to build five €100 million businesses that would help create the company's future, but it didn't succeed. Next, he was part of the GoGlobal initiative, which invited startups to pitch ideas to work with certain large Unilever brands. Seven pilot projects were commissioned with startups in 2014, such as an interactive cabinet for Magnum ice creams created by a startup called NewAer that allowed customers to find the nearest place to buy the product through a mobile app. This inspired Basset, who knew from his prior experience with the New Business Unit and GoGlobal that there was an appetite internally to try new things, to figure out a way to partner with startups and led to the creation of Unilever Foundry that year. He said, "The idea wasn't for Unilever to buy out these startups, because experience told us that would kill their entrepreneurial spark; rather, it was about creating a commercial opportunity that worked for both sides."[6]

While the Unilever Foundry was launched in London where Basset worked at the company's head office, in some other cases the initial effort may have to be situated in a locale *away* from the head office to ensure that it is taken seriously, both internally among key executives and externally with startups. Well-known entrepreneurial ecosystems like Silicon Valley, Israel, and Bangalore have

the advantage of being synonymous with innovation and entrepreneurship, and hence signal a genuine intent to partner with
startups. SAP and Microsoft, among many other corporations, leveraged Silicon Valley to initiate their BizSpark and Startup Focus
programs, respectively. Also, Israel has been an important context
for launching a startup partnering program. One such example is
Intel's Ignite program under the leadership of Zack Weisfeld, who
had achieved fame in local and global startup ecosystems for his
earlier work launching a Microsoft accelerator in Israel, which
became the blueprint for additional such accelerators around the
world (and which Weisfeld assumed global responsibility for).
Bangalore in India is another attractive location that hosts global
initiatives such as SwissRe's InsurTech startup accelerator and Cisco's LaunchPad.

As another example of an initiative that was launched at some
distance from the head office, when Coca-Cola initiated a program
to work with entrepreneurs, the corporation piloted it in a location that was believed to be large enough as a market to be taken
seriously but distant enough from headquarters to escape unhelp-
ful interference: Australia. Such locations are useful for initiating
startup partnering in that they facilitate good learning outcomes in
terms of learning the ropes of how to engage effectively with startups
while steering clear of the clutches of those corporate managers at
headquarters that are predisposed to kill new ideas emanating from
elsewhere in the organization. In sum, the overarching goal here is to
balance significance with nonintrusion.

Yet another impetus for startup partnering, especially in locations where the government plays a dominant role, is public policy measures promoting entrepreneurship. In China, the introduction of a policy imperative to promote what was referred to as "mass innovation, mass entrepreneurship" witnessed a flurry of activity within both Chinese companies and multinational corporations operating in China. Part Three of this book (Chapters 5 and 6) takes a more detailed look at some of the nuances of geographic location.

Allying with other gorillas to get started. Reaching out to startups to initiate startup partnering can be a challenge for corporations at the outset. These companies typically have extensive experience in dealing with other large corporates but find the adjustment to working with startups a nontrivial one. One trick that some large corporations pull off is to turn their adeptness at working with fellow large companies into an advantage for getting started with identifying and engaging with startups. Following are three strategies through which large corporations can work together to partner more effectively with startups.

First, *hunt in packs*. Especially when trying to get started, searching for the right startup partners can be akin to looking for a needle in a haystack, and is expensive in terms of time, money, and energy. One way to mitigate these costs is to share them with others in the same industry, which is why some companies band together – even if they are fierce rivals. For instance, pharmaceutical companies that compete with each other come together periodically as part of the heath sector program of Plug and Play, a Silicon Valley–based organization that connects corporations and startups. (More about such third-party specialists in the concluding section of this chapter.) Programs like this offer curated speed-dating or other pitching events that help large corporates find innovative startups to work with. The thinking of companies that take part in these programs, often for a subscription fee, seems to be that if the price for making this quest to move rapidly to a more viable process is to cooperate with fierce rivals, so be it. The rationale is that to cope with digital disruption and its accompanying uncertainties, it is more important to be exposed to the most innovative startups out there than to necessarily have exclusivity over the search process. Of course, once a partnership is forged, then nondisclosure and noncompete clauses are bound to come into play. But at the beginning, there can be mutual benefits of taking a peek at startup options alongside other companies in the industry.

Second, *collaborate in three-way partnerships*. It may be that startups simultaneously work with two gorillas in the same *project*. In highly innovative ecosystems, there is an opportunity for technology-based corporations to combine their expertise and those of their startup partners with the competencies of other large companies in more traditional industries. This is especially feasible when the latter is a heavy user of the former's technology. For example, the first cohort of the SAP.iO Foundries' three-month accelerator program in Tel Aviv included Youtiligent, an Israeli Internet-of-Things startup that helps large corporations to monitor and derive data-based insights from their appliances. Following the demo day,

Youtiligent, which had already collaborated with large corporates like Coca-Cola, actively explored partnering opportunities with SAP clients that would effectively be three-way collaborations. Of course, examples likes this are usually found in highly sophisticated ecosystems such as Israel's. But in more nascent ecosystems also three-way collaborations may be valuable as a more fundamental way of providing a platform for partnering in the ecosystem. In Nairobi, Kenya, which has one of the most vibrant startup ecosystems in Africa, I visited Nairobi Garage, a startup accelerator that is supported by two large corporates – Microsoft and Liquid Telecom, a broadband provider that is active in East and Southern Africa.[7] Startups in African hubs like this are, in effect, able to simultaneously engage with two large corporates with complementary expertise, one in software and the other in infrastructure.

Third, *feed one company's funnel with another's cohort.* Gorillas can also cooperate by joining forces through their respective startup partnering programs in a mutually beneficial way (see Figure 4.2). Walmart's collaboration with Microsoft in China illustrates this strategy. In 2019, Walmart China launched Omega 8, a partnering initiative that operates as a *funnel*, meaning that startups are progressively screened out in a competitive process until one is selected to pilot a new technological solution that addresses a pain point of that company. To jumpstart the search and collaboration process, Walmart worked closely with Microsoft, one of its major global technology partners, which has worked with numerous *cohorts* – groups of startups that co-mingle, typically for a few months – through its

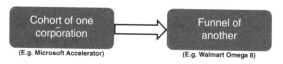

Figure 4.2 Cooperation Among Corporations in Startup Partnering

accelerator (now ScaleUp) program around the world. Startups that graduated from Microsoft's accelerator in China were among the first that Walmart turned to for proof-of-concept pilots through its Omega 8 program. The Microsoft for Startups team in China organized a weekend hackathon in which a few of its handpicked alumni startups interacted with Walmart executives, and as a result, suitable startups could be identified to participate in Omega 8. Thus Microsoft's cohort-based partnering activities fed Walmart's funnel. Such collaboration is mutually beneficial: Walmart was able to accelerate its search process while Microsoft could enhance the odds of success for its startup network by giving them access to a prospective marquee corporate client.

The Microsoft-Walmart example indicates that some corporations have had a head start over others in terms of developing expertise in startup partnering – and these companies are in a unique position to work with other gorillas to engage with startups. Walmart aside, James Chou, who leads Microsoft's engagement in East Asia, has regularly worked with well-known multinationals in a range of industries including healthcare, retail, and financial services on joint initiatives. These partnerships essentially allow corporations that might include relative latecomers to the startup world to leverage Microsoft's existing capabilities and, crucially, its pool of startup partners. Of course, Microsoft would value the opportunity for its startups to work with marquee clients and, in the process, utilize its technologies like Azure. Another example of a corporation that has been working with startups for a while now is the Spanish telecoms giant, Telefonica (through its innovation hub network, Wayra). During a discussion I had with Gary Stewart in London when he headed Wayra's activities in the UK, it was apparent that Wayra was, similar to Microsoft, in a position to work with other corporations that are interested to engage with startups. Furthermore, Wayra has engaged in joint efforts with leading academic institutions such as the University of Edinburgh, thus extending its reach well beyond the London ecosystem to include Scotland.

In sum, it is also worth noting that corporations don't have to necessarily do everything by themselves – other gorillas, even competitors in some instances, could be useful allies in working with startups.

Selecting suitable startup partners. The synergy-interface-exemplar framework helps inform the selection criteria for picking startups to work with since the choices made about each facet has a bearing on startup partner suitability. Of course, at an early stage partner selection may not be a very sophisticated process and, as will be noted, refinements can be made along the way. Still, being thoughtful from early on regarding the selection criteria for startup partners can help corporations make a promising start at startup partnering.

First, compatibility in terms of the synergy sought is the natural starting point – and points to a startup's *quality and commitment*. A key consideration is whether there is the requisite level of commitment to using the corporation's technology (when the synergy relates to building blocks) or if the startup delivers on what is being sought (when the synergy relates to pain points). The implication is that startups need to not only exceed a certain quality but also be genuinely inclined to engage with the corporation, as opposed to merely seeking kudos by being associated with a large corporation.

Second, the nature of the interface might suggest what type of startup is best suited in terms of its *openness to ambiguity*. Cohort-based interfaces, which have the virtue of potentially enabling serendipitous outcomes, would ideally attract startups with a founding team that is open to close mentoring and collaboration with peers. Funnel-based interfaces, which are good for generating more predictable outcomes, would typically welcome highly focused and efficiency-oriented startups. Of course, both sets of characteristics described here could coexist in the same startup – however, certain entrepreneurs might be more comfortable with relatively open-ended (cohorts) than tightly defined (funnel) objectives.

Third, the type of exemplars that the corporation identifies as most compatible with its strategic objectives and ones that it can add the most value to – and this assessment may evolve over time – can also help identify some of the *organizational attributes* of suitable startup partners. For instance, a corporation may realize over time that they are better suited to work with (that is, benefit from and add more value to) business-to-business (B2B) startups. Also, there may be a recognition of whether a broad or narrow range of technological specialisms is more suitable to work with. Another consideration is whether the startup is early-stage or more mature. The tradeoff, of course, is that the former can be shaped more while the latter is more likely to deliver solutions that will work in the near term.

In sum, initiating the startup partnering process entails being cognizant of the associated purpose, people, and process. Of course, corporations should avoid the danger of paralysis by analysis; being thoughtful is important, but overthinking things can be counterproductive. In the early stages of this process, as previously noted, one way to mitigate the risks of exploring what types of startups to work with is to piggyback on the efforts of other corporations that have already gotten deep into startup partnering. Getting started offers the basis for the further expansion of startup partnering efforts, as discussed next.

EXPANSION

To have meaningful organizational impact, the initiated partnering activity needs to be scaled and so, following the initiation of an initial activity or set of activities to interface with startups, there is scope to expand on this. The main purpose of this phase is galvanizing support from within the corporation. In terms of people, then, several internal actors need to get involved. Expansion might be in terms of the scope of activities or that of the audience – for instance, an expanded geographic coverage or involvement of a more diverse set of startups. Such expansion matters because it provides scope for the corporation to learn a new capability – how to partner with startups. This, in turn, calls for three actions by the managers driving startup partnering: repeating, refining, and routinizing. These facets of the process of expansion, which is firmly interrelated to the people involved, are discussed next.

Repeating – Getting Beyond a One-Off Activity

If there is support within the organization, it is feasible to repeat and expand the initiated startup partnering activity. Repetition is important because new capabilities are not built through one-off activity. In terms of building a new capability to partner with startups, repeating a startup activity – which may have instilled enthusiasm among the individuals and team driving it the first time round – is an important next step. In some ways, undertaking a startup engagement program for a second time is as big – if not bigger – an achievement in terms of progressing down the path of embedding such practices within the fabric of an organization.

Gaining traction within the organization can help corporations expand initial ad hoc startup partnering efforts. For example, Telefonica's startup accelerator Wayra was introduced in London, UK, where it has become a well-known entity in the startup ecosystem. Expanding startup engagement activities requires not only extensive networking with the startup community but also, just as crucially, if not more, wide engagement within the large corporation itself. In a sense, creating external interfaces with startups, important and challenging though it is, is merely the tip of the iceberg. As much, if not more, effort has to be directed to the invisible-to-the-world internal audiences of the organization.

As such, it is necessary to get buy-in from the wider organization. This calls for *spanning boundaries* – not just outside the organization but (especially) within – to multiply touchpoints and partnering incidences between the corporation and startups. A startup partner interface is only as good as its ability to bring relevant high-quality external startups in contact with appropriate internal managers. Such boundary-spanning calls for entrepreneurial behaviors and efforts on the part of startup engagement managers who run the partner interface.

It is critical for the startup interface team to span boundaries *inside* the company by reaching out to various people because, as noted, they might be skeptical of startup initiatives. A classic mistake that companies make is to devote all their energy to engaging with the external startup ecosystem while ignoring the company's internal audiences. Three problems arise as a consequence of insufficient internal communication. First, a coherent link between the startup partnering efforts being made and the company's strategic priorities may not be readily apparent to internal managers. Second, there is a dearth of meaningful collaborative opportunities for startups because potentially influential managers don't see the point or are not convinced. Third, the vast majority of employees end up being blissfully unaware of startup engagement efforts, resulting in their being embarrassingly ignorant when faced with (even informal) queries from external parties about such activities. While it is not uncommon for managers in one division of a large corporation to not know exactly what's happening in another, in the case of startup partnering it would be a missed opportunity to spread the word internally as this of itself could be a signal that the company is willing– or, indeed, is actively seeking – to be entrepreneurial.

Specialist managers running the partner interface who are effective in bridging the external startup ecosystem with their corporation need to get a range of internal actors on board. These intrapreneurs have to be effective at responding to external stimuli in the pursuit of new opportunities while *at the same time* coping with internal dealings (and politics) to ensure access to resources and approvals (or at least the avoidance of impediments).

A good illustration comes from the internal boundary-spanning efforts of Sheelpa Patel, co-founder of INFINITI LAB, one of Asia's first automotive corporate accelerators established by Renault/Nissan/Mitsubishi Alliance's premium brand, INFINITI Motor Company. This three-month Hong Kong-based accelerator program (combining a primarily pain point-based synergy with a cohort-based interface) was established in 2015, and evolved over time from its initial global branding focus to a much broader strategic role in terms of global cultural transformation. The experience of Patel,[8] and that of other similarly effective startup interface managers, suggests that three types of actors are important to win over (see Figure 4.3):

1. Internal champions (ideally senior managers)
2. Opportunity generators (primarily business unit managers)
3. Roving ambassadors (potentially including even more junior managers)

Internal champions. Patel worked hard to promote INFINITI LAB to the CEO and top management team. If they engaged with the process and made it a priority then that would be a valuable signal to other managers within the corporation. Patel diligently obtained their input on pain points that the startups could solve, persuaded them to become selectors and mentors of the startup participants,

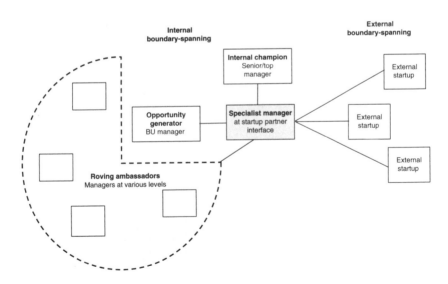

Figure 4.3 Internal Boundary-Spanning to Galvanize Support for Corporate-Startup Partnering

and take part in the demo day event that concluded the accelerator program. The demo day would of course not only be the culmination of the preceding three months but potentially the start of further engagement with the corporation to develop their ideas into a proof-of-concept or pilot project. What Patel and other startup partner interface leaders have found is that when senior executives explicitly support startup initiatives and back that up with their own participation then there is a valuable signal of legitimacy that cascades down within the organization. As Patel commented, "Such buy-in is important to connect the dots and provide the bigger picture of where the corporation is going."

Opportunity generators. In addition to engaging with the CEO and his team, Patel also spent a lot of effort in making several presentations to the business unit leaders across the Renault/Nissan/Mitsubishi Alliance. She engaged regularly with the Alliance's internal innovation steering committee comprising, for instance, leaders of the Connected Car team. This ensured that they became familiar with the startup initiative. Her efforts paid off and meaningful opportunities for startups to develop proofs-of-concept began to emanate and thereafter alumni startups were able to progress to larger-scale pilots and other forms of collaboration, with ongoing support from the startup interface team. And of course, this fed into a virtuous cycle of success stories being showcased, which in turn engendered further internal belief in the value of partnering with high-quality startups for mutual benefit. But none of this would have been possible had Patel not worked hard to convince business unit leaders of the potential benefits of working with startups and align the outcomes of startup engagement with the needs (and key performance indicators) of the business units.

Roving ambassadors. At a broader level of internal engagement, Patel's team made sure that stories relating to the startup program were featured in the (already existing) periodic employee newsletters as well as the CEO's presentations at employee town halls. Such efforts resulted in a large number of employees having a basic idea of the company's startup partnering program in terms of its objectives and, over time, some success stories. Furthermore, employees who had an inclination to get involved in some way were invited to "speed-dating sessions" whenever a new intake of startups commenced to identify potential internal mentors and suitably match them with the startup partners. Subsequently, some of these mentors participated in a one-off program for intrapreneurs that was conducted under the auspices of INFINITI LAB. Patel's experience suggests that by taking the trouble to reach out to a wider internal audience, there is a greater likelihood that people at least are aware of what's going on – and that some of them will be willing to act as mentors and informal ambassadors for the startup initiative.

Corporate innovation professionals have an important yet challenging role to play in corporations as they span both external and internal boundaries. In the early days of my research it appeared that their primary challenge was to get startups to take them seriously. Before long, however, this seemed to be less of a problem – indeed, many of them were treated like rock stars in the startup ecosystem, often being featured as sought-after speakers on panels about partnering between established firms and startups. Rather, the greater challenge that emerged was how to be taken seriously within the company and get access to resources to ensure that startup partnering wouldn't be regarded merely as a fad, but actually get taken seriously. Thus the skillset that any intrapreneur needs, which includes advocacy and diplomacy, can help greatly.

Of course, what this clearly implies is that startup partnering requires *much* more than external engagement in the startup ecosystem (important as that is), and highlights the importance of having genuinely interested intrapreneurs at the helm of startup partnering initiatives, who can adeptly deal with both external *and* internal audiences.

Refining – Making Adjustments Along the Way

Repeating the activity, in multiple locations[9] or business units, is an important part of the process of capability learning, especially if this leads to the refining of the company's startup engagement practice(s).

This may include fine-tuning the *process*. When Bosch initiated a startup partnering program, its formula of discover, nurture, and accelerate – abbreviated to DNA – seemed eminently sensible. However, as the concerned managers repeated the process, and reflected on it, they realized that some modifications to the process might help. The main adjustment they made was to add a step *prior* to what was previously the first step of discovery. They figured that at the beginning they had been very open to engaging with any type of startup – but this was a bit inefficient in that they ended up talking to a number of startups that were undoubtedly capable but not compatible, in terms of strategic focus, with Bosch. Therefore, in subsequent iterations of the accelerator program, a new prediscovery step was added to help screen out, at the very outset, startups that were not strategically compatible. While seemingly a minor change to the process, the impact was potentially great in terms of making that company's startup partnering activity more effective.

Another way to modify the process is to take a cohort- or funnel-based program and add elements of the *other* interface, thus allowing it to evolve into a somewhat hybrid interface. For instance, in one iteration, Bayer's accelerator program (cohort) had an added grand challenge competition for participants in parallel (funnel). Alternatively, a competitive process (funnel) may incorporate elements of a cohort, such as Unilever Foundry in Singapore, where some startups come together in a co-working space adjacent to the corporation's offices.[10]

There may also be refinement in the scope of *participants*. For example, over time, Microsoft changed its focus from early-stage startups to more mature ones as they recognized that they could gain more from and add greater value to the latter. In other cases, nonstartup participants may be included in the mix, as in the case of SwissRe, which decided to expand beyond startups when it repeated its accelerator in Bangalore for the third time.

Refining may also occur in terms of understanding better the *payoff* associated with startup partnering. This may include recognizing unanticipated benefits. For example, when Intel India reflected on its startup partnering effort, it became aware of an outcome that they had not expected: reverse mentoring. That is, while Intel's formidable team of engineers were able to provide technical mentoring to startup entrepreneurs, they in turn received mentoring from those entrepreneurs in aspects like business model innovation. Subsequent iterations of the startup partner program sought to harness these reverse mentoring benefits more explicitly and effectively.

In sum, the choices made around synergy, interface, and exemplar should be continuously revisited to gauge what the corporation is learning about what type of startups work best – in terms of what they can both give and get through the partnership. This may well be an evolving picture; partner selection criteria may change over time. Inevitably, there is a bit of trial and error.

Routinizing – Ensuring Repeatability

As refinements are made, there is scope to routinize the partnering activity – in other words, to make them repeatable. Ultimately, a new capability is woven into the fabric of an organization when it becomes routinized, not in the sense of people going through the motions but rather in terms of there being sufficient know-how to undertake the activity regularly and in a competent way.

The capability to partner with startups becomes routinized when it goes beyond the initial pioneering, entrepreneurial partnering efforts that typically characterize the initiation phase. Routinization solidifies the shift from ad hoc to systematic partnering practices and alignment with the overall strategy. In a sense, once it is taken for granted that the company undertakes a particular activity – in other words, embedded in the organization's processes and, more importantly, its culture – then it can be argued that its capability set and culture support startup partnering.

One of the frustrations expressed by well-meaning corporate managers and startup entrepreneurs alike is that in some cases, a number of small-scale pilots or experiments involving startups are undertaken – but rarely do these get scaled. At one level, this problem of "death by pilots" reflects the nature of the beast; by definition, only a subset of these efforts will succeed, and starting with pilots gives both parties the benefit of failing early and redirecting efforts into what might result in more productive efforts for each after parting ways.

At another level, however, what this frustration reveals is a lack of sincerity or ability. That is, in many cases, corporations are doing little more than going through the motions of innovation theater (lack of sincerity) and lacking in the wherewithal to move pilots that hold promise to the next level (lack of ability). Addressing both problems calls for genuine leadership both from senior and middle managers in corporations, which in turn can help companies to adopt more rigorous and vigorous efforts – particularly in relation to clarifying synergies and cultivating exemplars. In some ways, it is easy to be drawn to working on a startup interface. But a failure to come to grips in an intellectually honest way about the synergy can ultimately lead to efforts with a lack of clarity of purpose and eventually of sincerity. Similarly, when there is insufficient consideration of how to cultivate exemplars and the continuing role they might play, then again, it is very likely that many high-potential partnerships simply go nowhere, which is a wasted opportunity to the large corporation and a source of great disappointment to the startup. Ultimately, this will erode the corporation's street cred in the startup world as a partner of choice.

When routinizing a startup partnering activity, it is helpful to think of (and revisit) the considerations that must be taken into account while building an interface in the first place: the target audience, duration of engagement, and ownership of the interface. The difference between thinking of these factors when initiating the process and later when trying to routinize them is that there is now feedback on the process thus far. In terms of target audience, refinements may well have been made, as noted. In terms of duration, this has an effect on the possible frequency of the activity. For instance, some accelerator programs that host cohorts for a three- to four-month period may do this twice a year. This is the approach that Microsoft adopts. Others, like Bayer, do this annually. In both cases, there are clearly stated application deadlines for startups targeting a certain cohort.

By contrast, some funnel-like interventions happen on more of an ongoing basis, with expressions of interest made or received as and when opportunities (including identified challenges or pain points) arise. This would be true of BMW's Startup Garage or the Unilever Foundry. Of course, in other cases the engagement may be short tangos – a week or even a weekend. With regard to ownership of the interface, again this is important to ensure the continuity of the program. Over time, there may be assimilation of startup partnering into wider organizational processes – as discussed in the third part of the capability-building process: systematization.

SYSTEMATIZATION

Once there are clear routinized or programmatic partnering activities that are repeatable, then the purpose of the final stage, systematization, is to institutionalize these into a more coherent whole, which ensures the continuity and meaningfulness of startup partnering activity. A reasonable but tricky question that often comes up in my discussions with executives concerns whether it pays to engage in startup partnering. One way to view a question like this is to impute quantifiable output, in terms of cost savings accrued (especially for pain point-related synergies) or additional revenues gained (especially for building block-related synergies). Some corporations do this. And, without disclosing information shared with me in confidence, I can say unambiguously that there are managers out there who definitely view startup partnering as having a positive payoff. That said, I will also readily concede that there are some who remain skeptical.

However, a narrow financial perspective may, in fact, get in the way of seeing the bigger picture. For example, when it comes to corporate venture capital (CVC), the question as to whether startup engagement pays may appear to be more readily answered, since a factual result can be produced to estimate the return to investment made in the startup. But even in this case, there are other problems that muddy the water. Strategic outcomes such as gaining greater visibility on an emerging technology may justify engaging with a startup through CVC even if the return on investment, in purely financial terms, is modest. And therein perhaps lies the nub of the matter: a more holistic perspective may be more relevant than a narrowly financial one. This is because startup partnering should, in the end, not be viewed in isolation, but rather as an important component of larger strategic imperatives of the corporation.

In terms of the people involved, getting to that point would likely happen if there is strong support throughout the organization, and sufficient resources are committed to it. This means that startup partnering is no longer dependent on one or two people driving the process but has come to be viewed as an important, collective effort within the company. As indicated earlier, this involves more than just the startup engagement team; individuals within the organization need to continue to act as champions, generate opportunities, and provide mentoring support. This is especially important because often the individuals who drive the initiation of the startup partnering activity move on – to other roles or away from the company. Another important consideration is that the people who are most effective at initiating the startup partnering process may not be the ones who are most adept at consolidating. It may well be that for a given company, the initiating is done by a passionate individual and the systematizing by a more task-oriented plodder. Different processes in this journey require different skills and it is therefore not surprising that one manager may pass on the baton to another as the partnering process unfolds.

In terms of the process, systematization may take at least three different forms that are not mutually exclusive, and are discussed next.

Integrating with the Wider Corporate Innovation Effort

Systematizing may entail crystallizing a portfolio of startup partnering activities under a broader umbrella of corporate innovation. Startup partnering may become part of a wider corporate innovation agenda that includes other tools such as corporate venture capital and intrapreneurship activities. In some cases this may occur naturally, in that some interfaces may run their course. For example, SAP retired the Startup Focus program, merging it with its general-purpose flagship partner engagement program covering all types of partners.[11] Meanwhile, other forms of startup partnering have emerged at SAP such as SAP.io, which offers a combination of investment and incubation to select startups.

This transition may also reflect the need for a more mature or formal process of engaging in corporate innovation. This was the case with Bayer as a more formalized and structured program superseded and incorporated the startup accelerator program that had emerged from the initial G4A activities. Fujitsu's Silicon Valley open innovation platform is another example of a holistic program within which startup partnering can be subsumed. As another example, SwissRe's global startup partnering initiative, launched in Bangalore, has been expanded into a wider open innovation program. As Amit Kalra, managing director and head of SwissRe's Global Business Services explains, "While for underwriting and risk management Swiss Re group has over 150 years of expertise, when it comes to innovation, we are new. Since we had operations in the entire value chain in Bangalore, we launched a global accelerator to explore topics like IoT, which is extremely relevant . . . and now we are in the process of transforming the accelerator into an open innovation platform."

The philosophy of opening up innovation processes that allow collaborative working with a range of actors – including universities, licensors, and startups – that was advocated by Henry Chesbrough and others has taken root in many corporations.[12] As noted, a prominent example of this is the Fujitsu Open Gateway in Silicon Valley that provides that Japanese multinational the scope to co-innovate with multiple partners. When startup partnering is seen as an important open innovation tool, then its value can potentially be enhanced and valuable cross-fertilization could occur with, say, the corporation's partnerships with universities. For instance, engaging with engineering school incubators could allow a corporation to be simultaneously connected with both academia and the startup world. Of course, a key skill in open innovation is that of boundary spanning and when corporate managers are able to adeptly connect the dots with different partnering activities then there is even greater scope for startup partnering to make a valuable contribution to corporate innovation.

As such, it is important to consolidate the wider corporate innovation effort, and recognize what role startup partnering plays in it, as well as to capture synergies with other tools including intrapreneurship by sharing resources and also finding ways for internal and external entrepreneurs to work together, as was the case when an internal Intel China team worked alongside an external startup, as described before.

Integrating with Corporate Culture Transformation

The broader strategic imperative of partnering with innovative startups is the importance for an organization – whether big or small, for-profit or non-profit – to be entrepreneurial. In large established corporations, in particular, the need for entrepreneurial behavior has been emphasized by many management thinkers, including Gary Hamel in his co-authored book *Humanocracy*,[13] which decries the stifling effect that bureaucracy has on corporate managers' proclivity to be entrepreneurial. As discussed in Chapter One, entrepreneurs within large corporations are sometimes called intrapreneurs.

One practical way to think about how to cultivate interactions between corporations and startups – in a way that is systematic yet not overly straightjacketed – is to develop mastery at designing and executing what some sociologists refer to as *interaction rituals*. An interaction ritual does not necessarily have a religious connotation – although there are several religious rituals such as church services and wedding ceremonies. And the term "ritual" is not being used here in the pejorative sense of going through the motions meaninglessly. In fact, interaction rituals can be highly meaningful, as they bring together individuals in a shared space with a common focus for period of time.[14]

Part of the richness of my research over the past 15 years has stemmed from the opportunities I have had to be an observer of numerous corporate innovation-related events at the corporations I have studied, such as Bayer, IBM, Intel, Microsoft, Unilever, and Walmart in North America, Europe, and Asia. In the context of corporate-startup partnering these interaction rituals may take the form of highly choreographed events as part of, for example, the corporation's partner ecosystem gatherings. Alternatively, they may be relatively informal yet "religiously" followed rituals such as Wednesday night pizza for the startup participants in a corporate accelerator. I have observed both in the case of Microsoft, as I described before: a massive worldwide partner conference with over 10,000 partners attending and much-smaller-scale interaction rituals, such as heading to a pub with startups from one of Microsoft's accelerators.

Such examples highlight two facets of interaction ritual – the frontstage and the backstage. Being featured in a frontstage-centric glitzy ecosystem event has a different connotation than a more backstage-friendly gathering in a pub. Recognizing the relative significance of each can potentially help corporations to facilitate more useful interactions between their managers and people in their startup-partners. There are at least three valuable benefits arising through interaction rituals.

First, there can be useful *showcasing*. At a regular level, this happens on the demo day of an accelerator program. But there could be other special venues to showcase startups – for instance, within specific panel sessions or keynotes or exhibition spaces within a wider ecosystem event. Thus interaction rituals can be embedded within bigger ones. From the corporation's perspective too these ritualized events – in the sense that these are seen as special and distinct from the everyday – are valuable in that it becomes seen to be a desirable partner for startups.

Second, a valuable outcome could be *solidarity*. Particularly backstage interactions give startups and corporations' *people* the opportunity to have somewhat less formal discussions and interactions that enable them to gauge each other's trustworthiness and establish a sense of mutual goodwill and solidarity. Indeed, the backstage is also the setting where awkward situations in arriving at a satisfactory negotiated agreement could be resolved and intimate, empathetic mentoring meetings conducted. This can help a large corporation and startup find meaningful ways to engage, as Techstars' Dave Drach observes: "What we found is that when you start to engage corporate executives as mentors . . . this allows the corporations to learn more effectively from the startups, and for the startups to actually gain benefits from working with those corporations. The mentor ethos drops the barriers between the CEO of Disney and the founder of a 40-person company. Those two need to communicate as peers, without any feeling of 'I'm better than you' in either direction. When the two start to communicate as peers . . . that's where the real change starts to occur." Furthermore, the backstage is where forthcoming frontstage showcasing can be rehearsed and messaging clarified to avoid crossed wires and ensure alignment.

Third, unanticipated benefits could accrue through *serendipity*. The interplay between the front- and backstage – with showcasing and solidarity – could lead to unanticipated outcomes through brainstorming or multiple actors (not just two) coming together. One startup working with Microsoft was able to use discussions arising through the corporation's ecosystem events to land an unexpected offer to collaborate from Microsoft's retail arm. Another startup in the Disney accelerator ended up leveraging their spherical robotics expertise in Disney's Star Wars franchise.

Being mindful of the ritual-like nature of some interactions has some benefits, but it also can alert us to certain downsides. For instance, in highly ritualized settings – ones that are very different from the everyday – any fresh ideas or brainstorming that result may be exciting at the time, but difficult to implement later on because they are too removed from reality.[15] Also, relationships may break down if a ritual goes badly wrong. Thus designers and orchestrators of ritual-like interactions need to be mindful to mitigate these dangers and find ways to stay grounded when translating discussed ideas into concrete action by having follow-up meetings within the everyday context.

Integrating with the Overall (Evolving) Corporate Strategy

Ultimately, one of the most important ways to consolidate startup partnering is to mainstream it by connecting the dots between startup partnering and the corporation's core strategy. Microsoft illustrates this transformation in its startup partnering journey. In the Microsoft case, as discussed before, there is now close alignment between Microsoft's core strategy of maximizing Azure consumption and the prospect of co-selling with startup partners (to get to which stage startups can benefit from existing interfaces). Microsoft's sales force is incentivized to sell partners' products in the co-sell repository in the same way as they are to sell Microsoft's own products since the end result is the same: greater consumption of cloud computing, by the startup and/or the customer.[16] In a sense, Microsoft has come full circle from "business as unusual" – that is, figuring out specific ways to engage with startups – to business as usual, whereby partnering with startups is aligned with the corporation's overall cloud-first strategy. As Dan'l Lewin, the early pioneer of Microsoft's startup partnering, pointed out to me, Microsoft has been working toward a business model change over time, and the startup partnering activity of the company has co-evolved with this strategic transformation. In this sense, partnering with startups can be an important piece of a much bigger picture involving corporate strategic transformation.

A longstanding challenge for established corporations as they grow by doing what they are good at is that as the business environment changes – incrementally and discontinuously – there is a growing need to avoid strategic drift and embrace strategic renewal. Refreshing, sometimes drastically, the product-market mix of a company is an important part of this process. When partnering with startups transcends relatively simple fixes of pain points to include more radically new offerings, in terms of technology or business model, then there is potentially greater strategic significance of the startup for the corporation. Of course, this is where more involved forms of startup partnering, including corporate venture capital or outright acquisitions, may come into play. But it is plausible that candidates for investment or acquisition may be identified from the pool of startups that corporations engage with through non-equity partnering as a starting point.

Facing a new environment characterized by rapid digital transformation and business model innovation, it is clear that effecting cultural transformation, highlighted previously, is high on the agenda of many CEOs. In IBM CEO Arvind Krishna's first letter to his colleagues, he cited the need for developing an entrepreneurial mindset.[17] Startups, almost by definition, have a different culture from that of large corporations. Of course, this is a crucial driver of the asymmetry of paradox – the challenge arising from the fact that the very differences that make corporations and startups attractive to each other also make it difficult to work together. But when corporations are able to successfully utilize the synergy-interface-exemplar framework to overcome the challenges of asymmetry, at least partially, then the cultural differences can also be harnessed to the advantage of the corporation.

As noted in the preceding discussion on interaction rituals, intentionally facilitating conversations between corporate managers and startup founders can be a valuable educative experience for the former (and the latter). Of course, there is always the danger that bringing a group of startups into the ambit of corporate managers could end up being gimmicky and superficial attempts to infuse a bit of "startup magic" into a large company. But when done thoughtfully, with genuine interest and support from senior management, then being exposed to the mindset of startup founders can be inspiring, intimidating, and, almost inevitably, thought-provoking for corporate managers.

LEARNING FROM EXTERNAL SPECIALISTS

To conclude, getting the partnering process right takes time and effort – including learning by trial and error. When done right, there is scope to realize the promise of the division of entrepreneurial labor between corporations and startups. But getting to that point can be laborious in its own right. And here, the role of individuals bears emphasizing (again).

Before ending the chapter it is worth pointing out that corporations that are serious about partnering with startups are bound to come across third-party specialists that offer to help with this process – of course, for a fee or some other form of remuneration – that can help them in initiating, expanding, and systematizing the startup partnering process.[18] In my research I have heard differing views about third-party specialists – some balk at the fee, whereas others swear by their effectiveness. The key is to find a good fit with a third-party specialist, and for both parties to have clear expectations of the nature of the intervention or assistance provided.

Also, just because a corporation chooses to work with a third-party specialist doesn't mean that they are absolved from building a new partnering capability themselves – indeed, the success stories I have heard have entailed very savvy corporations that were able to work with third-party specialists astutely, in order to achieve mutually satisfactory partnering outcomes with startups. In the end, corporations must make the call about whether to work with specialists and, if so, which one has the best fit. Some corporations have used the services of such organizations as a one-off, others primarily during the initiation phase, and yet others have built longstanding comprehensive relationships. The key is for each corporation to honestly assess its needs and the availability of resources to spend on such specialist services. But working with specialists isn't a substitute for the hard work of building a new partnering capability with startups. More capable corporations are more likely to use these specialists' services more effectively.

When considering the prospect of engaging third-party specialists, three important issues ought to be considered that are discussed below.

What Is Their Unique Partnering Competence?

One of the important things to understand about a third-party specialist is its core competence. Is it good at scouting for startup partners? Or developing the partnering strategy? Or actually helping to execute a collaboration plan? Of course some specialists are (or at least claim to be) competent at more than one thing. Yet, like in any industry, reputations develop for different players around distinct aspects of being a good intermediary. Take two of the most prominent ones, Techstars and Plug and Play, which are a study in contrasts.

Plug and Play is, at its core, a *matchmaker* that connects corporations and startups. Founded in Sunnyvale, California essentially as a real estate provider for startups, it eventually pivoted to position itself as an intermediary that could expose corporates to cutting-edge startups. Its revenue model is subscription-based; companies pay an annual fee for the opportunity to have startups that are relevant to their vertical (industry) pitch to them periodically. Companies become part of various vertical-led consortia. An intriguing aspect of this approach is that rivals in the same industry sit together when startups pitch to them. From the corporations' point of view, when scouting early-stage startups there seems to be less apprehension about rivalry with each other and a greater emphasis on getting exposure to novel, potentially disruptive ideas quickly. Such managers seem willing to trade off exclusivity of access to speed of access to these startups.

Techstars, headquartered in Boulder, Colorado, is arguably the originator of the *corporate accelerator* concept. Originally founded as a founder-led accelerator that worked intensively with cohorts of 10 startups for a three-month period, Techstars went on to offer corporates the option of running an accelerator for them with the same format as a turn-key service. Although Techstars continues to run standard accelerator cohorts in different cities around the world – a relatively recent addition being the Techstars Bangalore program – corporate accelerators have become a mainstay of what they do, with former and current clients – such as Barclays, Disney, Ford, Metlife, and Target, to name a few – coming from a range of industries. Techstars invests in each of the 10 startups selected for a cohort on behalf of the client and takes equity in return. Over the three months, startups go through a program of intensive mentor interactions, executing a refined plan of action and preparing for fundraising, with the climax being a demo day at the very end.

Some specialists, like London-based Founders Factory, build ventures from scratch in conjunction with founders, with a view to meeting the strategic needs of a set of (noncompeting) corporations. Co-founded by Brent Hoberman (a co-founder of lastminute.com, one of the UK's biggest successes of the dot-com boom in the late 1990s), Founders Factory has built 50-plus startups from scratch in its venture studio backed by a set of noncompeting corporations, including L'Oréal, Aviva, and easyJet. For example, a startup called Guider was created to address a problem statement around inefficiencies in employee mentoring within corporates by developing an AI employee matching platform with Marks & Spencer and piloted by Aviva and Reckitt Benckiser.[19] The portfolio of startups is encouraged to find ways to engage with all the corporate sponsors.

Do They Specialize in Cohorts or Funnels?

While Techstars and Plug and Play essentially offer cohort-based interfaces, there is also now a set of third-party specialists whose work aligns more closely with funnel-based interfaces through which prospective startup partners are progressively screened out.

For example, 27 Pilots helps corporations adopt what they describe as the "venture client" model. Co-founder Gregor Gimmy had developed this concept at BMW Startup Garage where external startups were identified as partners that could work with specific innovation units of the corporation to address specific opportunities or pain points, and in the process, the corporation would become a client for the startup – hence the term venture client. As Gimmy explains in a *Harvard Business Review* article that he co-authored with a group of IMD professors, "In essence, the venture client, instead of equity, buys the technology of a startup when it is still a venture . . . partnering as the first big client with young companies that have either graduated from an accelerator or received professional VC funding. The first purchase is a 'minimum viable purchase,' since the incumbent buys just a sample of the startup's solution for validation in a real pilot project conducted by the business unit. Selected startups become real suppliers, with purchase orders and supplier numbers, from day one of the venture client program."[20]

As another example, Pilot 44 describes its mission as being to "help top brands leverage the power of emerging, startup technologies to accelerate digital innovation."[21] In particular, it helps companies to move fast in experimenting with new ideas, typically drawing on the expertise of external startups, by executing a pilot project. A pilot can be launched quickly – for example, within a month or two. The process involves design, development, and execution. To illustrate, the design may center around goals, learning plans, hypotheses, and key performance indicators (KPIs) associated with a corporation's intent to build a personal relationship with customers and guide them within a retail environment to the right option as they navigate a bewildering set of alternatives. The development phase would then involve coming up with a minimum viable product of, say, an artificial intelligence bot. Since the corporation itself likely lacks the capability to develop this, this is where Pilot 44 becomes an intermediary between that company and external startups. During the development phase, Pilot 44 would select a startup to work on the pilot by scouting, screening, shortlisting (say, five startups), and selecting one to work on the pilot

Where Is Their Geographical Strength?

Not all specialists can add value equally well across geographical locations. Some intermediaries – including ones founded by managers who previously ran startup programs – have real strength in North America or Europe, where some others are well placed to serve emerging markets. For example, in China, XNode is an example of a third-party specialist that helps multinationals connect with local startups. To illustrate, XNode worked with Pernod Richard to promote cocktails among young consumers by identifying a startup, Gin & Tommy, that developed a platform based on WeChat to build a community for cocktail lovers. The French multinational also became a corporate investor in the startup. ReHub, a Shanghai-based outfit, has been successful in connecting technology from Israeli startups with multinational corporations operating in China, especially in the retail sector. In India, Bangalore-based Kyron showed promise in being able to connect corporations and startups – and eventually, when Techstars decided to enter the Indian market, they partnered with Kyron's parent company, ANSR, and, in essence, transformed that organization into Techstars India. In South America, particularly Brazil, 100 Startups is a third-party specialist that connects startups and corporations.[22]

The geographic aspect of startup partnering is one that is of great importance for large multinational corporations. As indicated by several of the examples used in this book so far, for corporations operating in multiple locations, there are opportunities to engage in meaningful corporate-startup partnering around the world. To make the most of their global partnering opportunities, multinationals would do well to pay attention not only to the prospect of partnering with startups around the world, but also actively consider nuances associated with different types of locations – which we discuss next, in Chapter 5.

PART THREE

WHERE

CHAPTER FIVE

PARTNERING WITH START-UPS AROUND THE WORLD

Today the challenge is to innovate by learning from the world. And because innovation drives growth, those companies that fail to learn will be left behind.

— Professor Yves Doz (INSEAD)[1]

LEARNING FROM THE WORLD

A global mindset – which involves characteristics such as curiosity, connections, and the competence to deal with different cultural contexts – helps managers recognize the value of partnering with startups across multiple settings. The Microsoft case illustrates that traversing a wide range of geographic locations and tapping startup ecosystems around the world can be highly rewarding – but also demanding in terms of the resources and effort involved. For companies exploring how to build or strengthen an international dimension to their startup partnering, it can be useful to consider three perspectives that can be progressively layered on.

First, consistent with the "think global, act local" mantra,[2] while corporations recognize that partnering with local startups could help them be more effective in foreign markets by responding better to local needs, they should also consider how their startup partnering practices may have to be modified to suit the local context. This is especially true for corporations from advanced markets operating in emerging markets.

Second, consistent with a "think local, act global" logic, corporations should recognize that new partnering practices can be learned from innovation hotspots like Israel and applied elsewhere.[3] Also, diverse technological ideas that a corporation gains exposure to from international startups may be applicable in other markets as well. When Crowdz, a Silicon Valley-based startup, participated in Barclays' London accelerator, it was actively pursuing opportunities in East Asia.

Finally, combining these ideas, a "think global, act global" perspective could be thought of in terms of developing a portfolio of locations (including hotspots and non-hotspots in advanced and emerging markets) and aligning practices to the characteristics of these different contexts. Although not every multinational will necessarily partner with startups literally around the world, they are likely to encounter a range of different locations. For instance, Barclays has had corporate accelerator programs in London, New York, and Tel Aviv as well as Cape Town, South Africa. Several multinationals, including BMW and Unilever, have introduced their startup partnering programs in China. As such, it is useful to obtain an understanding of how to differently handle various locations that are part of a multinational's globally dispersed portfolio of startup partnering activities.

This chapter looks at each of these three perspectives, in turn:

1. Think global, act local
2. Think local, act global
3. Think global, act global

THINK GLOBAL, ACT LOCAL: ADAPTING PRACTICES

As a starting point, a global orientation to startup partnering needs to take into account differences between entrepreneurial ecosystems and calls for suitable *local adaptation* of startup partnering practices in the same way that many multinationals have had to adapt their product offerings significantly overseas. One of the most apparent cases of needing to *adapt* practices is when partnering practices are imported from advanced to *emerging markets*.

When startups from China and India enjoyed great success in the IBM Global Smartcamp competition of 2015, it was clear that the entrepreneurial ecosystems in these emerging markets were attracting attention from global multinationals. That year, the global winner of the competition was Insight Robotics, a Hong Kong-based startup that helps in firefighting through their technology in an automated detection system using robotics.[4] Another finalist was Stelae Technologies, a Bangalore-based AI startup, which later went on to participate in the Airbus BizLab global aerospace accelerator. In my conversations with Kevin Chan, CEO of Insight Robotics, in Hong Kong and Aruna Schwarz, Stelae's CEO in Bangalore, it was clear to me that the Asian startup founders had developed a camaraderie during the process and were rejoicing in each other's success, and felt that the spotlight was rightfully being turned to the East.

However, notwithstanding these success stories, emerging markets are a bit like startup partnering itself: they can be attractive *and* challenging at the same time. Furthermore, there are differences among emerging markets. Policy priorities may differ. For example, at a time when China was emphasizing the promotion of mass entrepreneurship, South Africa was focused on the empowerment of black communities and entrepreneurs. Also, the level of scale varies. The volume of entrepreneurship in large emerging markets like China and India greatly exceeds that in smaller ones. Furthermore, there are varying skillsets associated with different markets and, in certain areas (e.g. drones in China), the level of expertise may be on a par with advanced markets.

Nevertheless, these markets do have some broad similarities in terms of opportunities and challenges. Focusing on one of each, at the level of the country and of the company, yields four important factors:[5]

1. Country-level challenge: The immaturity of the startup ecosystem
2. County-level opportunity: The appetite for entrepreneurship
3. Company-level challenge: The "outsider" status of multinationals
4. Company-level opportunity: Proximity to novel technologies

Understanding these four factors (see Figure 5.1) helps identify four corresponding adjustments to startup partnering strategies and practices in emerging markets.

	Challenges	Opportunities
Country-related factors	Immaturity of the entrepreneurial ecosystem [Strategy: Compensate]	Considerable appetite for entrepreneurship [Strategy: Commit]
Company-related factors	MNCs are outsiders vis-à-vis emerging market startups [Strategy: Co-opt]	MNC proximity to novel technologies in emerging markets [Strategy: Co-innovate]

Figure 5.1 Partnering with Startups in Emerging Markets: Opportunities and Challenges

Compensate for Ecosystem Immaturity

In emerging markets, a key challenge at the country level is dealing with the relative immaturity of entrepreneurial ecosystems. As the next point indicates, there are often a *lot* of exciting developments in the leading startup ecosystems in emerging markets such as Bangalore and Shenzhen. However, multinationals will often find themselves dealing with first-time entrepreneurs (unlike in Silicon Valley or Israel, where many more entrepreneurs have worked on multiple startups). There are deficiencies in the institutional environment, including limitations in terms of access to market intermediaries or property rights. Also, the ease of doing business isn't always ideal.

In such circumstances, multinationals typically have to work harder to be discerning about identifying high-quality startups and make efforts to be more supportive. To illustrate, managers in Microsoft South Africa added more scaffolding to the standard

BizSpark program that was launched in the United States and globally. By partnering tapping local schemes for funding capacity building, they were able to add a great deal more mentoring support than the regular partnering program normally provided, and this was seen to be an important way to compensate for the immaturity of the entrepreneurial ecosystem. Also, IBM added certain modules to their Global Entrepreneurship Program in China that provided extra technical educational input and mentoring. And in Indonesia, Facebook launched a free-of-charge facility called Linov (Lab Innovation Indonesia) to enable collaborative learning among technology developers and innovators in the startup ecosystem.[6]

Commit Resources to Tap Ecosystem Energy

On the flip side, an opportunity at the country level in many emerging markets is the huge appetite for entrepreneurship, often due to policy support. The dramatic rise of startup creation in China since Premier Li Keqiang announced the "mass innovation, mass entrepreneurship" policy is a case in point. With a large amount of venture capital becoming available, a large number of startups aggressively pursued growth in the Chinese market, spawning the second-highest number of unicorns (startups valued at a billion dollars or more), next only to the United States. Although the initial frenzied pace of startup growth has quieted down (or, to put it differently, investors appear to have become more selective in terms of startup quality), it seems likely that even with the toll that Covid-19 has taken, emerging markets like China and India will remain vibrant sources of entrepreneurial opportunities and start-ups for the foreseeable future.

Multinational companies can respond to this opportunity by prioritizing emerging markets. As seen, when the Microsoft Accelerator initiative was launched, two of the first accelerators were located in Bangalore and Beijing. It was only subsequently that accelerators were opened in advanced market locations such as London. Also in India, it introduced a "partner in acceleration" initiative to help other actors, including key Microsoft customers, with their own startup engagement. One outcome of this was a Gen-Next Innovation Hub, a joint initiative between Reliance Industries Ltd., a Mumbai-based conglomerate, and Microsoft. Such efforts served as signals of Microsoft's commitment and interest to local startups in emerging markets. And in other Asian emerging markets that are also witnessing high levels of energy in their entrepreneurial ecosystems, Microsoft for Startups has launched its Emerge X Program, a competitive pitching event, as part of its "Highway to 100 Unicorns Initiative," which had winners from the Philippines, Singapore, Sri Lanka, and Vietnam.[7] Other multinationals are also increasingly active in these markets; for example, the Unilever Foundry Startup Battle has attracted over 500 startup participants from Asia, with over a third of them developing pilot projects with Unilever.[8]

Co-opt Insiders to Deal with Being an Outsider

Another challenge, which relates to the characteristics of the corporation, is that foreign multinationals face something of a liability as outsiders. This isn't to say that companies with strong global brand names don't have their own cachet; rather, the point is that it is not always easy for them to penetrate and form deep network connections in the local milieu compared to homegrown players. This may be especially true in emerging markets like China, which has a distinct set of ecosystem giants compared to those that dominate in most Western markets. Furthermore, foreign multinationals may be held to higher standards by various stakeholders, and also have the challenge of their own headquarters not fully grasping the reality on the ground facing its subsidiary executives in emerging markets.

One way to deal with this challenge is for multinationals to co-opt local "insiders" to help build bridges between themselves and local startups. As previously noted, some specialist intermediaries have strong connections in certain markets that can be usefully tapped. In the case of Target, when it opened its first accelerator in Bangalore, it partnered with an Indian specialist, Kyron, which later became Techstars' Indian presence. As another example, Amazon Web Services worked with the Dream T incubator in China. Dream T set up various three-way agreements involving the multinational, itself, and a local government to establish various startup hubs across China. In this way Amazon's outsider status – magnified by the dominance of Alibaba's cloud service – could be mitigated not only by having a local partner but also by having a close connection with the local government.

Co-Innovate with Startups to Access Novel Ideas

On the upside, by virtue of being outsiders, multinationals gain visibility to technologies and ideas that are novel to them. Although generally it is advanced markets that have superior technologies, because of the different institutional environment they face (with privacy, for instance, being viewed somewhat differently), emerging market firms may have made greater strides in the use of certain technologies, such as QR codes. Also, because historically these firms have had to contend with considerable constraints and did not have ready access to high-quality inputs, some of them have become adept at doing more with less, an approach to innovation that has been described as frugal, and to develop offerings using locally embedded know-how around nutrition, for instance.

To illustrate, AB InBev (the Budweiser company) sought to tap the culture of scanning QR codes in China to acquire data to aid customer engagement. Martin Suter, then a Shanghai-based executive at AB InBev, led the multinational to partner with ConvertLab, a local startup, to pilot a digital solution whereby customers could scan a QR code under a beer bottle cap, and the most loyal customers would get a free beer on their birthday.[9]

This led to a win-win situation for the corporation (a digital solution) and startup (a marquee client) through co-innovation. As another example, Starbucks has partnered with Indonesia-based Green Butcher, a startup making plant-based products, to offer vegan "beef" products – a unique local innovation – in that region.[10]

These examples highlight how working with local startups can help a large corporation in its efforts to localize and meet consumer needs better, in this case by addressing shifting consumer behavior in a digital world. But co-innovation can also result in new ideas that can be deployed in other markets of the multinational corporation. In the AB InBev example, that multinational not only developed new digital capabilities not readily available in its other markets, but also was able to leverage (albeit in a different format) its new capabilities in using QR codes to promote its leading beer brand in Brazil. The adoption of new partnering practices and technological ideas is more likely to happen with respect to innovation hotspots around the world, as discussed next.

THINK LOCAL, ACT GLOBAL: ADOPTING PRACTICES

Companies can benefit from the *global adoption* of practices originating in geographic locations far from a multinational corporation's home base by leveraging *innovation hotspots* around the world (see Figure 5.2). In innovation hotspots of both advanced and emerging markets – such as Silicon Valley, Israel, Beijing, Shanghai and Shenzhen in China, and Bangalore or Hyderabad in India – there is scope for large corporations to adopt new practices and ideas.

	Advanced market hotspots	**Emerging market hotspots**
Technological corporations	Global initiatives could be initiated, and global leadership of partner initiatives could be based in locations like Silicon Valley and Israel to signal a commitment to startups (e.g. Fujitsu, Intel, Microsoft, SAP)	Scope for tapping technologies that are well-suited for emerging markets; possibility of reverse innovation also (e.g. Qualcomm); also scope for global initiatives (e.g. SwissRe)
Traditional corporations	Even traditional companies have either located key initiatives or people who are part of key initiatives in Silicon Valley and Israel to "scout" for startup talent (e.g. Bayer, Ford)	Traditional corporations may also find locally relevant technologies (e.g. AB InBev) and in some cases even find uses for these in advanced market (e.g. Walmart; SwissRe)
Third-party intermediaries	Several third-party entities that position themselves as intermediaries between corporations and startups in Silicon Valley (e.g. Plug and Play, Silicon Foundry, Pilot 44) and Israel (e.g. The Floor for fintech)	Some local specialists that understand the context deeply (e.g. XNode and Chinaccelerator in China, THub and Kyron in India – the latter acquired by Techstars, Open 100 Startups in Brazil, etc.)

Figure 5.2 Tapping Hotspots for Corporate-Startup Partnering

Tapping Advanced Market Hotspots

In my research, I had the good fortune to meet managers and entrepreneurs in a range of interesting startup ecosystems. Silicon Valley was an obvious one to consider, and notwithstanding concerns of an exodus of firms to other locations (like Texas),[11] it is clear that this region has been a powerhouse of innovation and entrepreneurship. When I compare the onsite interviews I conducted in Silicon Valley in 2008 and then 2018 (in addition to several remote interviews over a longer period), I could not detect any letup in entrepreneurs' hunger for success, and a noticeable difference was the rise of players like Plug and Play, Silicon Foundry, and Pilot44 that was explicitly linking corporations with startups. Also, there were by now numerous corporations, including non-US multinationals, that had chosen to drive their startup partnering efforts out of Silicon Valley and establish "scouting units" or "innovation outposts" there.[12]

Corporations that are from outside Silicon Valley have long looked to this hotspot for inspiration, and drive their startup engagement out of places like Palo Alto, California. Corporations have been increasingly willing to engage with third-party specialists and even competitors to engage with the diverse talent represented by Silicon Valley startups. For an outsider, Silicon Valley could potentially have the benefit of being a locale that is distant away from headquarters to avoid undue interference but significant enough to signal to all relevant audiences that the effort to partner with startups was being taken seriously.

Of course, Silicon Valley has its challenges. For one, it is not cheap to operate out of there, in terms of personnel and real estate. Moreover, there is a danger of being caught up in innovation theater rather than making meaningful progress. And there is keen competition among corporations to win the hearts and minds of startups and other relevant actors. However, the key is recognizing that, in addition to legitimizing the startup partnering initiative, leveraging a location like Silicon Valley gives corporations access to the top talent available in terms of startups as well as expertise in partnering with the ecosystem. For instance, there is scope to engage with third-party specialists but also innovative initiatives of companies such as the Fujitsu Open Gateway. Through such interactions it may be possible to accelerate the initiation of the process of startup partnering more readily. This was the case with Microsoft, as well as SAP. Bayer also found it sensible to base the intelligence arm of its G4A initiative in the Valley.

Another iconic location that has been influential in the global corporate-startup partnering landscape is Israel. The "startup nation" that has one of the most vibrant entrepreneurial ecosystems in the world has also attracted many multinational corporations to establish research facilities as well as scouting units or innovation outposts. Since many Israeli startups get acquired by large corporations before they grow very big, corporate managers and startup entrepreneurs are keen to cross paths, and the rise of various intermediaries that link corporations and startups has made this readily possible. Importantly, intrapreneurs in Israel have had a profound impact on the startup partnering efforts of numerous corporations. Zack Weisfeld personifies this. Apart from driving Microsoft's global accelerator program, he later went on to have a similar impact on Intel. This is interesting because Intel has been a poster child of the success of multinationals in Israel, and prominently highlighted in the book *Startup Nation*.[13] Moreover, its corporate venture capital arm has been among the most successful (in terms of financial return) and prolific investors in startups. And yet, Weisfeld was able to persuade Intel to engage in non-equity partnering, broadly consistent with the model that Microsoft had pioneered, and to establish a new program, Intel Ignite, in Israel. Subsequently, accelerators have been established in the United States (Austin, Texas) and Europe (Munich, Germany).

Entrepreneurs around the world have been intrigued by the track record of Israel's entrepreneurs and seek to learn from them. A prominent feature of the narrative that one hears is the motivation to innovate stemming from an existential geopolitical threat, resulting in cutting-edge technologies in areas like cybersecurity. Rabbi Dr. David Mescheloff, who I met at the Hebrew University of Jerusalem, suggests that the entrepreneurial instinct is deeply embedded in Judaic tradition. Using a story of the Jewish patriarch Abraham who smashed his father's idols as a young boy, he argues that the roots of Israeli entrepreneurship lie in a deep and innate curiosity, and a willingness to take on big intellectual challenges.

Certainly, such status quo-challenging behaviors have been evident during the numerous interactions I have had with Israeli entrepreneurs over the years.

What has been especially striking is that the Israeli influence on corporate innovation practices such as corporate-startup partnering has been pervasive. In addition to prominent startup partnering activity by technology giants such as Microsoft and Intel that spread to other parts of the world, many companies in traditional sectors have built corporate accelerators in Israel first, before opening up others elsewhere. The proclivity for corporate managers and startup entrepreneurs to engage is uncommonly high, so much so that on one of my research trips to Israel, I learned of an Australian startup that was in advanced discussions with a US multinational about a potential collaborative project – something that was far more likely to happen in Israel than in that startup's home country. Furthermore, entities such as the world-renowned Sheba Medical Center in Tel Aviv (a role model for hospitals that take digital innovation seriously) have actively pursued startup partnering to enhance the efficacy of medical treatments.

As for other advanced market hotspots, it is worth noting that significant European startup ecosystems include London, Berlin, and Munich. Bayer's Grant4Apps (G4A) program initiated in Berlin and BMW Startup Garage located in Munich are testaments to those locations' importance – although in both cases, strong efforts were made to attract startups from further afield. And London, where Unilever Foundry's leadership is based, represents an incredible success story of how, with collective efforts from various stakeholders, startup ecosystems can be cultivated. Of course, London has some incredible advantages, resulting from history and circumstance, that cannot be easily replicated. But it shows that when a location is leveraged to incorporate a startup ecosystem, then there are enormous possibilities for corporate-startup partnering. The Spanish telecom multinational Telefonica demonstrated this through its Wayra accelerator in London under Gary Stewart's leadership. Barclays is another company that was able to launch an effective accelerator, Rise, in London (and elsewhere) in collaboration with Techstars. Barclays' accelerator program attracts startups from around the world; for example, a Silicon Valley–based startup, Crowdz, was part of one its London cohorts, and went on to collaborate with that corporation.

This is by no means an exhaustive list of advanced market hotspots; the point is that several exist and have attracted the attention of corporations seeking to partner with startups.

Tapping Emerging Market Hotspots

Important as advanced markets are, arguably the big story of the mobile and cloud computing era has been the rise of startup ecosystems in emerging markets. Bangalore and Beijing's Zhongguancun region have been longstanding sites for multinationals' research facilities, and with strong knowledge spillovers from such entities as well as the return of highly qualified people from the West, including

Silicon Valley, a startup revolution has emerged. Of course, these are not the only important locations in these markets. For example, in China, Shenzhen (with its hardware expertise) has rivaled Beijing's Zhongguancun (a longstanding bastion for software companies) for the title "Silicon Valley of China." Hangzhou is another Chinese city that spawned a large number of startups, following in the wake of Alibaba, which is headquartered in that city. Co-innovating with startups in emerging market hotspots could lead to the realization that some novel technologies accessed through this process can be utilized in other markets by the multinational, leading to the prospect of what Professor Vijay Govindarajan refers to as "reverse innovation," a process by which innovation is developed in emerging markets first and then exported to advanced markets (a reversal of the traditional direction in which innovations flow).[14]

Hotspots in emerging markets such as China and India offer the scope to access novel ideas. Take the case of Walmart China's Omega 8 initiative. Ben Hassing of Walmart is very much the kind of corporate manager I have come across in my research who takes startup partnering seriously: a good communicator who gets along well with different types of people. Hassing moved to China in 2015 and played an important role in shaping Walmart's digital strategy in that market. On Hassing's watch, with strong support from the subsidiary's leadership, Walmart also developed a partnering program to work with innovative Chinese startups to help them improve the customer experience in China. Andy Lei, a dynamic young Chinese manager mentored by Hassing, drove this new initiative, christened Omega 8.

This partner program allowed the retail giant to identify and work with Chinese startups, initially on a 60-day proof of concept (PoC) project that, if promising, would be piloted and then deployed at scale. Crucially, each PoC would be developed in conjunction with a business unit (BU) at the outset; thus there was a genuine pain point or opportunity driving the PoC. In this effort, Hassing and Lei found an ally in James Chou, head of startup partnering at Microsoft China. (Microsoft is a global strategic technology partner of Walmart's.) Chou organized a weekend hackathon for Walmart involving a small set of curated startups, mostly alumni of the Microsoft accelerator, which provided the initial pool of startups for Walmart to work with.

Clobotics is an example of a startup whose AI- and IoT-enabled offering enables retailers to obtain real-time dynamic market data ended up partnering with Walmart through this process.[15] Another Chinese AI startup helped Walmart address an in-store pain point. When customers buy loose vegetables or fruits, the process can often be a hassle: they must put the product in a plastic bag, have it weighed (which may require jostling with others in a queue) and then affix a sticky label obtained from the person who weighed the bag. The startup solved this problem by using image recognition technology that brings up images of fruit and vegetables on a screen, and the customer has a one-click solution whereby clicking on the relevant image generates a sticky label from the weighing machine itself. Intriguingly, Walmart was so impressed by this startup's technology that it even worked with the startup in the United States on a different problem, namely monitoring in-store theft – an intriguing example of reverse innovation via partnering with startups.

It was apparent that this subsidiary initiative in China had gained global attention within Walmart when its global CEO, Doug McMillon, spent 90 minutes learning about the program and three exemplar startups – including the one with the solution for weighing loose vegetables and fruit.

The Cisco LaunchPad in India offers another example of how emerging market hotspots can be tapped. Cisco LaunchPad was launched in Bangalore in 2016, the same year the Indian government launched its Startup India initiatives. Krishna Sundaresan, VP Engineering of Cisco Systems, observed, "At Cisco LaunchPad, what we bring to the table is sales expertise to take the startups to the market as well as engineering core competency on product scaling and deployment in the form of mentorship."[16] Rigorously selected cohorts of eight startups are supported for six months. They cover three broad areas: enterprise technology, digitization/IoT, and futuristic technologies. One source of the last-mentioned category is academic spinoffs, such as Astrome Technologies in space tech (Indian Institute of Science), Velmenni in LiFi connectivity (Indian Institute of Technology Delhi) and Qnu Labs in quantum safetech (Indian Institute of Technology Madras).

Cisco LaunchPad, which takes no equity in its startup members, provides support to startups by showcasing them at industry and their own events (like Cisco Live). Sruthi Kannan, who runs Cisco Launchpad, readily points to numerous exemplars from among the first 40 startups accelerated across five batches. These include Teslon, which partners with Greece's Health Ministry; Yellow Messenger, which also became a partner of SAP and WhatsApp; and Cloudphysician, whose remote ICU solution helped save a 13-year-old boy's life in Muzzafirpur, Bihar by suggesting an intervention never used in that hospital before. For Kannan this sort of impact is more important than a startup's valuation. As she observes, "We are interested in startups that create value for a billion, not a valuation of a billion."

Engaging with Startups in China and India: Some Similarities and Differences

Notwithstanding US-China trade tensions and the fallout of the Covid-19 pandemic, many multinationals operating in China have become aware of the potential for tapping into the rising innovation activities of local players, including startups. Another large emerging market where multinationals have also sought to engage with the startup ecosystem is India. A study by Tufts University's Fletcher School indicates that there is considerable digital momentum in these markets. As seen from various examples in this book, in some instances, corporations have brought their global startup programs to these markets (e.g. Bayer's G4A accelerator program being introduced in Shanghai, China) or launched new programs there (e.g. the Cisco LaunchPad created in Bangalore, India). Several other emerging markets across Africa, Asia, and Latin America are also proving to be of great interest but of these, China and India have the largest startup ecosystems. Therefore, these markets will remain vitally important to multinationals seeking to partner with startups on a global basis.

China and India reflect the influence of two important factors, which economic geographers refer to as "pipelines," and personal relationships, or "people". Pipelines represent connections to large multinational corporations; think of the subsidiaries for sales or research established in Bangalore and Beijing by the likes of IBM, Intel, and Dell. And the people reflect the "returnees" – those who come back to the land of their origin after stints abroad for education and employment. Triggered by personal circumstances or an interest in exploring new opportunities in the dynamic environment of an emerging economy, these individuals are often important sources of know-how, both technical and commercial. When Microsoft opened an accelerator in Shanghai, I was not surprised to find a number of the co-founders of startups in the inaugural cohort to be returnees, often from prestigious universities and companies.

Combining the ideas of pipelines and people, one can think of "people within the pipelines," such as returnees who play an important role as the country heads of multinational subsidiaries in these ecosystems.[17] And these individuals can be an important bridge between local startups and their wider multinational corporations. Skelta, one of the first Bangalore-based startups that Microsoft worked with closely, was able to engage closely with that multinational in the United States because Indian managers in Microsoft India were able to connect them with other (sometimes Indian-origin) managers in Microsoft in the United States. Of course, coethnicity of managers doesn't mean that collaboration will necessarily happen, but it might help to build rapport and allow smooth communication.[18] Such people in the pipelines have played an important part in Western multinationals recognizing the importance of, and tapping into, entrepreneurial ecosystems in emerging economies.

However, while China and India do have some shared characteristics as large emerging economies, they are a study in contrasts, and it is worth considering some of major differences between them.

First, the major technology giants that dominate the local business environment are different. China's Internet is dominated by Baidu, Alibaba, and Tencent – which originally could be thought of as the Google, Amazon, and Facebook of China, respectively, but have evolved into very large, complex organizations in their own right. While Western technology majors such as IBM, Microsoft, and SAP do have a major presence in China, especially in relation to enterprise solutions, local players dominate in the realm of the mobile Internet. By contrast, in India, the "Facebook of India" is Facebook and the "Google of India" is Google. In other words, the same global giants that dominate the Internet in the Western world are also the major players in India. This means that multinationals engaging with startups in China must recognize that their partners are more likely to be using Alibaba's cloud service than Amazon's, and will be inclined to build connections with both Western multinationals and Chinese homegrown giants. In that sense, they are competing more widely for startup partners than in most other markets. But this doesn't have to be a zero-sum game since startups can dance with many gorillas without evoking conflicts of interest by, say, having a different focus with different partners.

Second, in China, the government plays a major role in setting national priorities that businesses align with. This isn't to say that the government is insignificant in India, but rather to highlight the vastly different political systems that operate in these markets. Thus, when the Chinese government declares artificial intelligence to be a national priority, then that's what businesses focus on. By implication, startup partnering is likely to be more productive when such priorities are reflected. It is also important to understand that the role of the government at both the national and local levels matter in China. While Beijing sets the tone for national priorities and policies, it is local government officials – at the province, city, and district level (within large cities) – where policy is implemented. Thus, when Microsoft opened its second accelerator in China in Shanghai (after the one in Beijing), it was the result of entrepreneurial efforts by officials in the Caohejing district of Shanghai. Merck opened an innovation hub on Guangzhou International Biotech Island, a policy initiative aimed at promoting growth in the Guangdong-Hong Kong-Macao Greater Bay.[19]

In India too different state governments do have differing emphases and strategies to promote innovation and entrepreneurship with some, like Telengana's T Hub incubator with Ravi Narayan (formerly of Microsoft for Startups) as CEO, standing out for their proactive efforts. However, whereas in China various multinationals readily participated in efforts by the Zhangjiang district of Shanghai, home to a major national science park, to establish a "transnational" incubator, in India it is just as likely that a private sector trade body will play such a role. Over time, local governments in China develop a unique flavor or focus in their innovation and entrepreneurship policies, a nuance that is important for multinationals to grasp if they are to successfully tap into entrepreneurial ecosystems in China. The upshot is that one needs more than a catchall "China strategy"; it is important to have an approach that is fine-tuned at the level of the local government, after having worked out which one(s) to engage with.

Third, although many startups do have international aspirations, in China the focus is very much on the domestic market – and that is not surprising, because it is vast. While India undoubtedly also has a growing middle class, I have come across in my research many entrepreneurs who naturally gravitate toward finding opportunities overseas, including in Western markets. Thus, while multinationals partnering with startups in China seem to have a "pull of gravity" toward the domestic market, it is plausible that Indian startups will also actively seek to engage with other parts of the multinational as a pathway to going global themselves. Early in my research, I compared the best cases I found of Microsoft partnering with startups in China and India. In the Chinese case, a startup in Beijing called Gridsum founded by a brilliant computer scientist, Qi Guosheng, partnered closely with China, but predominantly in that market. By contrast, under the leadership of returnee entrepreneur Sanjay Shah, as previously noted, Bangalore-based Skelta went on to leverage its Microsoft relationship that originated in India in overseas markets. This is not to say that Chinese startups don't want to achieve, or are incapable of, internationalization, but rather, that their domestic market is so unique and vast that they are understandably highly focused on it. For multinationals partnering with startups in these two markets, the trajectory of the partnership is likely to unfold in somewhat different patterns.

* * *

In sum, for a think-local-act-global strategy to work, empowered leaders in local subsidiaries must act proactively and global headquarters need to have sufficient humility, born out of a recognition that they don't have all the answers, to give local subsidiaries the leeway to be entrepreneurial.[20]

THINK GLOBAL, ACT GLOBAL: ALIGNING PRACTICES

When companies pursue *both* the think-global-act-local and think-local-act-global strategies discussed above in tandem, they can elevate their startup partnering activity by connecting the dots globally. Each of the previous two sections has highlighted a distinction that can be made between specific local contexts at the level of a city or some other subnational region.[21] The first distinction is between advanced and emerging markets (discussed in the Think Global, Act Local section), the second between innovation hotspots and non-hotspots (implied in the Think Local, Act Global section).[22]

With regard to emerging versus advanced markets, as seen, there needs to be adaptation in emerging markets because their growth opportunities go hand in hand with weaker institutional environments in terms of less mature entrepreneurial ecosystems and intellectual property regimes. One way of summarizing the previously noted differences is to say that these contexts have higher *coordination costs* for collaboration with startups than advanced markets.

As for the distinction between hotspots and non-hotspots, it was seen that new practices and ideas can be adopted from innovation hotspots. Hotspots – the sort of startup ecosystems covered in Startup Genome reports like Silicon Valley, Israel, Bangalore, Beijing, Berlin, and London, to name but a few – differ from non-hotspots in terms of the access to firms that are good at both technology and entrepreneurship. The ease of attracting suitable partners is greater within hotspots; that is, the *search costs* for appropriate startup partners are lower.

Taking these two distinctions into account, we can think of a fourfold typology of locations:

1. Advanced market hotspots
2. Emerging market hotspots
3. Advanced market non-hotspots
4. Emerging market non-hotspots

It has been seen that partnering templates based on cohort or funnel interfaces may require adaptation in emerging market hotspots to contend with the greater coordination costs. This can be thought of as a difference between *facilitative* and *directive* templates. Whereas in advanced markets a facilitative approach to coordination suffices because of the strong institutional conditions, in emerging markets a more directive approach with, for example, greater intentional handholding is often called for. That said, as seen from several examples, corporations can have mutually rewarding outcomes when collaborating with startups in both advanced and emerging market hotspots.

Very many of the examples of corporate-startup partnering used in this book originate from advanced-market hotspots. Global initiatives such as Microsoft's BizSpark One program and SAP's Startup Focus were managed by teams in Silicon Valley. The Unilever Foundry program was headquartered in London, another innovation hotspot. These locations typify the "ideal" conditions of having access to a critical mass of startups in an institutionally strong environment. This allows corporations to orchestrate the startup ecosystem in a relatively loose, facilitative manner whereby opportunities are discovered as external startups and relevant actors within the large corporation are brought together. This isn't to suggest that the process is effortless – indeed, the major argument of this book is that corporate-startup partnering is effortful – but rather to highlight that the relative ease of facilitating collaboration in innovation hotspots doesn't necessarily translate to other location types.

In emerging market hotspots, this book has revealed numerous examples of successful outcomes in corporate-startup partnering. However, as this chapter has already indicated, the relative immaturity of startup ecosystems (albeit accompanied by huge growth and appetite) may require a somewhat tighter approach to orchestrating the startup ecosystem. That is, greater handholding for startups may be required, especially early on when a multinational takes its startup partnering activity to emerging markets. When Bayer brought its G4A startup accelerator to Shanghai, a lot of hands-on mentoring support was provided, with the then-Bayer China president Celina Chew being actively involved herself.

Similarly, when SAP introduced the Startup Focus initiative in Asia Pacific, its managers in Bangalore commented that startups needed much greater handholding during the go-to-market phase. This is not to say that emerging market startups are somehow inferior to ones in advanced markets; indeed, over time, China and India have seen some very sophisticated startups emerge, many with co-founders who are returnees from Silicon Valley. Rather, the point is that emerging markets will likely continue to have to cope with what Professor Tarun Khanna of Harvard Business School calls institutional voids[23] – deficiencies in institutions – and so providing extra support or involvement will remain a smart thing to do, while at the same time harnessing the palpable appetite for entrepreneurship, Covid-19 notwithstanding, in many emerging markets.

Much of the discussion thus far pertains to hotspots. But what about *non*-hotspots in advanced and emerging markets? While it is the case that most corporations confine their corporate innovation activities to hotspots, certain highly global corporations may well have operational subsidiaries in such locations that were established in the past or are being enticed by local policy makers from such regions who are keen to attract foreign direct investment.

IBM is an example of such a global company. In addition to its subsidiaries in hotspots such as London and Shanghai, it has subsidiaries in non-hotspots. One of its oldest foreign subsidiaries was established in a town called Greenock near Glasgow, a non-hotspot region in the UK. And one of its youngest is a research unit in Ningbo, a city in China's Zhejiang province. While the capital of Zhejiang province, Hangzhou, is an innovation hotspot (it's where Alibaba is headquartered), Ningbo is not. Yet IBM was able to reach out to innovative startups through both those subsidiaries.

How did this happen? The answer is purpose-built (as opposed to template-based) interfaces that were developed in collaboration with entrepreneurial local policy-makers. Whereas a template-based approach involving cohorts or funnels would normally work in a hotspot location, in non-hotspots where there is a lack of a critical mass of innovative startups a purpose-built approach – often working with an external party – seems necessary. Furthermore, these external parties may well be "non-market actors" such as local government officials who have a mandate to foster innovation in the local milieu and are willing to act entrepreneurially. Thus if some startups in non-hotspot areas do have valuable complementary capabilities for large corporations, it will likely take special mechanisms to get to them, a bit like hard-to-mine ore. While government officials can play a role even in hotspots, in non-hotspots the role of policy efforts can be particularly important, and it helps when local officials exhibit entrepreneurial behaviors themselves.

A good illustration of a purpose-built interface in an advanced market non-hotspot is offered by a public policy initiative, the Scottish Technology & Collaboration (STAC). It was jointly undertaken by Scottish Enterprise, the Glasgow-based economic development agency of Scotland, with ScotlandIS, a trade body for the software industry. The idea to set up an "honest broker" to help multinationals connect with local entrepreneurial firms was first proposed by a manager of Sun Microsystems' Scottish subsidiary, and received widespread support from other multinationals like IBM as well as local small firms. Multinational subsidiaries in the region, like Sun's, were keen to build up their innovative capabilities in order to convince their headquarters in the United States to give them more high-end work beyond manufacturing – much of which was being relocated to lower-cost regions.

These corporations were keen to tap into the engineering talent in Scotland, including that in local entrepreneurial firms. For the local firms, the opportunity to scale up their innovations in conjunction with a multinational was attractive. But in a non-hotspot, which typically lacks a critical mass of startups or the ubiquitous avenues for identifying partners such as the numerous accelerators in Silicon Valley, such a policy initiative can be helpful in matchmaking. Moreover, a purpose-built intermediary, like STAC, was in a position to reassure the large multinationals about the quality of the local partner while reassuring the latter of the good intentions of the former. Thus, the anxieties of both parties could be assuaged through an honest broker explicitly tasked with linking large and small firms. In one case, Sun Microsystems combined its hardware with the software expertise of a local software venture to co-develop a new product prototype that was successfully demonstrated to a prospective multinational client.

Non-hotspots in emerging markets have further challenges because, in addition to the lack of a critical mass of startups, there is also institutional immaturity. However, here too interesting partnerships can arise, especially when there are entrepreneurial local government officials to direct the process in a creative way. An interesting example I came across in my research was in Ningbo, China. There, local officials took a somewhat different approach compared to the STAC example mentioned earlier. They helped to create opportunities for engagement between large multinationals and local startups by leveraging an already existing policy initiative, the Ningbo Smart City program.

The entire smart city program – which entails the provision of digital services to improve local citizens' lives – was divided into a small number of large pieces, and each was awarded to a single company. The first to be tendered, smart logistics, was contracted to IBM. This meant that this multinational was now incentivized to establish a research unit in that city. However, it was clear that no single company could deliver the entire project on their own; they would have to work with local firms – and in Ningbo these were mainly startups. In the process, IBM ended up working closely with Ningbo Smarter Logistics, as well as other startups in the Internet of Things space, to develop a smart logistics solution that was showcased to IBM executives, including a high-ranking one from the United States.

Thus four types of partnering strategies can be identified, as shown in Figure 5.3. Taking a portfolio approach based on a nuanced understanding of locations around the world can draw attention to locations that could be easily overlooked – and yet may have more to offer than meets the eye. Of course, this doesn't imply that a company should be simultaneously active in every geographic location; for many corporations there will simply be neither the appetite nor bandwidth to engage with non-hotspots. But what it does mean is that companies should have a judicious mix of locations leading to a holistic *portfolio orientation* to their global footprint of startup partnering – which entails aligning partnering practices to different locational contexts.

	Innovation hotspot	Non-hotspot
Advanced market	In the "default" location for corporate-startup partnering, interface templates need to be applied to facilitate the attraction and nurturing of high-quality startup partners	Tapping public policy efforts to connect corporations and local startups can help for matchmaking in the absence of a critical mass of startups and a lot of partnering activity
Emerging market	Adaptations may be needed to compensate for ecosystem immaturity while harnessing innovative new business models arising from the appetite for entrepreneurship	The creative use of existing policy measures by entrepreneurial government officials can help to create nonobvious opportunities for corporate-startup partnering

Figure 5.3 Partnering with Startups Globally: Strategies Across Locations

∗ ∗ ∗

By no means am I suggesting that these models are the only ones that can work in each of the location types. Rather, what I am pointing out is that a holistic approach to identifying a locational portfolio draws attention to the fact that both advanced and emerging economies have regions outside hotspots where some global companies have a presence (say, a manufacturing facility set up in the past) or may consider having one (for example, because local policy-makers offer attractive incentives to make foreign direct investments). While those peripheral regions are unlikely to be the mainstream location for corporate-startup partnering, it is worth recognizing that productive collaboration *can* take place in those settings – provided there is creative and effective policy support from local governments.[24]

LOOKING
TO NEW FRONTIERS

To be clear, a global approach to startup partnering is not for every-one. But, a final thought to consider is that a global mindset that also considers non-hotspot regions draws attention to locations off the beaten track. These could include not only large emerging markets but others that may represent the next frontier for global corporate innovation – and offer the potential to have a positive societal impact. Indeed, beyond emerging markets such as China and India, there is excitement building – evidenced by announcements in recent years about research centers and other forms of investment – regarding what could be the next frontier of innovation: Africa.

On a research trip to Nairobi, Kenya I got a firsthand experience of this growing perception that there is considerable potential in the startup ecosystem there. In fact, a few years ago, it was a Kenyan startup that won IBM's global smartcamp competition.[25] Microsoft's 4Afrika initiative[26] is a signal of that corporation's commitment to the region, and provides a basis for engaging heavily with innova-tive local startups. The situation in Kenya is probably representative of Microsoft's broad strategy in Africa: there is breadth engagement in terms of community building and depth engagement in terms of cultivating partnerships with select promising startups.

But while this breadth-depth distinction is a familiar one in relation to Microsoft's startup engagement, the constraints on

Microsoft's managers in Africa seem somewhat greater since they are part of a primarily sales-oriented machine. Therefore managers tasked with startup engagement, especially under the umbrella of the Microsoft4Afrika initiative, work hard to understand how to make the most of the company's existing priorities and partnerships on the continent. As one manager put it, "We have a lot of meetings with a lot of people."

That said, the scope of such partnering is set to grow with Microsoft's development centers launched in Africa (one in Kenya, the other in Nigeria),[27] as well as two data centers in South Africa.[28] Part of the intent behind the development centers is to bring in more of an African perspective to product development with Microsoft, and seems to reflect a wider appetite for engaging with the local ecosystem. A case in point is the manner in which a strategic partnership with Liquid Telecom, a provider of fiber cable, has led to the establishment of a tripartite partnership between Microsoft, Liquid, and startup hubs – for instance, Nairobi Garage in Kenya. Similar arrangements have been made in multiple markets "from Cairo to Cape Town."

My observations in Africa have made me particularly cognizant of the potential for corporate-startup partnering to contribute to the achievement of the United Nations' Sustainable Development Goals.[29] For example, Ghana-based mPharma, a digital health startup that has played a key role in the battle against Covid-19 in that region, had previously been a participant in Microsoft's Israel accelerator.[30] In Kenya, Microsoft partners with Twiga Foods, a social enterprise that connects farmers with retail vendors.[31] And in one of its early startup partnering successes in South Africa, Microsoft partnered with WhereIsMyTransport, which maps informal public transport networks – about which there is often a dearth of reliable information – in emerging markets.[32]

Common to all of these startups is that they have a strong social mission, suggesting that, when done well, startup partnering on a global basis could well become a force for good, a prospect that Chapter 6 delves into.

CHAPTER SIX

PARTNERING WITH START-UPS AS A FORCE FOR GOOD

CEOs who quickly adopt a 360-degree view and become more attuned to their employees, value chains, and wider society will maneuver with a degree of sensitivity and humanity not open to those still focused solely on narrow financial returns.

– Paul Polman, ex-CEO of Unilever and Co-founder and Chair, IMAGINE[1]

DANCING WITH GORILLAS FOR THE SUSTAINABLE DEVELOPMENT GOALS

Many corporations are mindful about making a societal impact by helping to achieve the 17 Sustainable Development Goals (SDGs) that member states of the United Nations agreed in September 2015 to pursue, with a view to achieving them by 2030. Even before 2020 was overwhelmed by the Covid-19 pandemic, a clear intent to have social impact could be seen in the activities of many companies. While in some cases the companies are merely paying lip service, there are also clear examples of corporate leaders who have conveyed their commitment to sustainable development so vociferously that it's hard to doubt their sincerity. Royal DSM's honorary chairman, Feike Sijbesma, is unequivocal: "Delivering on the SDGs, the Global Goals, is a responsibility for all of us."[2] The Covid-19 pandemic arguably heightened this sense of societal orientation among responsible leaders. Paul Polman, ex-CEO of Unilever, who has consistently advocated a greater socially responsible role for business, observed: "The world which emerges from this COVID-19 crisis will look different. . . . In this undetermined future, agility will be a company's best asset . . . it's certainly plausible that firms which think beyond the next quarter, see the bigger picture, and display compassion and dexterity are on a better path."[3]

A professor at a Scandinavian business school once remarked that the genius of the SDGs is, in part, that there is little that is dramatically new in the issues covered – rather, what it is essentially offering is a *shared* global agenda for which there is a consensus of sorts. As Professor Jeffrey Sachs of Columbia University notes, "The SDGs have become the world's shared framework for sustainable development . . . businesses, science, and civil society must support SDG achievement."[4] The extent to which full-throated verbal support is matched by whole-hearted tangible actions is of course a whole other issue, which varies greatly across nations, companies, and individuals. But in terms of the purported agenda itself, it would be hard to argue with the fundamental importance of pursuing important social, economic, and environmental outcomes such as ending poverty and hunger (SDGs 1 and 2), facilitating good jobs and economic growth (SDG 8), and taking climate action to protect life below water and on land (SDGs 13, 14, and 15).[5]

Having a common vocabulary around the SDGs is useful in that it forces governments, organizations, and individuals to take stock of what *exactly* they are doing – for instance, which SDG(s) are being impacted, and precisely how, by their actions. It is increasingly common to see social responsibility reports explicitly highlight which SDGs are being impacted. A cynical response would be to view this as mere sugarcoating or window dressing, and that may well be true in some (even many) cases. But when done with serious intent, the clarity around the link between organizational activity and specific

SDGs can be enlightening and useful for both internal and external audiences.

Furthermore, it helps to recognize how one's actions vis-à-vis specific SDGs may (or may not) relate to those of others. This can lead to decisions about how to amplify one's efforts in concert with others', or to dial back on what one is doing in a certain area to avoid duplication. In the United Nations system, it is not uncommon to find agencies focusing on a specific SDG (for example, UN Habitat focuses on SDG 11, relating to sustainable cities) or a specific facet across multiple SDGs (such as UNICEF's emphasis on SDG targets as they relate to children). This clarity becomes helpful for businesses, including startups, in that they recognize that those multilateral organizations are potentially open for collaboration.

And of course, thinking about the SDGs forces deeper analysis of the efficacy of one's own goals. Honest self-reflection is important because although being associated with the SDGs might hold appeal for companies, as Jeffrey Sachs has observed, there is always the danger that corporations will simply "cherry-pick" the SDGs that they can more readily align with (and be seen as a good corporate citizen) while turning a blind idea to less convenient ones. The key, he argues, is for businesses to view the SDGs not as a straitjacket but rather as the major opportunity of the present era.[6]

Thus the role of business is crucial to achieving the Sustainable Development Goals, not least because pursuing the SDGs represents business opportunities. Professor Michael Porter talked about creating "shared value,"[7] which might take the form of pursuing what some thinkers like C. K. Prahalad conceived of as the "base of the pyramid"[8] or others, like Clayton Christensen, described as "market-creating innovation."[9] Whatever the specific manner in which companies go about seeking profitable yet socially impactful opportunities, it is worth paying close attention to the last of the 17 SDGs, which is "partnering for the goals."

Now, to be sure, SDG 17's remit is very broad and includes relationships involving governments, business, and civil society. However, the phenomenon of corporate-startup partnering potentially fits right in there. And this turns the spotlight particularly on social ventures that, by definition, seek to simultaneously pursue economic profit and social impact. This is about very different, nontraditional allies coming together to jointly create value. Arguably, this makes SDG 17 even more important: partnerships for the goals become critical in order to leverage complementary resources and capabilities to make headway in achieving the SDGs. When innovation through these partnerships has a positive impact on the SDGs, then its impact is all the more to be welcomed.

Microsoft's announcement of a global partner program for social entrepreneurs in February 2020 – just before Covid-19 became a full-blown crisis in the West – further underlines the attention being paid to achieving SDGs through the coming together of these very different sets of companies. One clear response has been in tackling the crisis itself. This has included efforts to provide solutions to the health-related consequences (for instance, making sanitizers and ventilators) as well as the business-related consequences (for instance, managing remote working and carrying out operations within the constraints of social distancing). And even beyond the immediate needs triggered by the crisis, there seems to be scope for some positive lingering effects in terms of companies contributing toward creating a better world – even if that sounds clichéd and a bit corny.

However, certain modifications of the process may be required. Whether corporate-startup partnering is pursued during a crisis or steady state, it is important to pay attention to certain contextual differences when dealing with an explicitly social outcome (alongside an economic goal). This may be less important if a Western social enterprise is working with a Western multinational based on an offering that has social impact. However, when the action takes place closer to the site of use, especially when the goal is to reach the less privileged, the synergy-interface-exemplar model will likely have to be suitably modified. And of course, this might take corporations further out of their comfort zone.

The material in this chapter is particularly influenced by work since September 2015, when the SDGs were adopted by the United Nations. By a happy coincidence, in the period since then I have been able to engage with Africa on a regular basis through my business school's campus in Accra, Ghana. My research on corporate-startup partnering in Africa opened my eyes to the prospect of positive social impact accruing through the coming together of nontraditional allies. The synergy-interface-exemplar framework still holds relevance but may be manifested somewhat differently

	"Regular" version	SDG-impacting version
Synergy	Win-win defined in economic terms with respect to building blocks or pain points	**Societal Synergy** Win-win defined not only in economic terms but also in terms of social impact
Interface	Typically manifests as a cohort or funnel run by a clearly identified startup engagement team; third-party specialists are also usually for-profit entities	**Inclusive Interface** May take the form of a cohort or funnel with the involvement of not only corporations but also noncommercial third parties such as NGOs or educational institutes
Exemplar	The success story is defined primarily in economic terms	**Hybrid Exemplar** The success story is ideally defined in both economic and social terms

Figure 6.1 Corporate-Startup Partnering for the SDGs: Adapting the Synergy-Interface-Exemplar Framework

when it comes to collaborations involving entrepreneurs and large organizations that have an impact on the SDGs; attention must be paid to (1) pursuing a *societal* synergy, and (2) using an *inclusive* interface that can (3) generate *hybrid* exemplars (see Figure 6.1). Each is discussed below.

SOCIETAL SYNERGY

When dealing with the realm of social outcomes, a broader interpretation of the concept of "synergy" is warranted, such that synergies – be they based on building blocks or pain points –incorporate a social dimension. In some cases, this is initiated by technology companies promoting their building blocks. In other cases, traditional-sector firms may take the lead in partnering with startups to contribute to addressing societal shortcomings such that when the situation improves over time, their services gain greater relevance or bigger opportunities. In either case, the win-win thus extends beyond mutual benefits for the corporation and startup to include a societal win.

Deploying Building Block Synergies to Address Societal Shortcomings

When applied to the realm of the SDGs, corporate-startup partnering may entail technological building blocks being deployed to help address societal pain points. A company like SAP or Microsoft may be keen to see that the usage of its platform technologies leads to societal value, not just economic impact for itself or the startup. This has come through often in my discussions with Microsoft managers, such as Muhammed Nabil, when he headed startup engagement under the auspices of the Microsoft4Afrika initiative. While there is also interest in the social impact of the partner in terms of helping overcome the lack of reliable market intermediaries[10] – for instance between farmers and the organized retail sector – there is undoubtedly a rational reason for this: the prospect of consumption of the corporation's cloud-based platform technologies. However, a challenge that Microsoft faces is weaning startups off a dependency on software credits and instead helping them reconsider how they might optimally engineer their products. This requires addressing a skills shortage, especially in terms of technological expertise. One way in which Microsoft deals with this is by connecting startups in

Africa with technology experts within Microsoft around the world who volunteer their time and expertise to these startups. Of course, here too, there is a longer-term benefit for Microsoft; as Kenya advances in terms of socioeconomic development, there will be further payoffs for Microsoft as more and more companies and individuals develop market demand for its offerings. Thus there is scope to "do well by doing good" and enact the company's social-minded values.

Overcoming Pain Points for the Corporation That Dovetail with Social Needs

Promoting greater financial inclusion leading to unbanked individuals gaining access to banking services is of natural interest to the financial sector because it addresses one of its own pain points, which is the inability to be relevant to many rural customers in developing countries. In November 2015, the MasterCard Foundation announced a six-year "Savings at the Frontier" initiative in partnership with Oxford Policy Management.[11] Its objective was to increase the range of financial services available to poor, rural populations in three African countries – Ghana, Tanzania, and Zambia – thereby connecting 250,000 people to the formal banking system by designing new financial products designed specifically for informal savings groups. By some estimates, approximately nine million adults in the three target countries participate in informal savings groups. Group saving involves low-income people, often women, pooling together small amounts that they save, from which loans may be issued to group members. Usually, one of them deposits the money in a rural bank – but since doing this often requires a long trek, that person initially safeguards the cash at home, where it may be stolen.

To address the objective of making financial services more inclusive, MasterCard Foundation is working with a Ghanaian venture that is digitalizing group saving. Founded as Interpay in 2014 by Saqib Nazir, a Ghanaian of Pakistani descent, the venture was eventually acquired at the end of 2018 by US-based Emergent Technology. The idea being pursued by the Ghanaian venture is to help these saving groups to use mobile money, which is a safer alternative than cash. Furthermore, this allows data to be generated on the relative amounts contributed by different individuals within the group. Such data can, in turn, now make it possible for the rural bank to target these individuals with customized offers of banking solutions, thus finally resulting in unbanked people becoming banked. The actual implementation of the project is carried out by Oxford Policy Management, and funds are dispersed in stages to Interpay (which is now Emergent Technology) based on the accomplishment of preagreed milestones.

Adding Societal Value by Meeting Crisis-Induced Challenges

Social impact may stem from the corporation's ability to create greater value for stakeholders that are important to it during a crisis by tapping the digital prowess of innovative startups. There were vivid examples of this during the Covid-19 pandemic. Indeed, in such a situation, when startups focus on achieving social impact (in addition to economic outcomes) – in some cases, resulting from some deft pivoting to address opportunities induced by a crisis – then this may open up new possibilities for partnering with a corporation. For example, Shanghai-based Hinonou added a mask and hand sanitizer to its health monitoring kit for elders, converted it into an anti-Covid 19 kit, and found an interested client in the French multinational Saint-Gobain. The sense of urgency created by the arrival of the crisis meant that Saint-Gobain could clearly see a synergy – in terms of a pain point, in relation to protecting its workforce.

Some gorillas may arise that are not the typical corporation – like Sheba Hospital in Israel, which partners with startups, and used this capability to organize hackathons to address the pandemic. Even the government may emerge as a gorilla, running funnel-like challenges to generate creative solutions to crisis-related needs. For example, SenseGiz, a startup that originated in the southern Indian town of Belgaum and a member of the alumni of the Cisco LaunchPad program in Bangalore, applied its expertise in monitoring home and office safety to create a social distancing and Covid-19 patient tracing application that won first prize at an innovation challenge organized by the government of India.

Corporate actors may also seek to augment or initiate partnering with startups during a crisis. The Covid-19 pandemic showed that startup ecosystem players could be directly involved in helping corporations and startups to collaborate. One standout effort was the Startups Against Corona initiative launched by the former co-founders of BMW Startup Garage who used their expertise in building interfaces between corporations and startups. Over 300 startups' solutions were made available to over 50 corporations. This example reiterates the importance of developing and deploying expertise in building corporate-startup partner interfaces.

INCLUSIVE INTERFACE

Even in relation to the SDGs, conventional partner interfaces could potentially yield effective results, if they are open to suitable social-minded startups joining the partnering initiative. Alternatively, a corporation may launch partner interfaces that specifically target social ventures. Additionally, the partner interface may involve other, nontraditional actors, such as NGOs, as a bridge between small and large organizations. All three possibilities are discussed next.

Conventional Corporate-Startup Interfaces

From time to time, regular corporate-startup interfaces enable collaborations that have a palpable societal impact. For example, IBM's Global Entrepreneurship Program gave rise to one of the first success stories from Africa that I learned about. IBM managers in Africa proudly talked about Kenya's inclusive fintech startup, Mode (later acquired by Singapore's TransferTo, now rebranded as DT One),[12] which became the first African startup to win IBM's global smartcamp competition, in 2014. Having reached the global final in Las Vegas as the regional finalist from Africa, pitted against other regional finalists from around the world, the Nairobi-based venture's success was an early indication of the immense potential of African startups as well as of the natural instinct of many African entrepreneurs to seek social impact. It also made clear the prospect that some large global companies would be interested to engage with such African startups.

Another example of a social enterprise that benefited from a conventional startup partnering program was a startup in Accra, Ghana that developed a mobile app called Bisa (the word means "ask" in the Twee language) that helps individuals obtain free medical advice from practitioners. Launched during the Ebola crisis of 2014 (which fortunately did not affect Ghana), the entrepreneurs behind this venture partnered with Bayer, specifically through participating in a 100-day accelerator program in Berlin. This partnership proved to be a major turning point for the venture, resulting in further collaboration with Bayer Foundation and thereafter with other influential organizations in West Africa, leading to a new office being opened in Senegal.

In a similar vein, existing corporate innovation efforts involving startups – such as the Cisco LaunchPad – helped current partners and alumni to pivot to make their offerings relevant to the Covid-19 crisis. Another way to promote inclusivity is to deliberately reach out to underrepresented constituencies. For example, following a study of diversity in the UK ecosystem, the former head of Wayra in the UK, Gary Stewart, led efforts to open up that corporate accelerator to entrepreneurs outside London, including women and ethnic minorities. Thus the involvement of the conventional corporate players discussed in the previous chapters of this book can be a force for good. Indeed, going forward, it may well be the case that corporations adopt a more compassionate and inclusive mindset – which, in turn, leads to more and more startup partnerships seeking to deliver social impact, in particular through partner interfaces that are dedicated to social ventures, as discussed next.

Dedicated Corporate Interfaces for Social Enterprises

While startups with the potential for significant social impact, such as Mode and Bisa, have been able to benefit from conventional partner interfaces, certain startup-oriented efforts have emerged that focus exclusively on *social* enterprises. Unsurprisingly, several of these involve corporate foundations as well as entrepreneurial ecosystem specialists and other nontraditional actors (such as government departments).

To illustrate, Shell Foundation sponsored the Powered Accelerator in Mumbai, India, in partnership with the UK Government's Department for International Development (DFID) and Zone Startups.[13] This initiative seeks to support women-led startups relating to energy as well as diversity through seed funding, mentoring, and access to networks for resources. Taru Naturals, a participant in this program, helps rural farmers undertake organic farming. Their work – which received a boost from the accelerator program – has benefited not only the farmers directly involved in the project but also others who act as suppliers, for instance a supplier of organic turmeric, thus helping to promote a fair trade supply chain.[14]

In some cases corporate foundations work with the incubators of prestigious business schools to offer programs for social enterprises. For example, the Dell Foundation supported the first cohort of social enterprises at IIM Bangalore. The Pernod Ricard India Foundation has partnered with the innovation park of IIM Calcutta to launch an SDG-oriented social incubation program for women social entrepreneurs in India.[15] As another example in India, Rakuten has brought its Japanese program for social ventures to India. Described by the company as a corporate social responsibility (CSR) collaboration program, the Rakuten Social Accelerator seeks to involve internal employees and external social entrepreneurs to address SDGs pertaining to ending poverty, protecting the planet, and promoting peace and prosperity.[16]

As noted in the opening account of Microsoft's startup journey, that multinational launched its global Social Entrepreneurship Program in February 2020.[17] Designed for B2B social ventures with less than $25 million in revenue and seven years of operations, the program provides access to technological building blocks (e.g. Azure), go-to-market support, leads to gain customers, and grants from

Microsoft Philanthropies. In selecting startups, the potential for both economic (magnitude of the market opportunity) and social impact (as a key business metric, not an afterthought) is evaluated. One of the early startups to be selected for this program was Zindi, a platform for data science scientists in Africa that seeks to ensure that there is sufficient talent to analyze and extract value from the vast amount of digital data being generated. During the Covid-19 crisis, Zindi enabled students and professionals from across the continent whose study or work had been disrupted to use their time and skills productively.

Interfaces Involving Noncorporate Gorillas and Specialists

In addition, it seems plausible that *noncorporate* actors that are not typically involved in corporate-startup partnering are able to facilitate such collaboration. This might include multilateral agencies of the United Nations, nongovernment organizations, corporate foundations, and academic institutions. There may be other, very different gorillas who are involved in the interface of startup partnering, such as NGOs and the United Nations. As seen in the case of emerging economy nonclusters (see Chapter 5), some new actors may have a role to play as a bridge between startups with innovative ideas and large organizations. In frontier regions like Africa, in particular, I found NGOs and corporate foundations to be especially involved.

To illustrate, in Africa, the Swedish NGO Reach for Change (RFC) has emerged as an important entrepreneurial ecosystem-enabler by offering valuable incubation and acceleration services. Under the leadership of the dynamic Amma Lartey in Africa, RFC sought to make an impact on social enterprise policy in Ghana and worked with UNICEF to help incubate a few social enterprises whose ventures aided the welfare of children. This endeavor has supported social enterprises with a focus on education, such as coming up with literacy solutions for children who speak local languages. When such solutions are found to be effective, they could potentially be scaled as part of other national programs that UNICEF rolls out in other developing countries. Environmental360, a Ghanaian social enterprise that runs recycling education campaigns, trains schools and communities to segregate waste at source and runs sustainable waste collection systems. By partnering with UNICEF through RFC in a three-way collaboration, the social enterprise was able to get incubation support for a two-year period that increased its odds of scaling.

In Ethiopia, RFC has been working with women social entre-preneurs in Ethiopia in partnership with the Ikea Foundation. Programs and formats range from incubation programs of two or three years for relatively early-stage social ventures to a "rapid-scale program" that seeks to accelerate the growth of more mature social ventures that already have revenue-generating activities. Fresh & Green is one of the social enterprises that RFC is working with through the incubator program. This social venture makes and sells Ethiopian flatbread (the revenue-generating activity), employs women living on the streets of Addis Ababa, enabling them to get off the streets, and uses the proceeds to fund a school for the children of the women. Whiz Kids Workshop – a children's television content producer – is a more established social enterprise being assisted through the acceleration program. Since advertising is not permitted on children's TV channels in Ethiopia, by gaining support and guidance from RFC's rapid-scale program this social enterprise is exploring other revenue streams by placing content on other channels (e.g. YouTube), pursuing merchandising opportunities, and exploring other markets in East Africa that do not restrict advertising on children's TV channels.

The UNDP's Accelerator Network seeks to create a powerful network that promotes rapid learning in the pursuit of solutions for sustainable development challenges. These include locations in advanced markets, like Denmark, and emerging ones, like Namibia. In Denmark, the program provides selected small firms with a six-month innovation "journey" to build and validate products, services, and business models associated with solutions that help achieve the SDGs. Through workshops and meetings with partner companies, UN experts, and potential investors, the partner firms have the opportunity to turn ideas into concrete action plans. Examples of ventures that have participated in this program include Bluetown, whose solar-powered WiFi hotspot systems provide Internet connectivity for deprived areas in developing countries, thus addressing SDG 9 (industry, innovation, and infrastructure). During the Covid-19 pandemic, the value of the offering could be seen in Ghana, where cloud users could freely access advisories from the WHO.[18] Other examples of participants in the SDG Accelerator are Aquaporin, who developed a wastewater purification and recycling solution for the textile industry in developing countries, and Unibio, which converts methane into protein for farming and fishing. In Namibia, through initiatives like its BOOST UP startup competition and online incubator, it has enabled local solution providers to be showcased,[19] such as AKA Nam-Kelp, which is turning seaweed into poultry feed, or Afridrones, which develops agricultural drones to help local farmers improve productivity.[20]

HYBRID EXEMPLAR

Exemplars that are relevant to the SDGs in terms of partnering between startups and corporations (as well as other relevant large organizations) are most likely to be effective when they showcase scope for hybridity in terms of both social *and* economic impact. This is because without the latter, it is unlikely that for-profit organizations that do have valuable resources will be motivated to get involved. That said, it is also important to articulate clearly the impact on the SDGs. Valuable inspiration can be obtained on these matters in emerging markets.

Showcase Social Impact *and* Economic Success

While there is an important role for non-profits in promoting the SDGs, the likelihood of scalable solutions emerging is greater when there is the involvement of for-profit businesses. As Harvard's Professor Michael Porter has observed in a TED talk, "Only business can create resources. So the question then is, how do we tap into that? Profit is the magic. You might say 'ugh' to that – but that profit allows whatever solution we have created to be infinitely scalable."[21] But part of the added challenge when social impact is incorporated in a for-profit organization's strategy is that dual – and, in a sense, opposing – agendas are involved.

Thus the trick is to be able to achieve both economic *and* social impact. Now, how this is achieved may vary; some organizations pursue opposing goals through separate endeavors (e.g. a for-profit arm to subsidize the non-profit activities) while others try to achieve both goals simultaneously (e.g. selling services to low-income market segments but at a profit or employing disabled people in a for-profit enterprise).

In either case, the key will be to demonstrate that both economic and social goals are being successfully pursued. In fact, I was intrigued to hear that in Ghana some people have become averse to the term "social enterprise" – because it has come to connote the pursuit of charitable grants, which then leads to a focus on the social outcomes at the expense of the economic. At Ashesi University's New Entrepreneurs

Xchange for Transformation: Idea to Impact Project (NEXTi2i) in Ghana, the term "hybrid entrepreneurship" – which is described as "doing good whilst doing well" – is used rather than "social entrepreneurship." This initiative, in collaboration with MIT's D-Lab and USAID, aims "to create a values-driven incubator to train entrepreneurs to build businesses with a focus on the Sustainable Development Goals."[22] The Ashesi Ventures Incubator (AVI), a program of NEXTi2i, is a one-year incubation experience for fresh graduates of Ashesi University.[23] One example is Ezekiel Senye Hormeku, whose venture "Tailored Hands" produces kaftans (loose-fitting traditional shirts worn by men in West Africa) and accessories such as African slippers; the intent is that the latter will be made by less privileged – for instance, disabled – people. While some might argue that the definition of "hybrid entrepreneurship" is entirely consistent with that of "social enterprise," the actual connotations of these terms on the ground in a context like Ghana are apparently a bit different.

When pursuing dual goals, actors have to be adept at paradox thinking – the capacity to embrace apparently contradictory ideas.[24] This does not mean that it's easy to pursue social and economic goals simultaneously, but rather that the goals are not viewed as mutually exclusive.[25] Of course, both sets of goals may not be achieved to an equal extent. Also some slack may be cut for social enterprises on the economic aspects by stakeholders such as investors if the social outcomes are outsized; but the economic outcomes remain important to achieve. And of course there will always be an important role for non-profits, some of whom may also engage with corporations. But, better still, if corporate-startup partnering can result in non-profits being assisted – for instance, a healthtech startup working with a large tech corporation to deliver a solution that a rural non-profit hospital can use to save lives – then social impact can be enhanced through the valuable work of the non-profit through added value addition from dancing with gorillas.

Bring SDGs into the Narrative

A startup that came up repeatedly during a field visit to Nairobi, Kenya was Twiga Foods. The venture was founded in 2014 by Peter Njonjo, a former executive of Coca-Cola in Africa, and an American, Grant Brooke, whose doctoral work at Oxford University led to the recognition of an opportunity to create the venture.[26] Cruchbase describes Twiga Foods as "a business-to-business marketplace platform that sources produce directly from farmers and delivers it to urban retailers."[27] One journalist describes Twiga Foods, in more elaborate terms, as "a business that delivers fresh produce to small-scale retailers, like mama mbogas [female vegetable hawkers], and finances small-to-medium-scale farmers who grow and supply the company with produce."[28] On its own website, Twiga Foods describes its story as follows: "Since 2014, Twiga has been bridging gaps in food and market security through an organised platform for an efficient, fair, transparent and formal marketplace. Today, we source quality produce from thousands of farmers, providing them with a ready

guaranteed market, and deliver from our pack houses to thousands
of vendors, at prices fair to everyone."[29]

Having attracted considerable funding, including from the
World Bank's IFC, one of Twiga Foods' strategic partners is Micro-
soft. Intriguingly, Twiga Foods was the first company that Somet
Kipchilat of Microsft4Afrika mentioned when I asked him to name
exemplar young companies that Microsoft was partnering with in
Kenya. Although it is not a classical independent software vendor
(ISV), Kipchilat has helped orchestrate Microsoft technological
resources – such as cloud computing capacity – making it available to
Twiga Foods, based on the belief that this company will grow into a
large account (i.e. paying user) of Microsoft technology in the future.
An exemplar like Twiga Foods has the advantage not only of attracting frequent media attention[30] but also readily relating its work to
specific SDGs such as SDG 8 (decent work), SDG 12 (responsible
consumption and production), and, since many of its small-scale
vendors are women, SDG 5 (gender equality).

As another example of corporate-startup partnering with clear
SDG outcomes, consider the case of Koa, a social enterprise based in
Switzerland and Ghana. This social venture works with cocoa farmers in Western Africa to help them increase their incomes by utilizing
the normally discarded cocoa pulp. Founded by Anian Schreiber, a
former professional rower, the startup has forged a partnership with
the multinational company Lindt & Sprüngli Chocolatiers to supply
their "Excellence Cacao Pure" Koa Powder, the dried form of cocoa
pulp, as a chocolate ingredient.[31] This is a good example of dancing

with gorillas for the SDGs, contributing to increased decent work (SDG 8) and responsible consumption through decreased wastage of natural resources (SDG 12).

Of course, actors will vary in terms of whether they specialize in specific SDGs or generalize across them. Certain organizations are associated with specific SDGs. For example, the United Nations Human Settlements Programme – known as UN-Habitat for short – focuses on human settlements and sustainable urban development, thus specializing in SDG 11 (sustainable cities and communities). It would seem highly plausible for organizations interested in exploring ways to work with startups in relation to SDG 11 to involve the UN-Habitat in some way. In other cases – such as the work of the UNDP through the SDG Accelerator – there is likely to be scope to create value across multiple SDGs. Whether to be specific or diffuse in relation to SDGs is a function of what the large organization's mission is. For healthcare corporations, SDG 3 (health and well-being) may be an obvious focus, whereas for a corporation like Microsoft it would be pointless to be overly restrictive.

In any case, the key is to explicitly bring SDGs into the narrative both as a way to gain greater visibility for the work being accomplished and to focus the mind in terms of the nature of the social impact sought. Professor Sachs and his coauthors have suggested that the 17 SDGs can be thought of as involving six major transformations: (1) Education, Gender, and Inequality; (2) Health, Well-being, and Demography; (3) Energy Decarbonization and Sustainable Industry; (4) Sustainable Food, Land, Water, and Oceans;

(5) Sustainable Cities and Communities; and (6) Digital Revolution for Sustainable Development.[32] It is helpful to be clear about which transformation is being fostered in a particular partnering program.

Harness Inspiration from Emerging Markets

While many frontier market ventures look to advanced economies of the West to learn from the experience of more established entrepreneurial ecosystems, they should recognize that they can also gain valuable insight by looking to emerging economies of the East. While it is useful to take entrepreneurs to Silicon Valley and dazzle them with the latest technologies and trends, ventures from developing countries will also find useful – and arguably, more relatable – experiences in emerging markets that they can learn from. The idea that social enterprises can have a bigger impact by partnering with large organizations is being actively explored in India, as seen, and in accelerators in China such as Impact Hub Shanghai.

Alibaba is one company that has stated an interest to contribute to the SDGs,[33] and has also demonstrated a willingness to support African entrepreneurs through initiatives such as the eFounders Fellowship program, in partnership with UNCTAD, which provides mentoring and support to highly promising entrepreneurs from the continent – including an intensive two-week stint in Hangzhou that helps these entrepreneurs understand and connect with the Alibaba ecosystem. (From Alibaba's point of view, there may be a potential win in that these entrepreneurs could be future partners if and when it becomes more active on the African continent.) Jack Ma has often spoken in public about his commitment to support "[Africa's] digital economy through local entrepreneurship" because, as he says, "I see Africa, full of problems, but full of opportunities."[34] This is illustrated by Tayo Bamiduro, a Nigerian entrepreneur whose venture Max.ng seeks to solve a major problem in Africa: making motorcycle taxis safe and accessible. Engaging with Alibaba helped him to refine his offering.[35]

Another eFounders fellow is Uju Uzo-Ojinnaka, a former student of mine from Nigeria whom I had taught at my school's campus in West Africa. She founded a pan-African e-commerce platform, Traders of Africa, a business idea that she first presented in my classroom. Participating in the eFounders program gave her an alternative source of inspiration to Silicon Valley – and arguably one that she could relate to well. Jack Ma's challenges of dealing with a nascent e-commerce market when he founded Alibaba 20 years earlier resonated with some of the issues in Africa, more so than what, say, Jeff Bezos had to deal with in the United States when setting up Amazon. She says: "I thought to myself, 'Jack felt the frustration and he did something about it. I also need to do something about it. Not just for me, but for my country, for Africa!'"[36] She also told me that through the Alibaba eFounders program, she had gained access to a network of ambitious, hungry, and high-caliber African entrepreneurs – who, ironically, might have been more accessible to her in Hangzhou during the eFounders program than would have been the case in Africa. And the validation for her idea and the greater credibility through the association with Alibaba were extremely valuable outcomes.

BUILDING SDG COALITIONS

The prospect of partnering between startups (including social ventures) and corporations (and other large organizations) is part of a much larger, and vitally important, reality: accomplishing the SDGs will take a (massive) collective effort. The Netflix documentary *Inside Bill's Brain: Decoding Bill Gates* offers insight into how the Gates Foundation has gone about tackling one of the biggest challenges in the developing world: providing affordable sanitation to the poor. The Foundation pursued a large number of collaborations – from NGOs in areas affected such as Côte D'Ivoire, to universities and entrepreneurs in advanced markets such as the United States and UK, and finally to potential manufacturers of low-cost toilets in China. These partnerships exemplify SDG 17 – partnerships for the goals.

What is required is coalitions of organizations. Indeed, an important contribution that influential organizations can contribute is to co-opt coalitions of partners – corporations, startups, multilateral organizations, and NGOs. Microsoft is one such coalition-builder. Muhammed Nabil of Microsoft4Africa saw his role as primarily helping to enable the ecosystem by partnering with others. He recognizes that Microsoft can open doors to other large organizations, foundations, and multilateral organizations like the World Bank – and is working on putting together coalitions of organizations that can help to develop and further strengthen entrepreneurial eco-systems across the continent, not just in a few hotspots. The rise of interest from global tech firms – with a for-profit motive – and the burgeoning social enterprise sector – not all of which has access to the resources available in Johannesburg, Lagos, or Nairobi – means that there is fertile ground for more multi-stakeholder collabora-tions that foster both innovation and entrepreneurship on the one hand and SDG-fulfilling outcomes on the other. This is especially pertinent on the African continent, which has a young population: 60% of the African population is under the age of 35. Furthermore, in areas of conflict around the world, entrepreneurship pursued by the youth is expected to have security benefits by reducing the regional instability triggered by unemployment. As Nabil puts it, one of the key challenges that Africa faces is the need to "democratize entrepreneurship."

There are already many encouraging signs of coalition-building. Catalyst 2030 is a network of social entrepreneurs and innovators from around the world that are committed to the SDGs. A different sort of coalition, involving businesses, is illustrated by the Fashion Pact, which involves commitments from leading companies in the industry to commit to address climate change, which Unilever ex-CEO Paul Polman has been instrumental in orchestrating, and is an example of the coalitions that are inevitably necessary to tackle the planet's challenges.[37]

Going forward, a key challenge remains the sheer differences between different types of organizations, especially for-profits and non-profits. They inhabit very different worlds. This is vividly seen in the case of healthcare. Consider CMC Hospital a large teaching hospital that was founded by an American missionary in Vellore, India. Her goal was to train women physicians and serve the poor. Later, even as the hospital gained renown for specializations such as neurology and cardiology, there was a strong emphasis on ensuring first-rate yet affordable treatment.[38] Community health development catering to nearby rural areas was an important focus alongside the activities of the main hospital. Now contrast this with Jiahua International Hospital, a large state-of-the-art for-profit hospital in Shanghai. Built in collaboration with one of the leading hospitals in the United States, this hospital is a far cry from the one in Vellore – in terms of the five-star quality of the infrastructure, the healthy ratio of medical staff to patients, and, of course, the price point of the treatment. Both organizations are key actors in the pursuit of SDG 3 – good health. Yet, they belong to two worlds: that of the not-for-profits and that of the for-profits. A key challenge is that the starting points and purposes of these sets of organizations are so different that finding common ground isn't easy. "Profit" can be viewed almost as a dirty word among some non-profits. Yet it is for-profit companies that often make the things – medicines, devices, and infrastructure – that allow non-profits to deliver value to their constituents.[39] And the Covid-19 lockdowns demonstrated how important the commercial activity of businesses is to generating livelihoods for people. Economic and social activity are thus inextricably intertwined. How the for-profit and non-profit worlds intersect in a synergistic way could be one of the keys to achieving the SDGs.

Of course, the idea that corporations and NGOs could collaborate has been around for a while.[40] Also, some non-profits have sought to add commercial activities to their scope of work and transform themselves into social enterprises. Moreover, not-for-profit corporate foundations have channeled corporate profits to worthy causes that have a positive social impact. The corporate foundation is an entity that appears in the mix when social ventures and the SDGs are involved. This was seen in the previously discussed case of Bisa, a Ghanaian social venture whose mobile app allows people to get free and confidential medical advice. Bisa was selected to be part of one of Bayer's G4A accelerator cohorts in Berlin. Subsequently as it sought to continue engaging with Bayer in order to strengthen its impact in west Africa's healthcare sector, it was able to do so through Bayer Foundation. It was this non-profit entity that gave the startup further visibility among organizations seeking to support socioeconomic development in poorer parts of the world, leading to Bisa's partnering with another German foundation that had close links to the Senegalese government. And this led to Bisa's opening a subsidiary office in Senegal and offering its app in that market. Also as seen, Reach for Change, an NGO that seeks to enhance societal well-being by supporting entrepreneurship and innovation, has worked with corporate foundations such as the Ikea foundation on a program that supports women social entrepreneurs in Ethiopia.

These developments need to continue apace and move up a gear or two in even more sophisticated ways so that untapped potential for nontraditional allies to work together is realized. For-profit new ventures that, for instance, seek to apply digital capabilities to health-care provision – a trend that got turbocharged by the Covid-19 pandemic in terms of, for instance, telemedicine – ought to be able to make their expertise available to non-profit hospitals in ways that fit the ethos and objectives of both. Getting to this point will require a lot of progress being made in each party's gaining trust in the other. Clearly, this will not be possible in the case of every single for-profit and non-profit; but in cases where there is a sufficient overlap of organizational purpose and mindset, such partnerships can be a valuable source of shared value being jointly created. Research by Acumen suggests that partnering with large corporations can yield different benefits, including access to new skills, channels, and joint business opportunities to organizations making a difference in developing countries under trying circumstances.[41]

And of course, in the short term, an important manifestation of corporations partnering with startups for the SDGs is collaboration between large firms and social enterprises. That partnering with startups can be a force for good – by contributing to the accomplishment of the SDGs, in particular – is very much on the radar of corporations, NGOs, governments, and the United Nations. Compared to the more conventional corporate-startup programs, it is too early to gauge the efficacy of the various socially oriented initiatives that have recently emerged. However, there is cause for optimism in that some of the core ideas encapsulated in this book about corporate-startup partnering ought to apply. And surely, the fine-turning of these initiatives that is required due to their differences from mainstream startup partnering will occur through further improvisation and reflective learning. The potential seems considerable.

To conclude, it seems appropriate to consider how dancing with gorillas may manifest as a way to address the SDGs. This is important because, as Paul Polman, former CEO of Unilever, has noted, solving some of the vexing problems that society faces requires multiple – often non-traditional – actors to come together. Addressing the SDGs is beyond the capacity of any single company, government, or sector. That is why SDG 17 makes eminent sense, and is likely to require nontraditional allies coming together. Social intrapreneurs and innovators within large corporations who seek to create social impact by leveraging their organization's capabilities would do well to engage with startups, including social ventures, to facilitate and amplify their efforts.

As a world battered by Covid-19 grapples with addressing the SDGs in the lead-up to 2030, it can do with all the ingenuity and creativity it can harness from high-quality startups as they dance with gorillas.

THREE MINDSETS FOR THE SDG DECADE OF ACTION

Real business success, in fact capitalism generally, cannot be just the surplus that you create for your own core constituency, but also the broader surplus that is created to benefit the wider society...

– Satya Nadella, CEO, Microsoft[1]

To say that 2020 went sideways for many is an understatement.

The material in Chapter 6 was always going to be relevant for 2020's Decade of Action. But as a consequence of the Covid-19 pandemic, the notion of dancing with gorillas for the SDGs takes on even greater urgency – and challenge. In this concluding section, I offer some thoughts on what lies ahead, and suggest that it is important to consider the three mindsets that this book highlights – entrepreneurial, collaborative, and global – that hold relevance for corporate innovation, organizational transformation, and social impact, by harnessing entrepreneurship *and* globalization via collaboration.

CONTRIBUTING TO THE SDG DECADE OF ACTION IN A POST-COVID WORLD

The opening account of the Microsoft story of startup partnering concluded with the announcement of a global program to work with social entrepreneurs in late February 2020. As it transpired, the timing proved to be ominous. Within days, Covid-19 was declared a pandemic. Few, if any, have been spared the tumultuous effects of this once-in-a-century event.

The effects of 2020 are likely to be felt for a long time to come.[2] The 2020s – dubbed the "decade of action" by the United Nations[3] – will be a period when the pursuit of the SDGs is even more important, and challenging, in the wake of the Covid-19 pandemic. To help make sense of where we are headed it might be useful to first briefly look back at what happened in the lead-up to this point (particularly at the 2008–2020 period) and consider what the 2020 pandemic changed.

2008–2020: A Period Bookended by Two Global Crises

In retrospect, as things panned out, my study of the phenomenon of corporate-startup partnering was bookended by two major worldwide shocks: the global financial crisis of 2008 and the Covid-19[4] pandemic of 2020.[5] Although the beginnings of my research on corporate-startup partnering resulted from my initial interactions with Microsoft in 2003–2004, it wasn't until 2008 – the year I published my preliminary results in an article titled "Dancing with Gorillas" in *California Management Review* – that I began to see full-fledged startup engagement efforts (other than corporate venture capital), notably with the launch of Microsoft's BizSpark program.

2008 proved to be a momentous year for the global economy. Subsequent years witnessed the rise of at least three macroenvironmental forces, with events during the third quarter (July-September) of 2008 portending each of these:

1. In July 2008, Apple launched its App Store, fueling the *rise of digitalization*, as smartphones – and the apps used on them – dramatically transformed the Internet, which had been commercialized in the PC era.[6]

2. In August 2008, the Beijing Olympic Games were held, an event that symbolized the *ascent of China*,[7] by offering an opportunity to showcase its economic progress in the preceding three decades since the opening up of the Chinese economy in 1978.[8]

3. In September 2008, Lehman Brothers collapsed, marking a pivotal moment in the onset of the global financial crisis. More broadly, this crisis threw into relief a *crisis of sustainability* in that in the pursuit of rampant growth, businesses seemed less mindful of their broader societal impacts.[9]

The rise of digitalization. In combination with the emergence of cloud computing, the mobile Internet would change the nature of digitalization. As lower-end handsets became available, the mobile Internet became accessible not only in advanced markets but also in emerging and frontier markets in Asia, Latin America, and Africa that leapfrogged the PC era. Furthermore, the rise of cloud computing dramatically reduced the IT infrastructure needs of startups, and heralded a startup boom. Brad Feld, co-founder of Techstars, notes that even as traditional companies were suffering in the wake of the financial crisis, technology-based startups were gaining success, resulting in entrepreneurship emerging as a mainstream interest in society. He observes: "As the macroeconomic impact of the financial crisis was felt throughout 2009 and 2010 . . . the startups kept being born, growing, and adding jobs. In early 2011 the world started to notice. . . . Overnight everyone started talking about entrepreneurship as the way to revitalize our global economy."[10]

The ascent of China. The lavish opening and closing ceremonies of the Beijing Olympics were a demonstration of what China had accomplished, and hinted at its growing aspirations in the decades ahead. From 2008 onward, emerging economies such as China attracted renewed attention from large multinational corporations – and became home to newly internationalized companies as well. While advanced Western economies suffered considerable hardship in the immediate aftermath of the 2008 global financial crisis, China continued to enjoy growth, supported by government policy measures to stimulate growth.[11] Many Chinese companies saw opportunities to acquire Western ones, such as medium-sized high-tech Mittlestandt companies in countries like Germany and Switzerland to access their technologies and brands.[12] The inexorable rise of China's mobile Internet since around 2011 (the year WeChat was launched) has witnessed a unique trajectory in which home-grown giants like Alibaba and Tencent dominate while global leaders like Google and Facebook are conspicuous by their absence. Eventually, trade tensions with the West (in particular, the United States) arose.

The crisis of sustainability. Although on the face of it, the financial crisis and concerns around sustainability might appear to be disparate issues, experts contend that they are linked,[13] not least through the growing inequality among the more and less well-off in society that the global financial crisis drew attention to and seemingly worsened.[14] That is, inequality is inextricably linked to sustainability.[15] The financial crisis triggered a period of societal turmoil that highlighted the problem of rising inequality because the pain of austerity measures disproportionately impacted lower-income sections of society, further exacerbating this divide. In the years following the 2008 crisis, as the world transitioned from the Millennium Development Goals (2000–2015) to the Sustainable Development Goals (2015–2030), the need to address this issue was explicitly recognized in the formulation of SDG 10 (reduced inequalities).[16]

Overall, this was a period in which digitalization went from being the domain of a select few companies to a mantra that every company was paying attention to, albeit with differing degrees of comprehension and efficacy. At varying speeds, large corporations – initially technology companies and eventually more traditional ones – came to consciously and explicitly recognize the prospect of a more "open" way of undertaking innovation that entailed close collaboration with external partners as well as intrapreneurship. This period also saw startup ecosystems emerge in places like Beijing in China (as well as in other emerging economies, such as Bangalore in India). Globally savvy multinationals like Microsoft were paying attention and opened accelerators in these regions, as previously noted. Also, concerns about sustainability became progressively incorporated in corporate-startup engagement, prominently in the case of the Microsoft global social entrepreneurship program announced in February 2020.

And then came the pandemic.

2020: The Exacerbating Effects of the Pandemic

In 2020, the world was struck a mighty blow in the form of the Covid-19 pandemic, arguably the biggest shock to the global economy since World War II.[17] The three forces noted earlier have been further impacted in one way or another.

First, in terms of digitalization, the pandemic had an unmistakable accelerating effect. As Covid-19 took hold around the world, many organizations and individuals demonstrated great agility in adjusting to remote work and study through the use of online tools.[18] As Microsoft CEO Satya Nadella noted after the first quarter of 2020, "We've seen two years' worth of digital transformation in two months."[19] The adoption of digitalization has very obviously been accelerated – from a wait-and-watch attitude that many companies have had, virtually overnight to plunge into a new world in which digital technologies represented the only way in which operations could, at least partially, be sustained.

Second, in terms of geopolitics, the pandemic – with which China is inevitably associated – has arguably seen an accentuation of a China-versus-the rest of the world perspective in many corporations. Global companies' local Chinese operations are likely to become even more "Chinese," with a somewhat delinked global value chain (with some, but not exclusive, Chinese suppliers involved) for the rest of the world.[20] This means that the disconnect between the Chinese and global Internet systems will likely remain pronounced, meaning that corporate-startup partnering will be somewhat different across these two contexts.

Third, in terms of sustainability, the already existing concerns encapsulated in the SDGs have only been heightened. In a post-Covid world the SDGs take on even greater urgency, necessity, and salience – yet will be even more difficult to achieve. Jacqueline Novogratz's book, *Manifesto for a Moral Revolution*,[21] was written prior to the onset of the pandemic – but its message arguably resonated all the more because the pandemic has forced many to recognize the social and economic havoc wrought by this once-in-a-lifetime tragedy and rethink their priorities.[22] As Elizabeth Boggs Davidsen, formerly of the UNDP, observed: "Even before this pandemic, progress against the SDGs was stalling. With the pandemic we find ourselves at a fork in the road. We cannot afford to take the path that leads us even further away from delivering on the SDGs. We must forge a new path that drives us towards that better future."[23]

The 2020s: The Urgent Need for Corporate Innovation in the Decade of Action

For society as a whole, the decade of the 2020s presents a mighty challenge. The timing of the pandemic was poignant – 2020 was going to be the year that would mark five years since the adoption of the 17 SDGs by the United Nations and, hopefully, infuse greater energy into the efforts of the 2020s decade. Turbulence that was already emanating from the US–China trade war and fallout from Brexit, in addition to various geopolitical tensions, reached gigantic proportions with the outbreak of the Covid-19 pandemic. Societal challenges embodied in the SDGs that were always going to be critical but challenging to address are even more so. The pandemic has made the "decade of action" even more difficult, yet even more important, with a strong need for agility and resilience. A big challenge is how to blur the boundaries between "doing well" and "doing good," since the latter appears to no longer be a "nice to have" but rather something that is essential.

In the SDG Decade of Action, everyone needs to do their part, bringing to bear different tools and approaches. This includes all those who, in one way or another, are engaged in corporate innovation. Corporate-startup partnering represents an approach to innovating that brings together nontraditional allies with complementary capabilities by overcoming the impediments posed by their interorganizational asymmetry to achieve win-win results. This principle, applied to a broader set of actors – including NGOs (e.g. Reach for Change), corporate foundations (e.g. Bayer Foundation), government actors, and multilateral agencies (such as the UN[24]) that are paying more and more attention to open innovation – has great relevance to the SDGs, in particular the last one, SDG 17, which pertains to partnerships for the goals (see Figure 7.1).

With the upsurge of digitalization during the pandemic came anecdotal evidence of the value of corporate-startup partnering in turbulent times. In some cases, startups have been adept at

	Forces arising during the 2008–2020 period	Complications due to the 2020 pandemic	Corporate-startup partnering in the 2020s (Decade of Action)
Digitalization	Rise of digital startups with the growth of cloud computing and the mobile Internet.	Digitalization accelerates due to remote working, telemedicine, and other applications.	Startup partnering will remain an important way of leveraging digital technologies for the SDGs.
Geopolitics	Rise of emerging economies, notably China, accompanied by US-China trade and technology tensions.	Geopolitical tensions and decoupling of global value chains accentuated.	Despite tensions, there will still be scope for gaining inspiration and resources from different locations.
Sustainability	Rising concerns about inequality that draw attention to a crisis of sustainability.	Societal difficulties – including inequalities and digital divide – exacerbated.	Social impact (less harm and more good) via startup partnering will be much needed.

Figure 7.1 The Decade of Action: Looking back and looking ahead

addressing pain points arising due to the pandemic. For example, through Startups Against Corona, a partnering initiative established by the former co-founders of BMW Startup Garage, the Swiss cement multinational LafargeHolcim partnered with an Indian startup, Leena.AI, to address workforce management issues caused by the Covid-19 crisis in Latin America.[25] Also, London-based ChargedUp, a mobile charging startup that pivoted to hand sanitizer stations (called CleanedUp) during the pandemic, partnered with Diageo to make its service available in pubs.[26] In other cases, corporations like Microsoft and Cisco proudly showcased alumni startups from their accelerator programs that were contributing to the fight against the pandemic. For example, Cloudphysician, a startup that participated in the Cisco LaunchPad accelerator program, was able to provide its telemedicine-based ICU solutions to hospitals in less affluent locations where hospital facilities were much needed.[27]

The steep learning curve around digitalization that the pandemic brought about presents an opportunity that ought to be built upon and harnessed. Jeff Sachs has noted that six transformations are key to achieving the SDGs, the sixth of which pertains to digital transformation.[28] And yet (as Sachs also notes) the digital divide that the pandemic has thrown into relief needs to be addressed. Also, environmental, social and governance (ESG) considerations become even more important, and in this regard, startups – especially ones with a clear social impact focus – can be important allies. To the extent that innovative solutions emerge that represent a win for the organizations involved and the constituents served, the more likely it is that ESG and social impact considerations will make headway during the 2020s.

Also, doing more with less will be important. Navi Radjou, a leading expert on frugal innovation, describes the efforts of the Financial Solutions Lab (FSL), an initiative launched by a non-profit, Financial Health Network, in partnership with JPMorgan Chase to help improve the financial health of people impacted by the global financial crisis in the United States. One of its activities is a fintech accelerator program, and the 2020 cohort addressed challenges to financial health arising from the Covid-19 pandemic while the 2021 cohort's remit is to help develop long-term financial stability.[29] Such efforts promote both agility and resilience in challenging times.

These examples highlight that it is important, and plausible, for organizations to recognize – not least because of the economic hardship brought about by the Covid-19 pandemic – the importance of looking beyond narrow profit considerations and pursuing the SDGs. In the Decade of Action, companies should not only seek to do less harm but also more good, particularly by leveraging digital technologies. Corporate-startup partnering, broadly defined, can be a force for good.

The odds of this will be greater when three important mindsets, which underlie the ideas in this book, are prevalent in the various organizations that have a role to play in fostering corporate innovation for the SDG Decade of Action: the entrepreneurial, collaborative, and global mindsets.

ENTREPRENEURIAL, COLLABORATIVE AND GLOBAL MINDSETS

There are certain core underlying principles that my book highlights which will outlast the nature of, or interest in, corporate-startup partnering per se. These are the three mindsets that are highlighted in this book, which matter not just for collectives but also, crucially, for individuals.[30] As Intel's Kapil Kane observes, "Transformation is happening at a furious pace. The only way to innovate is to experiment a lot. For this to happen, you need an entrepreneurial workforce at every level. Employees need to be given new skills, cultivate their mindset, and be empowered to think and act like entrepreneurs." The three enduring mindsets that this book draws attention to (see Figure 7.2) are the entrepreneurial mindset, the collaborative mindset, and the global mindset.

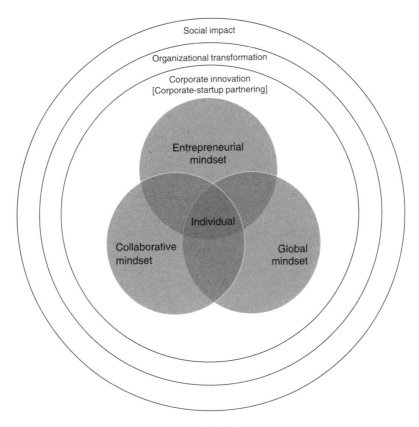

Figure 7.2 Three Enduring Mindsets

These mindsets form the basis for professional efficacy in multiple spheres: corporate innovation, organizational transformation, and social impact. In terms of *corporate innovation*, when these mindsets work in tandem in individuals, the results they produce are especially effective. Picking the right people to drive startup partnering is important. Some of the most effective managers at startup partnering that I have observed demonstrate these three mindsets. This is also true of the many outstanding entrepreneurs I've come across who've danced effectively with large gorillas. And it holds for enterprising individuals in non-profits, corporate foundations, government departments, and other organizations that may be involved in corporate innovation.

More broadly, these mindsets are relevant in contributing to *organizational transformation*. It has been my good fortune that for some of the companies that I've studied closely, such as Microsoft, partnering with startups was not a side hobby, but rather a fundamental contributor – thanks to a combination of astute leaders from headquarters and empowered actions by subsidiary managers – to organizational transformation. These companies show that at the intersection of these three mindsets lies the potential to collaborate with startups in a way that is closely aligned with their overall strategy. Inculcating these mindsets in individuals is a valuable contribution to managerial human capital that business leaders, professors, coaches, and consultants can provide.

Finally, as these competencies intersect, there is scope for organizations to have a positive *social impact* by creating shared value in a way that ensures that corporate innovation is undertaken with compassionate inclusivity. The value of social impact via corporate innovation seems especially relevant in the 2020s, as the world intensifies its focus on achieving the SDGs.

Entrepreneurial Mindset – Making Things Happen

The discussion of the *why* of corporate-startup partnering (Chapters 1 and 2) indicated that an important starting point is an *entrepreneurial mindset* that entails three key facets: proactiveness, innovativeness, and risk-taking. Proactiveness is evident in the recognition of potential win-wins in working with startups. Innovativeness can be seen in the creative efforts through which intrapreneurs incorporate startup engagement; out-of-the-box thinking can help save time and resources. Finally, there is an inevitable element of risk involved in embarking on startup partnering. Risks can be mitigated by starting small and under the radar, working hard to create quick wins, especially in the early stages, and enlisting support from formal and informal partners. A key message here is that the impetus to engage with external startups can't always be expected to come from on high. In fact, in numerous instances that I've studied, the driving force has been individual managers, often without a fancy job title or any mention of being entrepreneurial in their job description, that were the catalyst of startup partnering in their company. What they did have was an entrepreneurial mindset, and their proactive, innovative, and (calculated) risk-taking efforts made the difference.

Collaborative Mindset – Joining Forces with Others

The discussion of the *how* of corporate-startup partnering (Chapters 3 and 4) added the perspective that another important mindset that companies need is a *collaborative mindset*. My research reveals three important aspects of this mindset: leveraging networks proactively, discerningly, and reflectively. Leveraging networks proactively in relation to *how* goes beyond merely recognizing the *why* and is reflected in the threefold partnering process described in this book, which entails synergy clarification, interface creation, and exemplar cultivation. Leveraging networks discerningly – in terms of understanding which startups are more suitable than others – is inherent in making choices about who to engage with, how, and to what extent. Finally, in terms of leveraging networks reflectively, learning from startups is important in terms of identifying and cultivating certain success stories (the exemplars), and gaining feedback from startups in terms of how to enhance the partnering process.

Global Mindset – Engaging with the World

Finally, the discussion of the *where* of corporate-startup partnering (Chapters 5 and 6) highlighted the importance of a *global mindset*. This entails curiosity, competence, and connections. Curiosity is the basis for exploring novel technologies and ideas in other geographic contexts. Competence – particularly in terms of partnering capability – is an important basis for startup partnering globally, but there is also a need for cross-cultural competence to deal with both internal managers and external startups in entrepreneurial ecosystems in varied locations. An important manifestation is learning to adapt to other conditions. Connections can help to enrich the corporate-startup partnering experience for both parties. For instance, startup-partners' own global expansion can be enhanced and the global startup partnering capability of the corporation strengthened, thus adding to value co-creation through corporate-startup partnering.

Now, of course, this last-mentioned mindset could raise an eyebrow or two given the unmistakable slowdown of globalization in a world of geopolitical tension, disrupted global travel, and decoupling global supply chains. Even so, I submit that a global mindset still matters – which is my closing point, below.

HARNESSING ENTREPRENEURSHIP *AND* GLOBALIZATION VIA COLLABORATION

As a final thought, it is worth acknowledging that my emphasis on a global mindset might seem counterintuitive, even misplaced, in a world that appears to be deglobalizing. In the context of the three mindsets that are being highlighted here, some may argue that an entrepreneurial mindset is very relevant, a global mindset less so. That's because globalization is on the back burner while entrepreneurship is on the ascent. There has been a backlash against globalization in the aftermath of the 2008 financial crisis, with stunning political manifestations in 2016 (such as Brexit and Trump), and arguably reaching a crescendo in 2020 in a world battered by the Covid-19 pandemic.

However, even as I hear the phrase "globalization has had a good run" being oft-repeated, in a sense I see even more of a need for all three mindsets – *including* the global mindset – in these times. Globalization has undoubtedly produced losers, not just winners, and requires greater attention to be paid to inequities of wealth and knowledge creation outcomes within and across the nations of the world. And yet, it would be a colossal waste to miss out on the advantages that globalization can provide, such as employment generation. Of course, for this to happen, organizations must be able to demonstrate a spirit of inclusiveness and responsibility with respect to the local environment in which the multinational corporation operates. As Microsoft CEO Satya Nadella has observed: "More than half of Microsoft's revenues are from outside the United States. We can't do business effectively in 190 countries unless we prioritize the creation of greater local economic opportunity in each of those countries . . . to support local entrepreneurship and public sector services in North America, South America, Asia, Africa, and Europe. In each of these regions, we have to operate with responsibility."[31]

Without diminishing globalization's ill effects, it is worth recognizing that it has historically been intertwined with entrepreneurship. Consider the case of Lipton tea. I vividly remember coming across Lipton's Seat, amid tea plantations about a half-hour's drive from my grandmother's house in Sri Lanka, where I would visit as a boy. My mother's side of the family grew up on tea estates in very scenic parts of the island, and Thomas Lipton (who built the eponymous tea brand) was a major player in that world. Later, when I moved to Glasgow, Scotland – Tommy Lipton's birthplace – I became even more cognizant of how globalization and entrepreneurship were intertwined in the Lipton story. Rising from humble origins as a grocer in Glasgow in the nineteenth century, Lipton used practices he observed in the United States as a youth to build a successful retail business in the UK, before he discovered Ceylon tea during a stopover on a voyage to Australia. He turned what until then had been a niche product of the British elites into a beverage for the mass market.

Fast-forward to the present day. Lipton is a Unilever-owned brand that engages with startups in order to mitigate its negative impact on the environment. For example, it partnered with the startup Literatti, whose digital app and community help to identify and dispose litter, on a "cleanup challenge" in the Netherlands.[32] Lipton's parent, Unilever, set up Transform, an initiative to support social enterprises in developing countries in partnership with the UK government and, subsequently, other partners such EY and MasterCard.[33] While multinationals are rightly held to high standards by stakeholders with respect to sustainability and the environment – and many undoubtedly need to do more – it should also be recognized that these organizations have resources and networks that can be fruitfully harnessed by actors such as social ventures and non-profits. It would be a wasted opportunity if the social impact baby got thrown out with the globalization bathwater.

The pendulum of globalization may swing toward more sedate local economic activity, away from the more volatile global value chains toward a "new normal" of globalization. But rather than seeking to do away with globalization entirely, it may be more prudent to harness globalization, in whatever form it exists – in particular its entrepreneurial benefits by generating business opportunities – in a way that is more equitable and compassionate than before. In the same way that corporate-startup partnering has moved from the periphery to the core in Microsoft and several of the other companies featured in this book, so should the emphasis on social impact. And if this happens, it would be a wasted opportunity to not leverage opportunities and ideas from other parts of the world despite the slowdown of globalization and rise of geopolitical tensions.

A global mindset is just as important as an entrepreneurial one because it helps us look beyond our immediate context to identify potential ways to transcend our immediate sphere of influence and extend impact. It leads us to look to other places for inspiration and solutions (or components to the solution). In so doing, it may be more possible to find suitable allies; key actors like multinationals, global NGOs and foundations, and multilateral organizations (such as the United Nations) are inherently international entities. And it keeps us from forgetting a lesson brought home by the Covid pandemic: we cannot wish away how interconnected we all are on Planet Earth. Whatever geopolitical differences might exist, it would be a shame not to harness skillsets and resources from wherever these can be found.

The digital health startup mPharma embodies all three mindsets – entrepreneurial, collaborative, and global – and has looked for inspiration and input from around the world. Its founders came up with the idea in the United States, gained support from the Israel ecosystem, and launched the company in Ghana. During the pandemic, a board member with ties to Silicon Valley and networks around the world helped mPharma connect with a supplier in China that could provide affordable equipment to support its diagnostic efforts, which proved to be extremely timely in meeting the large demand for Covid-19 testing. A company like this is poised to continue contributing to SDG 3 (good health and well-being) in Africa and beyond.

What was discussed in Chapter 5 (partnering with startups around the world) is arguably about harnessing entrepreneurship *and* globalization, and Chapter 6 is about making globalization "good," notwithstanding its ill effects, by leveraging multinational corporations and other international organizations. The key to both is a collaborative mindset. It is in partnerships – between nontraditional allies – that valuable business opportunities can be pursued while generating societal value: in indirect ways like generating employment and, for a subset of collaborations, through deliberate efforts to generate societal value through, for example, more inclusive finance, more accessible healthcare, and more universal education.

The pandemic appears to have deepened the strong yearning of business professionals that I have come across to lead meaningful lives with a purpose that transcends the narrow pursuit of profit. One's personal mission can be enriched by considering the three enduring mindsets highlighted in this book. There is a need – and an appetite – to act now. And a truly global effort is needed.

* * *

As I reflect on the intellectual journey that produced this book, I feel fortunate to have chanced upon an intriguing phenomenon – the coming together of corporations and startups, highly dissimilar yet complementary actors – at a very early stage. I am glad that I stuck with it, as an academic researcher, for a decade and half.

The early promise I saw in what organizations could achieve via dancing with gorillas has begun to be realized, as the gorillas have become more adept at dancing with startups, and more and more large organizations look to startups for innovation. I was intrigued to learn that even La Liga, the world-famous Spanish football (soccer) league, has been engaging with startups as part of its digital transformation efforts! A startup competition organized with the Global Sports Innovation Center, with involvement from Microsoft, resulted in various pilot projects. For example, LaLigaSportsTV incorporated the social viewing technology of a startup called

Sceenic, which allows viewers to watch and comment online with friends, for a trial period.[34]

I was lucky to observe some of the most skilled companies in this area – and to watch them get to that point (since virtually no one starts out being good in something that takes them out of their comfort zone). The lessons derived from this process, which this book contains, will save time and effort for the relative novices among gorillas that are seeking to engage with startups.

Inevitably, some of the specifics of the corporate-startup partnering phenomenon will evolve with time. The nature of the dance may change. Who knows, perhaps working together may become so commonplace that a time will come when not many will need to be reminded of its potential, or even schooled in the nuances of the process. In other words, as open innovation becomes increasingly institutionalized (as a recent IBM CEO report suggests ought to be the case[35]), the market for a book like this may well disappear in years to come! Indeed, that will have vindicated efforts such as this to contribute to a better understanding of what it takes for asymmetric partners to collaborate.

And my sincere hope is that, in the process, social impact will become an integral outcome that is pursued through such collaboration, as a post-Covid world pursues the SDGs in the Decade of Action with agility and resilience.

ENDNOTES

Prologue: Microsoft's Startup Partnering Journey

1. http://allthingsd.com/20070531/d5-gates-jobs-transcript/ (accessed 22 March 2021).
2. The process of technological change at Microsoft, entailing cloud computing and artificial intelligence (AI), is insightfully described in Iansiti, M., and Lakhani, K. R. (2020). *Competing in the Age of AI: Strategy and Leadership When Algorithms and Networks Run the World*. Boston, MA: Harvard Business Review Press.
3. Kim, T. (2018). How Microsoft Beat Out Apple and Became the World's Most Valuable Company. https://www.barrons.com/articles/how-microsoft-beat-out-apple-and-became-the-worlds-most-valuable-company-1543623288 (accessed 22 March 2021).
4. CHM Editorial (2018). Changing Lanes: Meet New CHM President and Chief Executive Officer Dan'l Lewin. https://computerhistory.org/blog/changing-lanes-meet-new-chm-president-and-chief-executive-officer-danl-lewin/ (accessed 22 March 2021).

5. Monk, B. (n.d.). Making – and Preserving – History. https://www.microsoftalumni.com/s/1769/19/interior.aspx?sid=1769&gid=2&pgid=2066&sitebuilder=1&contentbuilder=1 (accessed 22 March 2021).

6. http://www.lettersofnote.com/2011/07/internet-tidal-wave.html (accessed 22 March 2021).

7. Martínez, A. G. (2018). What Microsoft's Antitrust Case Teaches Us about Silicon Valley. https://www.wired.com/story/what-microsofts-antitrust-case-teaches-us-about-silicon-valley/ (accessed 22 March 2021).

8. Wikipedia (2021). Halloween Documents. https://en.wikipedia.org/wiki/Halloween_documents (accessed 22 March 2021).

9. Rosoff, M. (2011). EXCLUSIVE: Microsoft's Top Dog in Silicon Valley Talks about Startups, Bubbles, and Pet Food. https://www.businessinsider.com/qa-with-danl-lewin-microsofts-top-dog-in-silicon-valley-2011-3 (accessed 22 March 2021).

10. Wikipedia (2020). Microsoft Innovation Center. https://en.wikipedia.org/wiki/Microsoft_Innovation_Center (accessed 22 March 2021).

11. Prashantham, S. (2013). Skelta and the Microsoft Partnership Ecosystem. Ivey Business School, case no. 9B12M122. London, Canada: Ivey Publishing.

12. Prashantham, S., and Madhok, A. (2019). Think Globally, Act Cooperatively: Entrepreneurial Partnering between INVs and MNEs. In: *Frontiers of Strategic Alliance Research: Negotiating, Structuring & Governing Partnerships* (ed. F. J. Contractor and J. J. Reuer), 337–352. London, UK: Cambridge University Press.

13. Prashantham, S., and Birkinshaw, J. (2008). Dancing with Gorillas: How Small Companies Can Partner Effectively with MNCs. *California Management Review* 51(1): 6–23.

14. Lewin, D. (2011). Microsoft BizSpark Accelerates 45,000 Startups Around the World. https://blogs.microsoft.com/blog/2011/11/16/microsoft-bizspark-accelerates-45000-startups-around-the-world/ (accessed 22 March 2021).

15. Somasegar's blog (2008). BizSpark – Software for Startups. https://docs.microsoft.com/en-us/archive/blogs/somasegar/bizspark-software-for-startups (accessed 22 March 2021).

16. Protalinski, E. (2009). Microsoft BizSpark Now Serves 15,000 Startups. https://arstechnica.com/information-technology/2009/06/microsoft-bizspark-now-serves-15000/ (accessed 22 March 2021).

17. Somasegar's blog (2010). BizSpark Graduation Offer for Startups. https://docs.microsoft.com/en-us/archive/blogs/somasegar/bizspark-graduation-offer-for-startups (accessed 22 March 2021).

18. BizSpark Group Blog (2013). BizSpark Celebrates Five Year Anniversary. https://docs.microsoft.com/en-us/archive/blogs/bizspark_group_blog/bizspark-celebrates-five-year-anniversary (accessed 22 March 2021).

19. Finley, K. (2019). Enemies No More: Microsoft Brings the Linux Kernel to Windows. https://www.wired.com/story/enemies-no-more-microsoft-brings-linux-kernel-windows/ (accessed 22 March 2021).

20. Oiaga, M. (2009). Microsoft BizSpark One, the Evolution. https://news.softpedia.com/news/Microsoft-BizSpark-One-the-Evolution-127280.shtml (accessed 22 March 2021).

21. MicroDocumentaries (2010). Microsoft BizSpark One: Matthew Clark, Senior Director, Startup Engagement. https://www.youtube.com/watch?v=yevH9xvT7YY (accessed 22 March 2021).

22. Nadella, S. (2011). Satya Nadella: Worldwide Partner Conference 2011. https://news.microsoft.com/speeches/satya-nadella-worldwide-partner-conference-2011/ (accessed 22 March 2021).

23. The nature of these services can be seen at https://azure.microsoft.com/en-us/services/storsimple/ (accessed 22 March 2021).

24. https://news.microsoft.com/2012/10/16/microsoft-reaches-agreement-to-acquire-storsimple/ (accessed 22 March 2021).

25. HuddleHQ (2012). Andy McLoughlin on Why Huddle Went to the SharePoint Conference 2011. https://www.youtube.com/watch?v=vwBemodGxJI (accessed 22 March 2021); and HuddleHQ (2012). Huddle Crashes the SharePoint Conference - Behind the Scenes Video. https://www.youtube.com/watch?v=rr8JMpMtmQI (accessed 22 March 2021).

26. Graham, P. (2007). Microsoft is Dead. http://www.paulgraham.com/microsoft.html (accessed 22 March 2021).

27. Dan'l Lewin emphasizes the importance of corporate involvement: "Israel had a corporate outpost in research. That's where Zack was able to do what he did with corporate oversight.... We gave people the right to try. If it worked we would scale this around the world."

28. Tsinghua University is widely regarded as China's equivalent of MIT or Cambridge.

29. Microsoft Startup Blog (2008). BizSpark Startup of the Day – Gridsum. https://blogs.msdn.microsoft.com/startup/2008/11/07/bizspark-startup-of-the-daygridsum/ (accessed 22 March 2021); and Prashantham, S. (2017). Dancing with Gorillas in the Land of the Dragon. http://www.ceibs.edu/new-papers-columns/dancing-gorillas-land-dragon (accessed 22 March 2021).

30. MicroDocumentaries (2010). Microsoft BizSpark One: Matthew Clark, Senior Director, Startup Engagement. https://www.youtube.com/watch?v=yevH9xvT7YY (accessed 22 March 2021).

31. Boyd, C. (2017). WeChat: The Evolution and Future of China's Most Popular App. https://medium.com/swlh/wechat-the-evolution-and-future-of-chinas-most-popular-app-11effa5639ed (accessed 22 March 2021).

32. Prashantham, S., and Zhao, L. (2017). Testin: Partnering with Multinational Corporations. Ivey Business School, case no. 9B17M127. London, Canada: Ivey Publishing.

33. Microsoft News Center (2013). Microsoft Introduces the 4Afrika Initiative to Help Improve the Continent's Global Competitiveness. https://news.microsoft.com/2013/02/05/microsoft-introduces-the-4afrika-initiative-to-help-improve-the-continents-global-competitiveness/ (accessed 22 March 2021).

34. Prashantham, S., and Yip, G. S. (2017). Engaging with Startups in Emerging Markets. *MIT Sloan Management Review* 58(2): 51–56.

35. Meisner, J. (2013). Announcing Microsoft Ventures for Startups to Build, Innovate and Grow. https://blogs.microsoft.com/blog/2013/06/25/announcing-microsoft-ventures-for-startups-to-build-innovate-and-grow/ (accessed 22 March 2021).

36. Shih, G., and Rigby, B. (2014). Microsoft CEO Signals New Course with Office for iPad. https://www.reuters.com/article/us-microsoft-office-ipad/microsoft-ceo-signals-new-course-with-office-for-ipad-idUSBREA2Q1MV20140327 (accessed 22 March 2021).

37. Kumar, D. K., and Roy, A. (2015). Microsoft Hangs up on Nokia Business, to Cut 7,800 Jobs. https://www.reuters.com/article/microsoft-redundancies/microsoft-hangs-up-on-nokia-business-to-cut-7800-jobs-idUSKCN0PI1KO20150708 (accessed 22 March 2021).

38. Griffith, E., and Primack, D. (2015). The Age of Unicorns. https://fortune.com/2015/01/22/the-age-of-unicorns/ (accessed 22 March 2021);

and CB Insights (2015). Unicorns are Breeding like Rabbits: Set to Double 2014's Record Pace. https://www.cbinsights.com/research/unicorn-update-2015/ (accessed 22 March 2021).

39. This program enabled Microsoft to work with more than 200 of the world's leading startup accelerators, allowing startups to receive generous Azure credits, technical support, and guidance from technical evangelists to help growth-stage startups bring their products to market. More details can be found in Prashantham, S., and Yip, G. S. (2017). Microsoft Starts Up. *strategy+business* 86: 10–12.

40. Vander Ark, T. (2018). Hit Refresh: How a Growth Mindset Culture Tripled Microsoft's Value. https://www.forbes.com/sites/tomvander-ark/2018/04/18/hit-refresh-how-a-growth-mindset-culture-tripled-microsofts-value/#8a4ebba52ade (accessed 22 March 2021).

41. Whitney-Morris, C. (2017). "Seriously, Call Anytime": Microsoft Loves Startups. https://news.microsoft.com/life/seriously-call-anytime-microsoft-loves-startups/ (accessed 22 March 2021).

42. Microsoft Startups (2018). 2016 – The Year of Microsoft Accelerator Startups. https://startups.microsoft.com/zh-cn/blog/2016-the-year-of-microsoft-accelerator-startups/ (accessed 22 March 2021).

43. https://startupsandplaces.com/shm2019-accelerator-rankings/ (accessed 22 March 2021); and https://gust-marketing-production.her-okuapp.com/accelerator_reports/2016/global (accessed 22 March 2021).

44. Yarkoni, C. (2018). Grow, Build and Connect with Microsoft for Startups. https://blogs.microsoft.com/blog/2018/02/14/grow-build-connect-microsoft-startups/ (accessed 22 March 2021).

45. Sawers, P. (2018). Microsoft Ventures Rebrands as M12 to Avoid "Confusion" about Its Purpose. https://venturebeat.com/2018/04/30/

microsoft-ventures-rebrands-as-m12-to-avoid-confusion-about-its-purpose/ (accessed 22 March 2021).

46. Lunden, I. (2016). Microsoft Confirms Microsoft Ventures VC Arm, Renames Old One "Microsoft Accelerator." https://techcrunch.com/2016/05/31/microsoft-confirms-microsoft-ventures-vc-arm-renames-old-one-microsoft-accelerator/ (accessed 22 March 2021); Kashyap, N. (2016). Ventures Reimagined. https://blogs.microsoft.com/blog/2016/05/30/ventures-reimagined/#sm.000003snpyrbeyelkq vjfmi3jk23u (accessed 22 March 2021); and Dirik, I. (2017). Microsoft's Startup Initiatives – "A Manual for Corporate Venture Capital." https://medium.com/@iskender/microsofts-startup-initiatives-a-manual-for-corporate-venture-capital-c131dbcd0eff (accessed 22 March 2021).

47. Courtois, J.-P. (2020). Creating a World of Good: Microsoft Launches the Global Social Entrepreneurship Program. https://blogs.microsoft.com/latinx/2020/02/21/creating-a-world-of-good-microsoft-launches-the-global-social-entrepreneurship-program/ (accessed 30 March 2021).

48. Courtois, J.-P. (2019). Why Investing in Social Entrepreneurship is Good for Business. https://www.linkedin.com/pulse/why-investing-social-entrepreneurship-good-business-courtois/ (accessed 30 March 2021).

49. Microsoft News Center (2019). Digital Advancements in the Healthcare Sector Brings Patients Closer to Doctors in Pakistan. https://news.microsoft.com/en-xm/2019/12/03/digital-advancements-in-the-healthcare-sector-brings-patients-closer-to-doctors-in-pakistan/ (accessed 22 March 2021).

50. Udoh, C. R. (2020). Microsoft Launches Global Social Entrepreneurship Programme for African Social Startups. https://afrikanheroes.

com/2020/03/03/microsoft-launches-global-social-entrepreneurship-programme-for-african-social-startups/ (accessed 22 March 2021).

51. https://startups.microsoft.com/en-us/social-entrepreneurship/ (accessed 22 March 2021).

52. Courtois, J.-P. (2020). Creating a World of Good: Microsoft Launches the Global Social Entrepreneurship Program. https://blogs.microsoft.com/latinx/2020/02/21/creating-a-world-of-good-microsoft-launches-the-global-social-entrepreneurship-program/ (accessed 22 March 2021).

53. Okwumbu, R. (2020). Microsoft Launches Global Social Science Entrepreneurship Programme. https://nairametrics.com/2020/03/10/microsoft-launches-global-social-science-entrepreneurship-programme/ (accessed 22 March 2021).

54. Prashantham, S., and Birkinshaw, J. (2020). MNE–SME Cooperation: An Integrative Framework. *Journal of International Business Studies* 51(7): 1161–1175.

Chapter One Why Entrepreneurship Matters for Large Corporations

1. China Europe International Business School (CEIBS) (2018). Techstars' Dave Drach on Partnering with Start-ups for Innovation. https://www.ceibs.edu/video-podcast/14391 (accessed 22 March 2021).

2. Ringel, M., Taylor, A., and Zablit, H. (2016). The Most Innovative Companies 2016: Getting Past "Not Invented Here." Boston, MA: The Boston Consulting Group (BCG). https://media-publications.bcg.com/MIC/BCG-The-Most-Innovative-Companies-2016-Jan-2017.pdf (accessed 22 March 2021).

3. The Unilever Foundry (2017). The State of Innovation: A Deep Dive into Corporate-Startup Partnerships from the Unilever Foundry. https://www.theunileverfoundry.com/sk-eu/content/dam/brands/foundry-unilever/gb/en/The-State-of-Innovation.pdf (accessed 22 March 2021).

4. Christensen, C. M., and Dillon, K. (2020). Disruption 2020: An Interview with Clayton M. Christensen. *MIT Sloan Management Review* 61(3): 21–26.

5. Stevenson, H. H., and Jarillo-Mossi, J. C. (1990). A Paradigm of Entrepreneurship: Entrepreneurial Management. *Strategic Management Journal* 11(4): 17–27.

6. https://www.mckinsey.com/business-functions/strategy-and-corporate-finance/how-we-help-clients/growth-and-innovation (accessed 22 March 2021).

7. March, J. G. (1991). Exploration and Exploitation in Organizational Learning. *Organization Science* 2(1): 71–87.

8. Dess, G. G., and Lumpkin, G. T. (2005). The Role of Entrepreneurial Orientation in Stimulating Effective Corporate Entrepreneurship. *Academy of Management Perspectives* 19(1): 147–156.

9. Somers, M. (2018). Intrapreneurship, Explained. https://mitsloan.mit.edu/ideas-made-to-matter/intrapreneurship-explained (accessed 30 March 2021).

10. Demott, J. S. (1985). Here Come the Intrapreneurs. http://content.time.com/time/magazine/article/0,9171,959877,00.html (accessed 22 March 2021).

11. Lubenow, G. C. (1985). Jobs Talks about His Rise and Fall. https://www.newsweek.com/jobs-talks-about-his-rise-and-fall-207016 (accessed 30 March 2021).

12. Swearingen, J. (2008). Great Intrapreneurs in Business History. https://www.cbsnews.com/news/great-intrapreneurs-in-business-history/ (accessed 30 March 2021).

13. Prashantham, S., and Birkinshaw, J. (2008). Dancing with Gorillas: How Small Companies Can Partner Effectively with MNCs. *California Management Review* 51(1): 6–23.

14. Birkinshaw, J. (2000). *Entrepreneurship in the Global Firm: Enterprise and Renewal.* London, UK: Sage.

15. Murphy Jr., B. (2020). Google Says It Still Uses the "20-Percent Rule," and You Should Totally Copy It. https://www.inc.com/bill-murphy-jr/google-says-it-still-uses-20-percent-rule-you-should-totally-copy-it.html (accessed 30 March 2021).

16. Samsung Newsroom (2016). How Samsung Helps Its Internal Innovators to Spread their Wings. https://news.samsung.com/global/how-samsung-helps-its-internal-innovators-to-spread-their-wings (accessed 22 March 2021).

17. Kim, Y. W. (2018). TagHive Tackles Smartphone Addiction of Kids. http://www.theinvestor.co.kr/view.php?ud=20180228000673 (accessed 30 March 2021).

18. Prashantham, S., and Cao, Z. (2021). Intel GrowthX: Partnering with Entrepreneurs for Growth. China Europe International Business School, case no. CC-320-105. Shanghai: China Europe International Business School.

19. Prashantham, S. (2020). Partner with Entrepreneurs Inside and Out. *MIT Sloan Management Review* 61(2): 80–81.

20. Chesbrough, H. W. (2003). The Era of Open Innovation. *MIT Sloan Management Review* 44(3): 35–41.

21. Adner, R. (2012). *The Wide Lens: A New Strategy for Innovation*. London, UK: Penguin.

22. Microsoft News Center (2012). Steve Ballmer and Stephen Elop: Microsoft and Nokia Press Conference. https://news.microsoft.com/2012/09/05/steve-ballmer-and-stephen-elop-microsoft-and-nokia-press-conference/ (accessed 22 March 2021).

23. Buckley, P. J., and Prashantham, S. (2016). Global Interfirm Networks: The Division of Entrepreneurial Labor between MNEs and SMEs. *Academy of Management Perspectives* 30(1): 40–58.

24. Ibid.

25. To be sure, the prospect of some level of competition coexisting with cooperation is often recognized by both parties. But this, of itself, hasn't proved to be an impediment to corporations and startups beginning to work together, in my observation. Equally, there are many (more, perhaps) that seem to be claiming that they wish to work with startups but are appearing to pay only lip service to that intent.

26. Interestingly, today many of these intrapreneurs have left their company to become consultants to other companies seeking to work with startups; such third-party specialists are discussed in the concluding section of Chapter 4.

27. Birkinshaw, J., and Meghani, S. (2016). Unilever Foundry. London Business School, case no. CS-18-015. London, UK: London Business School Publishing.

28. Arthur D. Little (2016).The Age of Collaboration: Startups and Corporates Need Each Other. https://www.adlittle.com/sites/default/files/viewpoints/ADL_MatchMaker_The_Age_of_Collaboration.pdf (accessed 22 March 2021).

Chapter Two Why Partnering with Startups Isn't Easy

1. Birkinshaw, J., and Meghani, S. (2016). Unilever Foundry. London Business School, case no. CS-18-015. London, UK: London Business School Publishing.

2. March, J. G. (1991). Exploration and Exploitation in Organizational Learning. *Organization Science* 2(1): 71–87. For an insightful discussion of how the exploration-exploitation distinction relates to established corporations' challenge to be entrepreneurial, see Hamel, G., and Zanini, M. (2020). Humanocracy. Boston, MA: Harvard Business Review Press.

3. Putnam, R. D. (2000). *Bowling Alone: The Collapse and Revival of American Community*. New York: Simon & Schuster.

4. Sarasvathy, S. D. (2009). *Effectuation: Elements of Entrepreneurial Orientation*. Cheltenham, UK: Edward Elgar Publishing.

5. Adner, R. (2012). *The Wide Lens: A New Strategy for Innovation*. London, UK: Penguin.

6. Decreton, B., Monteiro, F., Frangos, J. M., and Friedman, L. (2021). Innovation Outposts in Entrepreneurial Ecosystems: How to Make Them More Successful. *California Management Review*. https://doi.org/10.1177/0008125621996494.

7. Doz, Y. L. (1987). Technology Partnerships between Larger and Smaller Firms: Some Critical Issues. *International Studies of Management & Organization* 17(4): 31–57.

8. Prashantham, S. (2019). The Two Ways for Startups and Corporations to Partner. *Harvard Business Review* Digital Article. https://hbr.org/2019/01/the-two-ways-for-startups-and-corporations-to-partner

(accessed 30 March 2021); and Prashantham, S. (2021). Partnering Effectively with Innovative Small Firms in Ecosystems. https://business-ecosystem-alliance.org/2021/04/28/gorillas-can-dance-partnering-effectively-with-innovative-small-firms-in-ecosystems/ (accessed 30 April 2021).

Chapter Three How to Partner with Startups Systematically

1. Saran, C. (2015). Satya Nadella: Every Business Will Be a Software Business. https://www.computerweekly.com/news/2240242478/Satya-Nadella-Every-business-will-be-a-software-business (accessed 22 March 2021).

2. Holmes, M. (2019). Microsoft CEO: "Every Company is now a Software Company." https://www.satellitetoday.com/innovation/2019/02/26/microsoft-ceo-every-company-is-now-a-software-company/ (accessed 22 March 2021).

3. Ziegler, C., and Patel, N. (2016). Meet the New Ford, a Silicon Valley Software Company. https://www.theverge.com/2016/4/7/11333288/ford-ceo-mark-fields-interview-electric-self-driving-car-software (accessed 22 March 2021).

4. McKendrick, J. (2011). How Cloud Computing Is Fueling the Next Startup Boom. https://www.forbes.com/sites/joemckendrick/2011/11/01/cloud-computing-is-fuel-for-the-next-entrepreneurial-boom/#33e9c0471db8 (accessed 22 March 2021).

5. Stephen, C. (2009). Enduring Ideas: The Three Horizons of Growth (Interactive Presentation & Audio File). *McKinsey Quarterly*.

https://www.mckinsey.com/business-functions/strategy-and-corporate-finance/our-insights/enduring-ideas-the-three-horizons-of-growth (accessed 22 March 2021).

6. Miller, J., and Kagan, J. (2021). *Designing the Successful Corporate Accelerator*. Hoboken, NJ: Wiley.

7. Prashantham, S., and Yip, G. S. (2017). Microsoft Starts Up. *strategy+business* 86: 10–12.

8. Prashantham, S. (2017). Lessons from Bayer & BMW on Partnering with Startups. http://viewswire.eiu.com/index.asp?layout=ebArticleVW3&article_id=1405361324&channel_id=&category_id=&refm=ebHome&page_title=Latest++management+thinking (accessed 22 March 2021).

9. Bansal, M. (2018). SAP Startup Focus – The Journey Continues. https://www.linkedin.com/pulse/sap-startup-focus-journey-continues-manju-bansal/ (accessed 22 March 2021).

10. Gimmy, G., Kanbach, D., Stubner, S., Konig, A., and Enders, A. (2017). What BMW's Corporate VC Offers That Regular Investors Can't. https://hbr.org/2017/07/what-bmws-corporate-vc-offers-that-regular-investors-cant (accessed 22 March 2021).

11. HuddleHQ (2012). Andy McLoughlin on Why Huddle Went to the SharePoint Conference 2011. https://www.youtube.com/watch?v=vwBemodGxJI (accessed 22 March 2021); and HuddleHQ (2012). Huddle Crashes the SharePoint Conference - Behind the Scenes Video. https://www.youtube.com/watch?v=rr8JMpMtmQI (accessed 22 March 2021).

12. Prashantham, S., and Birkinshaw, J. (2008). Dancing with Gorillas: How Small Companies Can Partner Effectively with MNCs. *California Management Review* 51(1): 6–23.

Chapter Four Building the Capability to Partner with Startups

1. Executive Insights (2013). The Story of a Startup: The Drivers behind the SAP Startup Focus Program. *SAPinsider*. http://www.sapinsider-digital.com/sapinsider/april_may_june_2013?pg=9#pg9 (accessed 22 March 2021).

2. Prashant, K., and Harbir, S. (2009). Managing Strategic Alliances: What Do We Know Now, And Where Do We Go From Here? *Academy of Management Perspectives* 23(3): 45–62.

3. Prashantham, S. (2017). Lessons from Bayer & BMW on Partnering with Startups. http://viewswire.eiu.com/index.asp?layout=ebArticleVW3&article_id=1405361324&channel_id=&category_id=&refm=ebHome&page_title=Latest++management+thinking (accessed 22 March 2021).

4. China Europe International Business School (CEIBS) (2017). The Making of BMW's Startup Garage. https://www.youtube.com/watch?v=zAlu4aV9cuw (accessed 22 March 2021).

5. Stevenson, H. H. (1983). Perspective on Entrepreneurship. Harvard Business School, case no. 384131-PDF-ENG. Boston, MA: Harvard Business School Publishing.

6. Birkinshaw, J., and Meghani, S. (2016). Unilever Foundry. London Business School, case no. CS-18-015. London, UK: London Business School Publishing.

7. Kenyan WallStreet (2017). Liquid Telecom to Provide Free Internet to Co-working Space Nairobi Garage. https://kenyanwallstreet.com/

liquid-telecom-provide-free-internet-co-working-space-nairobi-garage/ (accessed 22 March 2021).

8. Prashantham, S., and Patel, S. (2019). Winning over Internal Stakeholders to Make External Startup Engagement Work. http://viewswire.eiu.com/index.asp?layout=EBArticleVW3&article_id=457941229&channel_id=788114478&category_id=&refm=ebCh&page_title=Latest&from=singlemessage&isappinstalled=0 (accessed 22 March 2021).

9. Thus expansion may involve a geographic aspect – and this is explored further in Chapter 5.

10. Tegos, M. (2017). Unilever Just Launched Its Own Co-Working Space in Singapore. https://www.techinasia.com/unilever-level3-co-working-space-launch (accessed 22 March 2021).

11. Bansal, M. (2018). SAP Startup Focus – The Journey Continues. https://www.linkedin.com/pulse/sap-startup-focus-journey-continues-manju-bansal/ (accessed 22 March 2021).

12. Chesbrough, H. W. (2003). *Open Innovation: The New Imperative for Creating and Profiting from Technology*. Boston, MA: Harvard Business School Press.

13. Hamel, G., and Zanini, M. (2020). *Humanocracy*. Boston, MA: Harvard Business Review Press.

14. Johnson, G., Prashantham, S., Floyd, S. W., and Bourque, N. (2010). The Ritualization of Strategy Workshops. *Organization Studies* 31(12): 1589–1618.

15. Ibid.

16. Mahtani, V., and Evers, D. (2021). Co-sell with Microsoft Sales Teams and Partners Overview. https://docs.microsoft.com/en-us/azure//marketplace/marketplace-co-sell (accessed 22 March 2021).

17. Krishna, A. (2020). My First Day as CEO – Our Journey Together. https://www.linkedin.com/pulse/my-first-day-ceo-our-journey-together-arvind-krishna/ (accessed 29 March 2021).

18. As with the corporations discussed in the book, I did not have any commercial relationship with any of the third-party specialists mentioned here while conducting the research that this book is based on.

19. This sequential approach of working with different gorillas is sensible. One corporate innovation manager who attended a talk I gave commented that his organization had built a consortium with five other (noncompeting) corporations with a view to identifying startup partners that would build proofs-of-concept or pilot projects that could be relevant to all of them. Clearly, this has its limitations. While the idea of hunting in a pack can make sense, it might be more realistic to ensure that a startup has one workable idea that has a good fit with the needs of at least one of the corporations in the consortium and then shopping it around to the others; trying to find a solution that works for everyone from inception might be a frustrating and inefficient process for all concerned.

20. Gimmy, G., Kanbach, D., Stubner, S., Konig, A., and Enders, A. (2017). What BMW's Corporate VC Offers That Regular Investors Can't. https://hbr.org/2017/07/what-bmws-corporate-vc-offers-that-regular-investors-cant (accessed 22 March 2021).

21. https://www.linkedin.com/company/pilot44-labs/ (accessed 22 March 2021).

22. Prashantham, S., and Kumar, K. (2019). Engaging with Startups: MNC Perspectives. *IIMB Management Review* 31(4): 407–417.

Chapter Five Partnering with Startups Around the World

1. Fisher, L. M. (2002). Yves Doz: The Thought Leader Interview. *strategy+business* 29: 115–123.

2. Prahalad, C. K., and Doz, Y. L. (1987). *The Multinational Mission: Balancing Local Demands and Global Vision*. New York: Free Press.

3. Doz, Y. L., Santos, J., and Williamson, P. (2001). *From Global to Metanational: How Companies Win in the Knowledge Economy*. Boston, MA: Harvard Business School Press.

4. https://www.insightrobotics.com/press_releases/insight-robotics-named-entrepreneur-of-the-year/ (accessed 26 March 2021).

5. Prashantham, S., and Yip, G. S. (2017). Engaging with Startups in Emerging Markets. *MIT Sloan Management Review* 58(2): 51–56.

6. TIA Bot (2019). In brief: Facebook Launches Hub for Developers, Startups in Jakarta. https://www.techinasia.com/facebook-launches-developers-startups-hub-jakarta (accessed 22 March 2021).

7. Microsoft Stories Asia (2020). Four Startups Win Inaugural Microsoft Emerge X Pitch Competition in APAC. https://news.microsoft.com/apac/2020/12/03/four-startups-win-inaugural-microsoft-emerge-x-pitch-competition-in-apac/ (accessed 22 March 2021).

8. Akhaya, P. (2019). Kora, Rytle Crowned Joint Winners of Unilever Foundry Startup Battle 2019. https://e27.co/kora-rytle-crowned-joint-winners-of-unilever-foundry-startup-battle-2019-20190701/ (accessed 22 March 2021).

9. Prashantham, S., Eranova, M., and Khamisani, V. (2019). How Entrepreneurs and Managers Can Find Common Ground in Big Data. http://viewswire.eiu.com/index.asp?layout=ebArticleVW3&article_

id=1537657937&channel_id=&category_id=&refm=ebHome&page_title=Latest++management+thinking (accessed 22 March 2021).

10. Mastup, F. (2021). Starbuck in Indonesia Partners with Green Butcher to Launch Their New "Plant-Based" Menu. https://jakartaveganguide.com/post/vegan-buzz/starbuck-in-indonesia-partners-with-green-butcher-to-launch-their-new--plant-based--menu/149 (accessed 22 March 2021).

11. Folger, J. (2020). Why Silicon Valley Companies Are Moving to Texas. https://www.investopedia.com/why-silicon-valley-companies-are-moving-to-texas-5092782 (accessed 29 March 2021).

12. Decreton, B., Monteiro, F., Frangos, J. M., and Friedman, L. (2021). Innovation Outposts in Entrepreneurial Ecosystems: How to Make Them More Successful. *California Management Review*. https://doi.org/10.1177/0008125621996494.

13. Gunn, D. (2009). How Did Israel Become "Start-Up Nation"? https://freakonomics.com/2009/12/04/how-did-israel-become-start-up-nation/ (accessed 22 March 2021).

14. Govindarajan, V., and Trimble, C. (2012). *Reverse Innovation: Create Far from Home, Win Everywhere.* Boston, MA: Harvard Business Review Press.

15. Clobotics (2019). Walmart X Clobotics: The Secret Sauce of Off-Line Retail Digitalization. https://medium.com/@clobotics/walmart-x-clobotics-the-secret-sauce-of-off-line-retail-digitalization-8af28d8f2136 (accessed 22 March 2021).

16. Team YS (2019). Cisco LaunchPad is Building a "Bridge to Possible" for B2B Tech Startups. https://yourstory.com/2019/08/cisco-launchpad-building-bridge (accessed 22 March 2021).

17. Prashantham, S., Kumar, K., and Bhattacharyya, S. (2019). International New Ventures from Emerging Economies: Network Connectivity and Legitimacy Building. *Management and Organization Review* 15(3): 615–641.

18. Prashantham, S. (2011). Social Capital and Indian Micromultinationals. *British Journal of Management* 22(1): 4–20.

19. http://eng.gdd.gov.cn/2019-11/22/c_426675.htm (accessed 29 March 2021).

20. Birkinshaw, J., and Hood, N. (2001). Unleash Innovation in Foreign Subsidiaries. *Harvard Business Review* 79(3): 131–137.

21. One exception is Israel, which is small enough as a country to be thought of as a single ecosystem.

22. For a more academic treatment, see Prashantham, S. (2021). Partnering with Startups Globally: Distinct Strategies for Different Locations. *California Management Review*. https://doi.org/10.1177/00081256211022743.

23. Khanna, T., and Palepu, K. G. (2010). *Winning in Emerging Markets: A Road Map for Strategy and Execution*. Boston, MA: Harvard Business Review Press.

24. For an academic treatment of this issue, see Prashantham, S., and Bhattacharyya, S. (2020). MNE–SME Co-innovation in Peripheral Regions. *Journal of International Business Policy* 3: 134–153.

25. Staff Writer (2013). Kenyan's MoDe Wins IBM Smartcamp Global Finals. https://innovation-village.com/kenyans-mode-wins-ibm-smartcamp-global-finals/ (accessed 22 March 2021).

26. https://www.ifc.org/wps/wcm/connect/5bac0326-8f59-4c35-86ab-9915de92ecf5/Digital+Skills_Final_WEB_M4A.pdf?MOD=AJPERES (accessed 22 March 2021).

27. Microsoft News Center (2019). Furthering Our Investment in Africa: Microsoft Opens First Africa Development Centre in Kenya and Nigeria. https://news.microsoft.com/en-xm/features/furthering-our-investment-in-africa-microsoft-opens-first-africa-development-centre-in-kenya-and-nigeria/ (accessed 22 March 2021).

28. Keane, T. (2019). Microsoft Opens First Datacenters in Africa with General Availability of Microsoft Azure. https://azure.microsoft.com/en-in/blog/microsoft-opens-first-datacenters-in-africa-with-general-availability-of-microsoft-azure/ (accessed 22 March 2021).

29. https://www.un.org/sustainabledevelopment/sustainable-development-goals/ (accessed 22 March 2021).

30. Shamah, D. (2014). Microsoft to Bring Start-Up Nation to the "Next Level." https://www.timesofisrael.com/microsoft-to-bring-start-up-nation-to-the-next-level/ (accessed 22 March 2021).

31. Prashantham, S. (2020). Global Meets Local as Multinationals Pair with Start-ups. https://www.ft.com/content/5a715eca-1a78-44ab-a23e-a5282037d532 (accessed 22 March 2021).

32. Prashantham, S., and Yip, G. S. (2017). Microsoft Starts Up. *strategy+business* 86: 10–12.

Chapter Six Partnering with Startups as a Force for Good

1. Polman, P. (2020). The Coronavirus Pandemic May Be a Turning Point for Responsible Business. https://fortune.com/2020/04/14/coronavirus-responsible-business-leadership-covid-19/ (accessed 22 March 2021).

2. https://www.dsgc.nl/en/sdgs (accessed 31 March 2021).

3. Polman, P. (2020). The Coronavirus Pandemic May Be a Turning Point for Responsible Business. https://fortune.com/2020/04/14/coronavirus-responsible-business-leadership-covid-19/ (accessed 29 March 2021).

4. Maddox, C. (2019). "Six Transformations to achieve the Sustainable Development Goals" Lays Out Integrated Framework for Implementing the SDGs. https://www.unsdsn.org/news/2019/08/26/six-transformations-to-achieve-the-sustainable-development-goals-provide-cross-cutting-framework-for-action (accessed 22 March 2021).

5. The 17 SDGs are: (1) No Poverty, (2) Zero Hunger, (3) Good Health and Well-being, (4) Quality Education, (5) Gender Equality, (6) Clean Water and Sanitation, (7) Affordable and Clean Energy, (8) Decent Work and Economic Growth, (9) Industry, Innovation, and Infrastructure, (10) Reduced Inequalities, (11) Sustainable Cities and Communities, (12) Responsible Consumption and Production, (13) Climate Action, (14) Life Below Water, (15) Life on Land, (16) Peace, Justice, and Strong Institutions, and (17) Partnerships for the Goals. https://sdgs.un.org/goals (accessed 8 May 2021).

6. Sachs, J. D., and Sachs, L. E. (2021). Business Alignment for the "Decade of Action." *Journal of International Business Policy* 4: 22–27.

7. Porter, M., and Kramer, M. (2011). Creating Shared Value. *Harvard Business Review* 89 (1/2): 62–77.

8. Prahalad, C. K. (2012). Bottom of the Pyramid as a Source of Breakthrough Innovations. *Journal of Product Innovation Management* 29(1): 6–12.

9. Christensen, C. M., Ojomo, E., Gay, G. D., and Auerswald, P. E. (2019). The Third Answer: How Market-Creating Innovation Drives Economic

Growth and Development. *Innovations: Technology, Governance, Globalization* 12(3–4): 10–26.

10. Tarun Khanna refers to this as an institutional void, which refers in particular to the absence of market intermediaries in emerging markets. Khanna, T., and Palepu, K. G. (2010). *Winning in Emerging Markets: A Road Map for Strategy and Execution*. Boston, MA: Harvard Business Review Press.

11. MasterCard Foundation (2015). The MasterCard Foundation Launches US$17.6 Million Initiative with Oxford Policy Management to Connect Rural Populations in Africa to Financial System. https://mastercardfdn.org/the-mastercard-foundation-launches-us17-6-million-initiative-with-oxford-policy-management-to-connect-rural-populations-in-africa-to-financial-system/ (accessed 22 March 2021).

12. DT One (2019). DT One Advances Mobile Technology Capabilities with Acquisition of MODE. https://www.dtone.com/dt-one-advances-mobile-technology-capabilities-with-acquisition-of-mode/ (accessed 22 March 2021); and Wakoba, S. (2019). Kenya's MODE Acquired by Singapore's TransferTo (DT One) to Bolster Its Global Mobile Top-Up Solutions. https://techmoran.com/2019/09/05/kenyas-mode-acquired-by-singapores-transferto-dt-one-to-bolster-its-global-mobile-top-up-solutions/ (accessed 22 March 2021).

13. http://powered.org.in/accelerator/#sectioninfo_dt (accessed 22 March 2021).

14. https://shellfoundation.org/app/uploads/2019/08/TARU-NATURALS-Case-Study.pdf (accessed 22 March 2021).

15. http://www.iimcip.org/prif-we/ (accessed 22 March 2021).

16. https://corp.rakuten.co.in/rsa-rakuten-social-accelerator/ (accessed 22 March 2021).

17. Courtois, J. P. (2020). Creating a World of Good: Microsoft Launches the Global Social Entrepreneurship Program. https://blogs.microsoft.com/latinx/2020/02/21/creating-a-world-of-good-microsoft-launches-the-global-social-entrepreneurship-program/ (accessed 30 March 2021).

18. SDG Accelerator for SMEs (2020). SDG Accelerator Solution at the Forefront of Response to COVID-19. http://www.sdg-accelerator.org/content/sdg-accelerator/en/home/news-centre/news/BLUETOWN-covid19.html (accessed 22 March 2021).

19. https://www.we.com.na/news/boost-for-start-ups2020-09-16 (accessed 31 March 2021).

20. Kampulu, M. (2019). A First Mapping of Local Innovators in Namibia: The Power of Good Ideas. https://acclabs.medium.com/a-first-mapping-of-local-innovators-in-namibia-the-power-of-good-ideas-d406469f303f (accessed 31 March 2021).

21. Walters, H. (2013). Got Social Problems? Business Can Help: Michael Porter at TEDGlobal 2013. https://blog.ted.com/got-social-problems-business-can-help-michael-porter-at-tedglobal-2013/ (accessed 22 March 2021).

22. www.nexti2i.com (accessed 22 March 2021).

23. NEXTi2i. Announcing the Ashesi Venture Incubator Fellows. https://www.nexti2i.com/ashesi-venture-incubator/announcing-the-avi/ (accessed 22 March 2021).

24. Prashantham, S., Eranova, M., and Couper, C. (2018). Globalization, Entrepreneurship and Paradox Thinking. *Asia Pacific Journal of Management* 35(1): 1–9.

25. An intriguing feature of both social ventures and corporate foundations is their hybrid nature. Both sets of organizations must simultaneously come to grips with a social logic that is predicated on "doing

good" and an economic logic of "doing well." This creates tensions that, when creatively handled, can deliver valuable outcomes for the SDGs. But this, of course, is easier said than done. Managers are typically comfortable with linear logic, not paradoxical cognition; most MBA programs produce professional managers that are adept at making tradeoffs through either-or thinking rather than leaders who use both-and (or even both-or) thinking as they continuously grapple with the imperative to handle competing tensions.

26. One of the many positive press stories describes the founding story thus: "The revolutionary business is the brainchild of Grant Brooke, a researcher, and Peter Njonjo, the former Coca-Cola President for west and central Africa. The son of public officials from Texas, USA, Brooke was educated at Princeton before first coming to Kenya in 2008 seeking to understand how religion affects purchasing and credit decisions of small business owners in Nairobi. So high was the potential he saw in Kenya that he returned even after postgraduate studies at the University of Oxford, this time for the long haul where he and Njonjo would begin laying the foundation for the business that has shaken the industry to its roots and attracted billions of shillings in investments in less than five years"; and Sigei, J. (2019). The Men Changing Face of Food Business. https://hakipensheni.blogspot.com/2019/06/the-men-changing-face-of-food-business.html (accessed 22 March 2021).

27. https://www.crunchbase.com/organization/twiga-foods (accessed 22 March 2021).

28. Ombogo, M. (2019). Twiga Foods: The Disruptors in the "Mama Mboga" Market. https://www.standardmedia.co.ke/business/article/2001315412/twiga-foods-the-disruptors-in-the-mama-mboga-market (accessed 22 March 2021).

29. https://twiga.ke/twiga-story/ (accessed 22 March 2021).

30. Not all external commentary on social ventures is necessarily positive – but this scathing analysis of the venture appears to be the exception rather than the rule since much more coverage of this venture that I came across was very positive; and Nyakundi, C. (2019). Twiga Foods Sinking with Billions: How Marikiti Mothers Fought and Won against White Monopoly Capital. https://www.cnyakundi.com/twiga-foods-sinking-with-billions-how-marikiti-mothers-fought-and-won-against-white-monopoly-capital/ (accessed 22 March 2021).

31. https://www.candyindustry.com/articles/89551-koa-partners-with-lindt-on-chocolate-bar-sweetened-with-cocoa-pulp-powder (accessed 30 March 2021).

32. Sachs, J. D., Schmidt-Traub, G., Mazzucato, M., Messner, D., Nakicenovic, N., and Rockström, J. (2019). Six Transformations to Achieve the Sustainable Development Goals. *Nature Sustainability* 2(9): 805–814.

33. Wang, J. (2019). Alibaba a Major Contributor to Sustainable Development Goals. https://www.alizila.com/alibaba-a-major-contributor-to-un-sdg/ (accessed 22 March 2021).

34. Chutel, L. (2018). Jack Ma Explains Why Africa Offers Opportunities for Entrepreneurs. https://www.weforum.org/agenda/2018/08/jack-ma-s-sermon-to-entrepreneurs-captured-just-why-african-business-looks-to-china (accessed 22 March 2021).

35. Prashantham, S. (2018). Lessons from West Africa: Partnering outside the Box. http://viewswire.eiu.com/index.asp?layout=ebArticleVW3&article_id=837244667 (accessed 22 March 2021)

36. Hsu, J. W. (2019). "Believe in Yourself and Just Do It" – Advice from Female Entrepreneurs. https://www.alizila.com/believe-in-yourself-and-just-do-it-advice-from-female-entrepreneurs/ (accessed 22 March 2021).

37. Roberts-Islam, B. (2020). Fashion Pact 2020: Diverse and Inclusive Enough to Protect People and Planet? https://www.forbes.com/sites/brookerobertsislam/2020/10/13/fashion-pact-2020-diverse-and-inclusive-enough-to-protect-people-and-planet/?sh=330f71e172b4 (accessed 25 March 2021).

38. For more insight into what businesses can learn from non-profits like CMC Hospital, see Prashantham, S. (2020). When Business as Usual Isn't Working, Look to Nonprofits for Inspiration. *Harvard Business Review* Digital Article. https://hbr.org/2020/09/when-business-as-usual-isnt-working-look-to-nonprofits-for-inspiration (accessed 30 March 2021).

39. Porter, M. E., and Kramer, M. R. (2011). Creating Shared Value. *Harvard Business Review* 89(1/2): 62–77.

40. Yaziji, M., and Doh, J. (2009). *NGOs and Corporations: Conflict and Collaboration*. Cambridge, UK: Cambridge University Press.

41. Zaidman, Y. (2016). *Beyond Dialogue: Building Sustainable and Inclusive Business Models in Partnership with Social Entrepreneurs*. New York: Acumen.

Epilogue Three Mindsets for the SDG Decade of Action

1. Nadella, S. (2017). *Hit Refresh*. London, UK: HarperCollins.

2. Bryant, N. (2020). The Year 2020: A Time When Everything Changed. https://www.bbc.com/news/world-us-canada-55353178 (accessed 25 March 2021).

3. https://www.un.org/development/desa/dspd/2020/09/decade-of-action/ (accessed 25 March 2021); and https://www.undp.org/content/

undp/en/home/stories/decade-of-action.html (accessed 25 March 2021).

4. Although Covid-19 itself was first detected in late 2019 – hence the name – its consequences became global only in 2020.

5. The last conventional field trip I undertook was in March 2020 when I visited Bangalore and Hyderabad in India. Those were the last flights I took before the pandemic became officially recognized as a global problem that resulted in widespread disruption of international travel for individuals and global value chains for companies. Shortly before that trip took place, at the end of February 2020, Microsoft announced the latest addition to its startup partnering arsenal, which was a global social entrepreneurship program. Although I still had numerous subsequent interactions with my research informants via Zoom, it certainly was the case that the bulk of the research reported in this book was bookended by two global crises, one in 2008 (the global financial crisis) and the other in 2020 (the Covid-19 pandemic).

6. Apple Newsroom (2008). iPhone App Store Downloads Top 10 Million in First Weekend. https://www.apple.com/newsroom/2008/07/14iPhone-App-Store-Downloads-Top-10-Million-in-First-Weekend/ (accessed 25 March 2021).

7. Leach, M., Reyers, B., Bai, X., et al. (2018). Equity and Sustainability in the Anthropocene: A Social–Ecological Systems Perspective on Their Intertwined Futures. *Global Sustainability* 1: E13. https://doi.org/10.1017/sus.2018.12.

8. USCBC (2008). The 2008 Olympics' Impact on China. https://www.chinabusinessreview.com/the-2008-olympics-impact-on-china/ (accessed 25 March 2021).

9. Lash, J. (2009). From Financial Crisis to Sustainable Global Economy. https://www.wri.org/blog/2009/01/financial-crisis-sustainable-global-economy (accessed 25 March 2021).

10. Feld, B. (2012). *Startup Communities: Building an Entrepreneurial Ecosystem in Your City*. Hoboken, NJ: Wiley.

11. Yu, Y. (2009). China's Policy Responses to the Global Financial Crisis. Richard Snape Lecture, Productivity Commission, Melbourne (25 November).

12. I speculate that without the financial crisis and accompanying economic distress, many of those Western companies may not have considered being acquired.

13. CIGI Working Group on Environment and Resources (2009). Environmental Sustainability and the Financial Crisis: Linkages and Policy Recommendations. https://www.cigionline.org/sites/default/files/environmental_sustainability_and_the_financial_crisis_0.pdf (accessed 25 March 2021).

14. Kuhn, M., Schularick, M., and Steins, U. (2018). Research: How the Financial Crisis Drastically Increased Wealth Inequality in the U.S. *Harvard Business Review* Digital Article. https://hbr.org/2018/09/research-how-the-financial-crisis-drastically-increased-wealth-inequality-in-the-u-s (accessed 25 March 2021).

15. Leach, M. (2016). 27. Inequality and Sustainability. In: *World Social Science Report* (ed. UNESCO and Institute of Development Studies (Brighton, England)), 132–134. Paris: UNESCO Publishing.

16. Ironically, one of the reactions to (justified) perceptions of inequality was the rise of populism which, in some markets like the United States, led to an administration being voted in that withdrew from the

Paris Climate Agreement; this decision has since been reversed. The point is that the post-financial crisis period has seen the crisis of sustainability become an ever-growing concern.

17. Wolf, M. (2021). Hopes and Fears of the Global Recovery. https://www.ft.com/content/cf2d5ad5-2b60-4398-a6d3-cbec8716d9ec (accessed 25 March 2021).

18. I witnessed this new-found agility firsthand as a business school professor (in somewhat amusing circumstances). A peculiar personal experience of mine illustrates how even education establishments, not always the quickest to embrace change, had to make rapid adjustments to the pandemic. In January 2020, prior to the pandemic, I had explored the possibility of delivering one of my classes by video link because of a – false, as it turned out – suspicion that I had chicken pox. (The doctor suggested I may have to be quarantined, a term that seemed so alien at the time, but one that became widely used as the year unfolded!) Unfortunately, I was told, this could not be arranged. Fortunately, this proved to be a momentary hiccup, as I resumed my regular teaching after missing just one lecture once my health was cleared. However, just a few weeks later, drastic changes were required owing to Covid-19. All of a sudden, with amazing dexterity, the students, administrators, and professors were able to switch to teaching on Zoom. This was an experience replicated around the world.

19. Spataro, J. (2020). 2 Years of Digital Transformation in 2 Months. https://www.microsoft.com/en-us/microsoft-365/blog/2020/04/30/2-years-digital-transformation-2-months/ (accessed 25 March 2021).

20. That said, it would be a missed opportunity if global companies didn't seek to use interesting digital ideas developed in China or they didn't

leverage their ESG expertise in Western markets, especially in Europe, by explicitly importing them to the Chinese context, which is still rather nascent in this domain. For more on this line of thinking, see Candelon, F., Puri, A., and Prashantham, S. (2021). Your Company Needs a New China Strategy in the "Decoupling" Era. https://fortune. com/2021/01/28/china-strategy-multinationals-chinese-decoupling-market-consumers-trade-manufacturing/ (accessed 25 March 2021).

21. https://acumen.org/blog/press-releases/manifesto-moral-revolution/ (accessed 25 March 2021).

22. Ibid.

23. Boggs-Davidsen, E. (2020). A Pandemic Gives Permission for Change. https://www.undp.org/content/undp/en/home/blog/2020/a-pandemic-brings-permission-for-change.html (accessed 22 March 2021).

24. https://www.unige.ch/formcont/en/news/a-study-on-innovation-in-ios/ (accessed 25 March 2021).

25. Niessing, J. (2020). How Corporates Can Leverage Start-ups against COVID-19. https://knowledge.insead.edu/blog/insead-blog/how-corporates-can-leverage-start-ups-against-covid-19-13756 (accessed 25 March 2021).

26. Key, A. (2020). CleanedUp: How a Mobile Charging Startup Pivoted to Hand Sanitiser under Lockdown. https://inews.co.uk/news/business/cleanedup-how-a-mobile-charging-startup-pivoted-to-hand-sanitiser-under-lockdown-569595 (accessed 25 March 2021).

27. Prashantham, S., and Krishnan, R. T. (2020). Harness Digital Tech for Inclusive Healthcare. https://www.thehindubusinessline.com/opinion/harness-digital-tech-for-inclusive-healthcare/article32197390.ece (accessed 25 March 2021).

28. Sachs and his coauthors argue, "six SDG Transformations as modular building-blocks of SDG achievement: (1) education, gender, and inequality; (2) health, well-being, and demography; (3) energy decarbonization and sustainable industry; (4) sustainable food, land, water, and oceans; (5) sustainable cities and communities; and (6) digital revolution for sustainable development." Sachs, J. D., Schmidt-Traub, G., Mazzucato, M., Messner, D., Nakicenovic, N., and Rockström, J. (2019). Six Transformations to Achieve the Sustainable Development Goals. *Nature Sustainability* 2(9): 805–814.

29. Radjou, N. (2021). Frugal Solutions. https://ssir.org/articles/entry/frugal_solutions# (accessed 25 March 2021).

30. One of the comments I received on earlier drafts of my write-up on Microsoft (see the Prologue) was that although the story was a fascinating one, spanning many locations and a large period of time, there were too many individuals identified by name and so it wasn't easy to remember everyone in the story. While I think that's a very natural reaction, that was actually an important point I wanted to make – partnering with startups ultimately comes down to the actions of specific individuals. One of the great joys of researching how corporations have grappled with the opportunity and challenge of partnering with startups has been the opportunity to engage with a number of outstanding individuals who broke new ground, on behalf of their companies, to forge pathways to make startup partnering more feasible and systematic than before.

31. Ibid.

32. https://www.lipton.com/co/new-sustainability/supporting-communities.html (accessed 25 March 2021).

33. https://www.unilever.com/news/news-and-features/Feature-article/2020/new-organisations-will-help-boost-our-support-for-social-enterprises.html (accessed 25 March 2021).

34. Carp, S. (2019). La Liga's OTT Platform Trials Social Viewing Feature in Sceenic Tie-up. https://www.sportspromedia.com/news/la-liga-sportstv-ott-social-streaming-sceenic (accessed 31 March 2021).

35. https://www.ibm.com/thought-leadership/institute-business-value/report/ceo (accessed 25 March 2021).

ACKNOWLEDGMENTS

There are far too many people to thank for their support and assistance during my journey of over 15 years as an academic researcher that has resulted in this book. So this is an inevitably partial list of acknowledgments.

I owe a debt of gratitude to Stephen Young and Neil Hood, pioneering international business scholars, whose research center in Scotland is where my journey began as a doctoral student, and where I first observed the prospect of startups partnering with large multinational corporations.

As coauthors and mentors, Julian Birkinshaw and George Yip, two renowned global strategy professors, helped me develop my ideas further and provided valuable advice as I wrote this book manuscript and pitched it to publishers. I am most thankful.

Numerous corporate managers and startup entrepreneurs, as well as professionals in NGOs, UN agencies, government bodies, and other experts, have generously shared their stories and experiences with me. Many are quoted or referred to in the book. Without them, this book would simply not have been possible. A particular word of thanks to Dave Drach who has contributed greatly to my research insights for over a decade, and helped to make possible David Cohen's wonderful Foreword. Thank you, Dave and David.

My deans and other colleagues at Glasgow University, Nottingham University (China campus), and CEIBS have also been a source of steadfast support, which I greatly appreciate.

Several coauthors in my academic work have enriched my thinking over the years, as have my various doctoral students. Some hardworking research assistants have supported my work along the way, including Rhea Li (who helped greatly with finalizing the book manuscript), Li Meng, Wing Wang, and Stella Yu.

To Bill Falloon at Wiley, thank you for believing in this project. And to Purvi Patel, Samantha Enders, and the rest of the team, your efforts to bring this book to life are sincerely appreciated.

I remain grateful to my wife, Deepali, for her unstinting support, as well as to my father, brother, in-laws, and the wider family and my friends for their constant encouragement of my writing endeavors.

Finally, a special nod to my children, Diya and Aditya, who have unwittingly lived through my research journey over the past decade and a half, and who are a constant reminder that purpose-driven corporate innovation – which this book is intended to support – matters greatly not only for today, but for their generation and the ones ahead.

ABOUT THE RESEARCH

I conducted over 400 interviews with corporate managers, startup entrepreneurs, entrepreneurial organizations (e.g. accelerators and other third-party specialists), policy-makers, and industry experts (e.g. academics and consultants). Initially many of the corporations that featured in my interviews were information technology multinationals – notably, Microsoft, but also others such as IBM, Qualcomm, and Texas Instruments. Thereafter, several non-IT corporations – including Bayer, BMW, Ford, Nissan, Unilever, and Walmart – featured in my interviews.

My research interviews were conducted during multiple field trips (see the following list) and several teleconferences in a range of geographic locations across Asia, Europe, and North America – and, more recently, Africa. Where possible, I also observed events and meetings (e.g. corporate accelerator demo days).

Date	Location	Examples of company studied (illustrative, not exhaustive)
June 2003	Seattle, Washington, United States	Microsoft
February 2004	Bangalore, India	Microsoft
February 2006	Edinburgh, UK	IBM Sun Microsystems
July 2006	Bangalore, India	Microsoft IBM
March 2007	Lahore, Pakistan	Microsoft
April 2007	London, UK	Microsoft
August 2008	Silicon Valley, California, United States	Microsoft The Indus Entrepreneurs
May 2009	Bangalore, India	Microsoft Qualcomm
April 2010	Geneva, Switzerland	United Nations
October 2010	Silicon Valley, California, United States	Microsoft Silicon Valley Bank
March 2011	Bangalore, India	Qualcomm Texas Instruments
July 2011	Los Angeles, California, United States	Microsoft
October 2011	Shanghai, China	Microsoft
April 2012	Glasgow, UK	IBM
July 2012	Bangalore, India	Bosch Microsoft
February 2013	Beijing, China	Microsoft
April 2013	Bangalore, India	Microsoft
October 2013	Ningbo, China	IBM
February 2014	Los Angeles, California, United States	Esri
July 2014	Vancouver, Canada	Microsoft
June 2015	Bangalore, India	Intel
September 2015	Beijing, China	Microsoft IBM

Date	Location	Examples of company studied (illustrative, not exhaustive)
December 2015	London, UK	Microsoft
February 2016	Bangalore, India	Microsoft IBM; SAP
February 2016	Hong Kong, China	IBM
February 2016	Johannesburg, South Africa	Microsoft IBM
June 2016	London, UK	Microsoft
July 2016	Shanghai, China	Unilever Intel
January 2017	Shanghai, China	Microsoft Ford
March 2017	Berlin, Germany Munich, Germany	Bayer BMW
April 2017	Accra, Ghana	Google Social Impact Hub
October 2017	Shanghai, China	Bayer Unilever
June 2017	London, UK	Unilever
December 2017	Tel Aviv, Israel	Microsoft The Floor (fintech accelerator)
January 2018	Bangalore, India	SwissRe Bosch
February 2018	Shanghai, China	AB InBev
March 2018	Lagos, Nigeria	Microsoft
March 2018	London, UK	Barclays Telefonica
August 2018	Silicon Valley, California, United States	SAP Fujitsu
November 2018	Hong Kong, China	Nissan (Infiniti)
March 2019	Shanghai, China	Walmart
August 2019	Zurich, Switzerland	F10 Incubator (launched by the Swiss Stock Exchange)
November 2019	Beijing, China	Intel

Date	Location	Examples of company studied (illustrative, not exhaustive)
October 2019	Bangalore, India	Cisco
October 2019	Nairobi, Kenya	Microsoft
December 2019	Tel Aviv, Israel	Intel
March 2020*	Bangalore, India Hyderabad, India	NSRCEL Incubator T-Hub Accelerator

* Travel was subsequently restricted owing to the Covid-19 pandemic. Nevertheless, I still conducted numerous remote interviews with research informants, especially to obtain updates during the writing of this book.

Over the years, ideas from my research analyses were written up in outlets such as the *California Management Review*, Economist Intelligence Unit, HBR.org, *MIT Sloan Management Review*, and *strategy+business*, among others. While various brief articles and teaching cases have resulted from my fieldwork over the years, this book represents the most comprehensive articulation of my research output. The primary approach to data collection and analysis was based on the case study methodology. These case studies were written up and analyzed longitudinally to derive an understanding of how the startup partnering process unfolded. Individuals cases were compared with each other to derive patterns and distinctions, for instance in terms of the differences between various partner interfaces, which gave rise to key insights. While I declined to undertake any paid consulting activity with the companies I studied to avoid any conflict of interest, I regularly shared my key findings with research informants and other experts to gain their feedback and validate my perceptions and emergent ideas.

ABOUT THE AUTHOR

Shameen Prashantham is Professor of International Business & Strategy, and Associate Dean (MBA), at China Europe International Business School (CEIBS) in Shanghai, China. A China-based, India-born British national, his research focuses on what he calls "dancing with gorillas" – how new ventures and large multinationals partner with each other. He has published numerous journal articles in outlets such as *California Management Review*, HBR.org, *Journal of International Business Studies, Journal of Management Studies, Journal of Business Venturing*, and *MIT Sloan Management Review*, as well as two books (Routledge, London). He holds a PhD from Strathclyde University in Glasgow, UK.

INDEX

Page numbers in *italics* represent figures.

Asymmetry
  between corporations and startups,
    lix, lxii, 26, 27–30, 139
  overcoming, 58–60
  paradox of, 52–53, 139
  See also Attention asymmetry; Goal
    asymmetry; Structure asymmetry
Attention asymmetry, 46
  confidence in startups, 47–48, 86
  ecosystem partnering, 50–52
  executing, 46
  learning outcomes, 48–50, 86
  reliability-oriented, 50–52
Australia, 110, 164, 237
  Sydney, liv
AVI. *See* Ashesi University (Ghana)
Aviva, 143

Baidu, 171
Ballmer, Steve, xxxii, xxxiv,
    xxxix, xlix, li
Bamiduro, Tayo, 212
Bansal, Manju, 20
Barclays, 4, 142, 151, 165
Barnes & Noble, 7
Basset, Jeremy, i, 18, 21, 27, 33, 109
Bayer, 5, 20
  engaging with digital startups, 5
  equity participation, 20–21
  Foundation, 199, 216, 227
  G4A (grants4apps), 74, 90,
    100–101, 103, 125, 132, 162, 164,
    169, 177, 216
  interaction rituals, 134
  routinization, 128

Belgaum, 197
Bezos, Jeff, 212
Bing, li
Birkinshaw, Julian, 12
Bisa, 199, 200, 216
Blockbuster, 7
Bluetown, 204–205
BMW Startup Garage, 74, *75*
  adopting new technologies,
    4, 19–20, 25, 66, 74–75
  concept of, 25, 104, 143
  ecosystem location, 164
  entrepreneur-manager duos, 20, 108
  interface ownership, 80–81
  routinization, 129
  venture client model, 19, 63, 71
Bonding ties, 31–32
BOOST UP, 205
Borukhovich, Eugene, 101
Bosch, 124–125
Boundary spanning, 20, 45,
    75, 108, 119–121, 133
Brady, Gerald, 21
Brazil, 145, 159, *160*
Brexit, 227, 236
Bridging ties, 31–32
Brooke, Grant, 208, 267n26
Buckley, Peter, 17
Building block-based synergy,
    61, 62, 63, 82
  cohort, 73–74
  funnel, 74
  elements of other synergy, 67–69
  for societal shortcomings,
    194–195